A Prisoner of the

Twelve Years Captivity at

Charles Neufeld

Alpha Editions

This edition published in 2024

ISBN 9789362514066

Design and Setting By
Alpha Editions
www.alphaedis.com
Email - info@alphaedis.com

Contents

INTRODUCTION

Within seventy-two hours of my arrival in Cairo from the Soudan, I commenced to dictate my experiences for the present volume, and had dictated them from the time I left Egypt, in 1887, until I had reached the incidents connected with my arrival at Omdurman as the Khaleefa's captive, when I became the recipient of a veritable sheaf of press-cuttings, extracts, letters, private and official, new and old, which collection was still further added to on the arrival of my wife in Egypt, on October 13.

My first feelings after reading the bulk of these, and when the sensation of walking about free and unshackled had worn off a little, was that I had but escaped the savage barbarism of the Soudan to become the victim of the refined cruelty of civilization. Fortunately, maybe, my rapid change from chains and starvation to freedom and the luxuries I might allow myself to indulge in, brought about its inevitable result—a reaction, and then collapse. While ill in bed I could, when the delirium of fever had left me, and I was no longer struggling for breath and standing room in that Black Hole of Omdurman, the Saier, find it in my heart to forgive my critics, and say, "I might have said the same of them, had they been in my place and I in theirs." But the inaccuracies written and published in respect to my nationality, biography, and, above all, the astounding inaccuracies published in connection with my capture and the circumstances attending it, necessitate my offering a few words to my readers by way of introduction; but I shall be as brief and concise as possible.

I have, both directly and indirectly, been blamed for, or accused of, the loss of arms, ammunition, and monies sent by the Government to the loyal Sheikh of the Kabbabish, Saleh Bey Wad Salem. Some have gone so far as to accuse me of betraying the party I accompanied into the hands of the dervishes; a betrayal which led eventually to the virtual extermination of the tribe and the death of its brave chief. The betrayal of the caravan I accompanied *did* lead to this result; it also led me into chains and slavery.

According to one account, I arrived at Omdurman on the 1st or 7th of March (both dates are given in the same book), 1887; yet, at this time, to the best of my recollection, the General commanding the Army of Occupation in Egypt, General Stephenson, was trying in Cairo to persuade me to abandon my projected journey into

Kordofan. In a very recent publication, in the preface to which the authors ask their readers to point out any inaccuracies, I am credited with arriving as a captive at Omdurman in 1885, when at this time I was attached as interpreter to the Gordon Relief Expedition, and stood within a few yards of General Earle at the battle of Kirbekan when he was killed. It is probable I was the last man he ever spoke to.

The guide and spy who reported my capture and death on the 13th or 14th of April, 1887, only reported what he thought had actually happened, as a possible result of arrangements he had made; while the refugee Wakih Idris, who reported in August, 1890, that I was conducting a large drapery establishment in Omdurman, must have been a Soudanese humorist, and, doubtless, hugely amused at his tale being believed in the face of the Mahdi's and Khaleefa's crusade against finery and luxuries (although the tenets may have stopped short at the entrance to their hareems), and when every one, from the highest to the lowest, had to wear the roughest and commonest of woven material. A drapery establishment is generally associated with fine clothing, silks, ribbons, and laces; in Omdurman, such an establishment, if opened, would have been consigned to the flames, or the Beit el Mal, and its proprietor to the Saier (prison).

Yet again, when I am more heavily weighted with chains, and my gaoler, to evidence his detestation of the Kaffir (unbeliever) entrusted to his charge, goes out of his way to invent an excuse for giving me the lash, I am reported as being at liberty, my release having been granted on the representations of some imaginary Emir, who claimed it on the ground that I had arranged the betrayal of Sheikh Saleh's caravan.

There is one subject I must touch upon, a subject which has made the life of my wife as much of a hell upon earth during my captivity, as that captivity was to me; and a subject which has caused the most poignant grief and pain to my near relatives. I refer to my Abyssinian female servant Hasseena. The mere fact of her accompanying the caravan opened up a quarry for quidnuncs to delve in, and they delved for twelve long years. It is needless to dilate upon the subject here; suffice it to say that if, when my critics have read through my plain narrative, they have conscience enough left to admit to themselves that they have more injured a woman than the helpless, and in this particular connection, ignorant captive, who has returned to life to confront them, and if they try in future to be as charitable to their own flesh and blood as some of the savage fanatics were to me in the Soudan, I shall rest content.

My narrative, and here I wish to say that it is presented as I first dictated it, notwithstanding my being confronted with, as it was put to me, "contradictions" based upon official and semi-official records and reports, may be depended upon as being as correct a record as memory can be expected to give of the events of my twelve years' existence, from All Fools' Day, 1887, when, in spite of all warnings, I rode away from life and civilization to barbarism and slavery.

At the beginning of 1887, Hogal Dufa'allah, a brother of Elias Pasha, a former Governor of Kordofan, came to me at Assouan and suggested my accompanying him to Kordofan, where large quantities of gum were lying awaiting a favourable opportunity to be brought down, he possessing a thousand cantars (cwts.). The owners of the gum were afraid to bring it to the Egyptian frontier, believing that the Government would confiscate it. Hogal was of opinion that if I accompanied him, we should be able to induce the people to organize a series of caravans for the transport of the gum, he and I signing contracts to buy it on arrival at Wadi Halfa, and guaranteeing the owners against confiscation by the Government. Letters and messages, he said, would be of no avail; the people would believe they were traps set for them by the Government, and it was out of the question for us to attempt to take with us the large amount of money required to purchase the gum on the spot. I being looked upon as an Englishman, and an Englishman's word being then considered as good as his bond, Hogal was sure of a successful journey; so it was finally agreed that Hogal and I should make up a small caravan, and get away as early as possible. At this time, February, 1887, the loyal sheikh, Saleh Bey Wad Salem, of the Kabbabish tribe, was holding his own against the Mahdists, and had succeeded in keeping open the caravan routes of the Western Soudan.

Hogal and I came to Cairo to make various business arrangements, and while here I called upon General Stephenson and Colonel Ardagh, and asked permission to proceed. They tried to persuade me to abandon what appeared to them a very risky expedition; but, telling them that I was bent upon undertaking it, permission or not, I was asked if I would mind delivering some letters to Sheikh Saleh, as a visit to him was necessary to procure guides for the later stages of the journey. I was also to inform him verbally that his request for arms and ammunition had been granted; that he should send men at once to Wadi Halfa to receive them; and that a number of messages to this effect had already been sent him. General Stephenson evidently gave the matter further consideration, for, on calling for the letters, they were not forthcoming. He said he would write to me to Assouan; but, he continued, he would be glad if I would encourage Saleh, or any of the loyal sheikhs I met, to continue to harass the dervishes, and let him have what information I could on my return respecting the country and the people.

The precise circumstances under which I received his letter I have forgotten, but my former business manager tells me that, one evening at Assouan, he found lying on the desk an official envelope, unaddressed, opened it, and was still reading the letter it contained when I walked in, and exhibited great annoyance at his having seen it. This was the letter from General Stephenson to me, referred to by Slatin and Ohrwalder. I remember it but as a sort of private communication, not in any way official; and I think it well at an early moment to state so, as it has been borne in upon me that there is an impression in certain quarters that I might, on the strength of references made to it in Father Ohrwalder's and Slatin Pasha's books, make some claim against the British Government, and I consider it advisable to say at once that no such idea ever occurred to me.

Completing our arrangements in Cairo, Hogal and I started south, Hogal going to Derawi to buy camels for the journey to Kordofan, and I going to Assouan and Wadi Halfa to make final arrangements and prepare food for the desert journey.

CHAPTER I
I START FOR KORDOFAN

Before leaving Assouan for Cairo, I had made an agreement with Hassib el Gabou, of the Dar Hamad section of the Kabbabish tribe, and Ali el Amin, from Wadi el Kab, to act as guides for us as far as Gebel Ain, where we hoped to find Sheikh Saleh. Gabou was in the employ of the military authorities as spy, receiving a monthly gratuity or pay. He and Ali el Amin were each to receive three hundred dollars for the journey, a hundred and fifty dollars each to be paid in advance, and the remainder at the end of the journey. On arrival at Gebel Ain, they were to arrange for guides for us from amongst Saleh's men. The route we had chosen is shown on the accompanying plan, taken from a map published by Kauffmann, a copy of which I had with me, and another copy of which I have been fortunate enough to find since my return.

AN ARAB GUIDE.

On arriving at Derawi, Hogal set about at once buying camels. Our party was to consist of Hogal, Hassib el Gabou, Ali el Amin, my Arabic clerk Elias, my female servant Hasseena, myself, and four men whom Hogal was to engage, to bring up our party to ten people, so that we might be prepared to deal with any small band of marauding dervishes. Hogal was to purchase camels from the Ababdeh, who possessed, and probably still do, the best camels for the description of journey we were undertaking. He was to take them into the desert to test their powers of endurance, as, from the route chosen, they might have to travel fifteen days without water. He was also to purchase extra camels to carry water, so that if the necessity arose, we could strike further west into the desert than arranged for, and be able to keep away from the wells for thirty days. We were to take with us only such articles as were essential for the journey; food, arms and ammunition, three hundred dollars in cash, and our presents of watches, silks, jewellery, pipes, and ornaments for the sheikhs we met.

Hogal was to leave Derawi on or about the 20th March, and bringing the camels through the desert on the west of the Nile, was so to time his last stage as to reach Wadi Halfa at sunset on the 26th or 27th. The guides, my clerk, servant, and myself were to slip over by boat, and our caravan was to strike off west at once. Our departure was to be kept as secret as possible.

On my reaching Shellal after leaving Hogal at Derawi, I was overtaken by an old friend, Mohammad Abdel Gader Gemmareeyeh, who, having learned in confidence from Hogal the reason for his purchasing the camels, hurried after me to warn me against employing Gabou as guide, as he knew the man was not to be trusted. He told me that Gabou was acting as spy for friend and foe, and was being paid by both, but this I did not then credit. I laughed at the man's expressed fears, and telling him that as Hogal and I were to direct the caravan, and Gabou was to accompany us as guide, I had no intention of abandoning a journey, at the end of which a small fortune awaited me. I knew very well that not a single person was to be trusted out of sight and hearing, but as there was no reason why Gabou should not be kept within both, there was equally no reason why I should have any fears. Besides this, I was vain enough to believe that perhaps I might, as a result of my journey, be able to hand to the military authorities a report of some value, and the halo of romance, which still hung over everything Soudanese, was in itself no little attraction.

I reached Wadi Halfa about March 23, and set to work quietly with final arrangements. Hasseena had elected to accompany us, and this on the suggestion of Hogal, his reasons being first, that being accompanied by a woman, the peaceful intentions of our little caravan would be evidenced; secondly, that Hasseena, when the slave of her old master of the Alighat Arabs, had on a number of occasions made the journey between El Obeid, Dongola, and Derawi, and would be of great use to us in hareems in very much the same way that a lady in civilized countries, having an *entrée* to a salon, is occasionally able to further the interests of her male relatives or friends; and in the East, *all* women have the *entrée* to hareems.

The morning after my arrival at Wadi Halfa I heard that forty of Sheikh Saleh's men, led by one of his slaves, Ismail, had already arrived to take over the arms and ammunition. Gabou came to me the same day, and suggested our abandoning the proposed expedition, as he was afraid that the dervishes might hear of Saleh's men coming in, and send out bands to intercept the caravan on its return, and we might fall into the hands of one of them. Believing that Gabou was simply trying to induce me to add to his remuneration for the extra risks, I told him I should hold him to his agreement. A day or two later, seeing that I was determined to go on, he suggested that we should, for safety, accompany Saleh's men, but this I objected to. The Kabbabish were fighting the dervishes, and lost no opportunity of pouncing down upon any small bands, and I had no particular wish to look for more adventures than my expedition itself was likely to provide. There was also the question of time; Sheikh Saleh's baggage camels would only move at the rate of about a mile an hour, while ours would cover two and a half to three miles easily.

On March 24, I received a telegram from Hogal, then at Assouan, announcing his arrival there with the camels, and his intention to come on at once, so that he should have reached Wadi Halfa on the 28th or 29th of the month. Gabou now exhibited particular anxiety that we should join Saleh's party, and took upon himself to make an arrangement with them. On my remonstrating with him, he said that if the dervishes were on the road, they would certainly be met with between Wadi Halfa and the Selima Wells, or, maybe, at the wells themselves, and this was the only part of our route where there was any likelihood of our coming in contact with them, our road, after Selima, being well to the west. "Now," said he, "if Saleh's caravan goes off, and the dervishes on the road are not strong enough to attack, they will allow the caravan to pass, but wait about the roads either in the hope of getting reinforcements in time to attack, or with the hope of attacking any smaller parties." He believed the dervishes might go on to the wells, and encamp there, so that in either case we should fall into their clutches. It was Gabou's opinion that Sheikh Saleh's caravan was strong enough to annihilate the dervish bands, which he *now* said he had heard were actually on the road. This decided me. I asked him why he had not told me of this before. He had forgotten to do so!

The 28th, 29th, 30th, and 31st of the month passed, and still no appearance of Hogal and the camels. Ismail was impatient to be off, and Gabou suggested, that as my camels must be close at hand, Hasseena, Elias, El Amin and I should start with Saleh's caravan, he following us as soon as our camels arrived. My camels being in good condition, and unloaded, would, he said, overtake the caravan in a few hours, and he was very anxious to test them for trotting speed while overtaking us. We were joined at Wadi Halfa by about twenty Arabs of different tribes, bringing our caravan up to sixty-four men and about a hundred and sixty camels. Gabou gave us as guide for Selima, a man named Hassan, also of the Dar Hamads. Crossing to the western bank of the Nile early on the morning of April 1, 1887, by ten o'clock we had loaded up and started on that journey to the Soudan, which was to take me twelve long years to complete.

When we had been two days on the road, I began to feel a little uneasy at the non-appearance of my camels; but thinking that maybe Gabou had purposely delayed starting so as to give them a stiff test in hard trotting, I comforted myself with this reflection, though as day after day passed, my anxiety became very real. On the night of April 7, we judged we must be close to Selima Wells, and sent out scouts to reconnoitre; they reached the wells, and returned saying that they could not find traces of any one having been there for some time. Our caravan reached the wells between nine and ten o'clock in the morning, and about midday, while we were occupied in watering the camels and preparing food, we heard a shot fired from the south-east, and shortly afterwards one of our scouts came in saying that he had been sighted by a party of about twenty men on camels; one of the men had fired at him at long range, and the whole party had then hurried off to the south.

A hurried conference was held; it was the general opinion that this party must be scouts of a larger one, and that they had gone off for the purpose of apprising their main body. Ismail decided upon pushing on at once. There was little time for me to consider what to do; to return to Wadi Halfa was out of the question, as Ismail could not spare any of his men as a bodyguard; to wait at the wells was not to be thought of, and the only other alternative was to go on with the caravan. I told Elias to write out short notes for Hogal and Gabou, which I had intended to leave at the wells; but as Ismail pointed out, I should have to leave them conspicuously marked in some way to attract attention, and, if the dervishes got to the wells first, or if those we had seen returned with others, they would be the first to get the notes, which would endanger our caravan, and the little party I was so anxiously expecting. There was nothing for it but to go on and hope for the best. If the worst came to the worst, it meant only that my gum expedition was temporarily delayed, and that I should, after reaching Sheikh Saleh, take my first opportunity of getting north again.

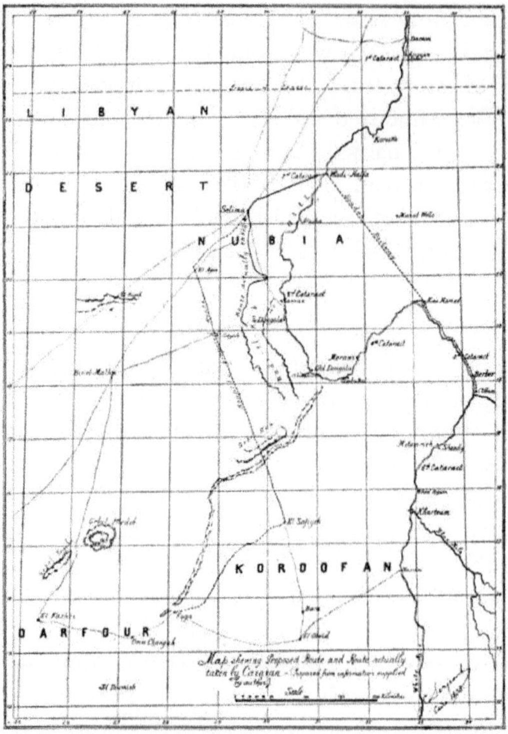

Map showing Proposed Route and Route actually taken by Caravan

see better image

CHAPTER II
BETRAYED BY GUIDES

There are five caravan routes running from Selima Wells—that furthest west leading to El Kiyeh, the next to El Agia, and the one in the centre leading to the Nile near Hannak, with a branch running to Wadi el Kab. Our objective being to meet Sheikh Saleh at Gebel Ain, we should have taken the route leading to El Agia, and this we had selected, because, as it was well out in the desert, there was little likelihood of our encountering any roving bands of dervish robbers. When we had been on the road a few hours, I ventured the opinion that we had taken the wrong route, and a halt was called while I examined the map I had with me, after which examination I felt certain that we were marching in the wrong direction. The guide Hassan was equally certain that we were on the El Agia road. A discussion ensued, which was ended by Hassan telling me, with what he intended to be withering sarcasm, "I never walked on paper" (meaning the map); "I have always walked on the desert. I am the guide, and I am responsible. The road you want us to go by leads to El Etroun (Natron district), sixty marches distant; if we take your road and we all die of thirst in the desert, I should be held responsible for the loss of the lives, and your paper could not speak to defend me." Hassan's dramatic description of the scene of his being blamed by the Prophet for losing these valuable lives if he trusted to a "paper," had more to do with his gaining his point than pure conviction as to whether we were on the right road or not. From El Agia, as Saleh's men said, they knew every stone on the desert, but in this part they had to trust to Hassan.

During the whole of this first day we forced the baggage camels on at their best pace, travelling by my compass in a south and south-easterly direction. The arrangement I had made with Gabou for my own caravan, which arrangement Ismail had agreed to when Gabou suggested our travelling with them, was that we should travel a little to the west of the El Agia camel tracks, but keep parallel to them. When we halted that night I spoke to Ismail about this, and asked him to keep to this part of the agreement—that is to say, to travel parallel to, and not on, the track. Hassan objected, as it meant slower travelling. Still pressing on after a short rest, Hassan zigzagged the caravan over stony ground with the object of losing our trail, as our caravan, consisting of about 160 camels, was an easy one to track up.

We travelled fast until mid-day of the 10th, when we were obliged to take a rest owing to the extreme heat. We were in an arid waste; not the slightest sign of vegetation or anything living but ourselves to be seen anywhere. Off again at sunset, we travelled the whole night through, my compass at midnight showing me that we were, if anything, travelling towards the east, when our direction should certainly have been south-west. At our next halt I spoke to Ismail again, but Hassan convinced him of his infallibility in desert routes. The following morning, the 11th, there was no disguising the fact about our direction: the regular guides travel by the stars at night-time, but they laugh at the little niceties between the cardinal points, as Hassan laughed at me when I tried to get him to believe in the sand diagram I showed him, with the object of proving to him that a divergence increases the further you get away from the starting-point. El Amin now joined me in saying that he thought we were on the wrong road, but Hassan was prepared. He had, he said, during the night, led us further into the desert to again break our trail, and that he was now leading us to the regular road. El Amin replied that it was his opinion that Hassan had lost the road in the night, and now was trying to find it. This led to a lively discussion and an exchange of compliments, which almost ended in a nasty scuffle, as some were siding with Hassan and others with El Amin.

Acting upon my advice, men were sent out east and west to pick up the regular caravan route. Hassan declared that a branch of the regular road would be found to the east, Amin and I declared for the west. Hassan took two men east, and Amin, accompanied by two others, went west. About an hour after sunset both parties returned. El Amin arrived first, and reported that they had failed to find any trace of the road. Hassan came shortly afterwards, and, having heard before reaching Ismail of the failure of the others, came up to us jubilant and triumphant, as a road had been picked up where he said it would. They had not only picked up the road, but had come to the resting-place of a caravan of fifteen to twenty camels, which could only be a few hours ahead of us, as the embers of the caravan's fire places were still hot. I judged it best to be silent on the subject of the route now, though Amin, jibed and scoffed at by the victorious Hassan, was loud in his declarations that we were on the wrong route, and that Hassan had lost his way;

this nearly led to trouble again between him and the two men who had accompanied Hassan, as they considered their word doubted.

We travelled east during the night, and crossed the road which Hassan had, during the day, picked up. But there was a feeling of uncertainty and unrest in the caravan. One after another appealed to me, and I could but say that I was still convinced my "paper" was right and Hassan wrong. El Amin, pricked to the quick, spread through the caravan his opinion that Hassan had not lost his way, but was deliberately leading us in the wrong direction. When we halted on the 12th, Ismail, noticing the gossiping going on, and the manner of his men, decided upon sending out scouts to the east to see if they could pick up anything at all in the way of landmarks. El Amin joined the scouts, who were absent the whole day. They returned at night with the news that we were nearer the river than El Agia Wells, and on this, our fourth day from Selima, we should have been close to El Agia. This report, coming not from El Amin only, but from Saleh's own people who knew the district, created consternation. Again the "paper" was called for, and on this occasion Hassan was told that the paper knew better than he did.

That night scene of betrayed men, desperate, with death from thirst or dervish swords a certainty, can be better imagined than described. There had been no husbanding of the drinking-water, and it was almost out; many, in the hurry of departure from Selima, had not filled their water-skins. There was no doubt now that we were, as I had said from the beginning, on the road to Wadi el Kab, and travelling in the enemy's country. But Hassan, threatened as he was, had still one more card to play. He acknowledged that he had lost his way, but said this was not altogether his fault; we, he said, had been travelling hard, and, feeling sure he was on the right track, he had been careless, or had neglected to look out for the usual marks, and that this was because Amin and I had annoyed him at the beginning of the march, as to the road. He now said that we were well to the west of El Kab, and on its extreme limits where the wady disappeared into desert water could be found, and being so far west, it was most improbable that we should find any dervishes there. Another council was held. Hassan was for continuing in an easterly direction; I proposed west, believing now that the wady would be found to the west; while Ismail, advised by Amin, elected for a southerly direction. At last it was agreed that Ismail, Hassan, and some men should ride hard in a south-westerly direction, in the hopes of picking up some branch caravan route leading to El Agia. The remainder of the caravan, with myself and

Amin, were to travel easily in a southerly direction for five hours, and then halt and await the return to us of Ismail.

We halted between three and four in the afternoon, but no sooner had we done so, when a heavy sandstorm burst upon us. There are varieties of sandstorms as there are of most other things, but this was one of the worst varieties. The air becomes thick with the finest particles, which gives one more the idea of a yellow fog in the north than of anything else I might liken it to. We were obliged to wrap our own and the camels' heads in cloths and blankets to protect ourselves, if not from suffocation, from something very near it. The storm lasted until after sunset, and as it must have obliterated all traces of our tracks, scouts were sent out to sight Ismail. Up till midnight no signs of him were forthcoming. Breaking up what camel saddles we could spare, we lit fires to attract his attention to our position, and as these burned low, shots were fired at intervals of five minutes. After ten or twelve shots had been fired, I recommended that volleys of five should be fired at the same intervals, and when I believe six had been fired, we heard Ismail calling to us from the darkness. He had encountered the sandstorm, but evidently had had a worse time of it than we had. He had heard our volleys, and had replied with single shots, but these we had not heard.

On reaching the caravan, Ismail ordered the fires to be put out, and the camels to be at once loaded and their fastenings well looked to. The rifles were cleared of the sand which had accumulated on them, and Ismail went round inspecting everything for himself. I called him aside and asked him what he had discovered. He whispered one word, "Treachery," and returned to his inspection of the animals. When he had satisfied himself of the arms being in readiness, and the cases so secured that if the camels bolted they would not be able to throw off their load very easily, he gave the orders to march. Ignoring Hassan completely, he led us west, sending out as scouts, on fast camels, Darb es Safai and El Amin, my guide; but at sunrise they came back to us, saying that not a trace of road could be found.

I cannot weary my readers with a day-to-day record of our zigzagging in the desert—one day Hassan in the ascendant as guide, another day El Amin, and from this time I cannot pretend to remember the exact day on which particular incidents happened. There were too many incidents to attempt a complete record, even with a diary, had I kept one.

El Amin had confided to me and Ismail his firm conviction that Hassan was doing all this purposely, and that he knew precisely whereabouts we were, as he had noticed him making some sort of calculations, and drawing lines with his camel-stick in the sand.

Perhaps it was because I did not wish to, that I could not credit the implied treachery. Gabou and Hassan belonged to the Kabbabish tribe, and as the rifles and ammunition we were carrying were to assist Sheikh Saleh to fight the common enemy, what object could there be in betraying us? Saleh's men would certainly fight to the death; betrayer and betrayed would run equal risks of being killed—indeed, the betrayer would almost certainly be killed instantly by those he was leading. I therefore dismissed the idea from my head, took it for granted that the man had actually lost his way, and declined to fall in with El Amin's suggestion to say "good-bye" to the caravan, make straight for the Nile, and take our chances of passing clear as merchants, should we meet any people on the road.

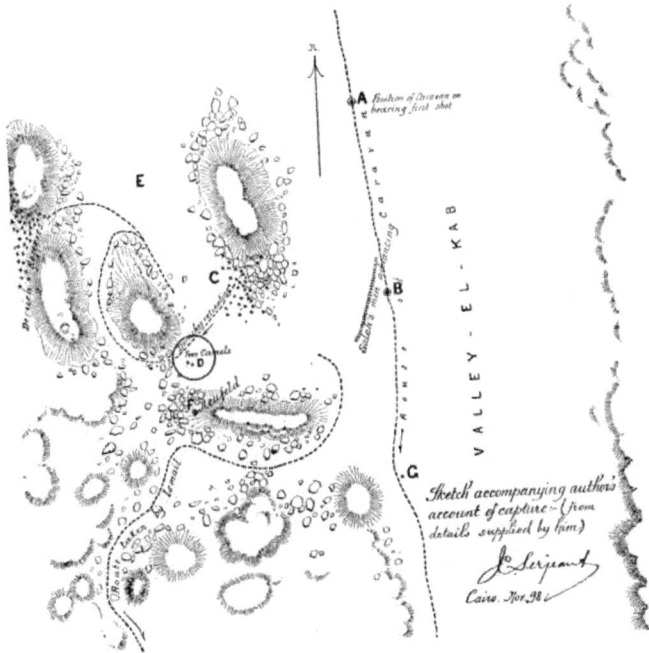

Sketch accompanying author's account of capture

see better image

On, I believe, our sixth day out from Selima, we crossed a caravan route running east and west, and, referring to my map, I had no hesitation in telling Ismail that this must be the caravan route between El Kab and El Agia, but on which part of the road we were I could not imagine. I wanted to attempt travelling along this road, but Hassan declared it led to El Kiyeh. That we must now be close to Wadi el Kab, every one knew. A "council of war" was held, at which it was decided to risk going on, as we must be travelling towards the wells on the extreme edge of the wady. We were to try and pick up the wells, water the camels, fill our skins, and then strike direct west and encamp at night-time, not to remain near the wells. While we were discussing the situation, some men had been sent along the road to try and discover anything in the way of marks or tracks which would give an idea as to our exact position, and they reported that there could be little doubt of this being El Kiyeh road, and that El Kiyeh must be six days distant. This news decided us. Our water-supply was out. A six days' march over that desert under such conditions meant perishing of thirst, and there was, again, the uncertainty as to whether we should be, after all, on the road to El Kiyeh or El Etroun.

One of the camels was ailing, so it was decided to kill it, and let the men have a good meal of meat. Early the next day, I believe our eighth or ninth day from Selima, an Alighat Arab was sent scouting to the west; he never returned. We halted and waited for his return as arranged, and lost the night's travel in consequence. On the following day, unmistakable landmarks were picked up, which proved that we were but a few hours distant from the Wadi el Kab, and it was believed we could reach the wells by sunset. Unloading the camels, and leaving four men in charge of the baggage, we started off for the wells, expecting to return the same night. We travelled without incident until about two o'clock in the afternoon, when we reached the broken ground skirting the wady proper. My guide, El Amin, and two men, had been sent on ahead to reconnoitre. The place is dotted with sand-dunes and hillocks from fifty to a hundred feet high, and on nearing the first hillock, and when approximately at "A," we heard a shot fired. El Amin and his companions had then reached the spot marked "G" on the accompanying plan; we believed the shot to be a signal that they had found water, and pressed on until we reached "B," when shot after shot was fired, the bullets whistling over our heads. At this moment we saw Amin and his companions hurrying back to us. Next came some broken volleys, but all the shots were high. Up to now we had not seen our assailants, but the smoke from the rifles now discovered their whereabouts—the hillock marked "C."

I was slightly ahead of the main body, with Hassan, the guide, some yards away on my right. Being mounted on a large white camel, well caparisoned, and wearing a bright silk Kofeyeh on my head, I offered an excellent mark, and shot after shot whistled over me. I was turning my camel round to hurry back to the main body, when I saw Hassan fall to the ground. Calling to my clerk Elias, who was nearest to him, to help him back on the camel, or make the camel kneel to cover him, I tried to get mine to kneel so that I could dismount, but the brute was startled and restive. Elias called out that Hassan was "mayat khaalass" (stone dead). Our men were now quickly dismounting and loading their rifles. Bullet after bullet and volley after volley came, but no one was struck as yet except Hassan. Making the camels kneel, as a precaution against their bolting, we advanced in open order towards the hillock from whence the shots came, I on the extreme left, Ismail in the centre, and Darb es Safai on the right. Rounding the hillock "C," we caught the first glimpse of the enemy, about fifty strong, and then rapidly retiring. We fired a volley into them, on which they turned and replied, and a pretty hot fusilade was kept up for some minutes, but the firing was wild on both sides. I saw two of our men fall, and about eight to ten of the dervishes. Picking up their dead or wounded, they hurried off again, leaving two camels behind. Darb es Safai, who was leading the right, and was now well in advance, was the first to reach the camels, and discovered that they were loaded with filled water-skins. Calling out, "Moyia lil atshan;* Allah kereem!" ("Water for the thirsty; God is generous!"), he commenced to unfasten the neck of one of the skins. A mad rush was made for the water; arms were thrown down, and the men struggled around the camels for a drink. I tried for a few seconds, when I reached them, to counsel moderation, knowing the effect of a copious draught on the system under the circumstances and condition they were in. Some of the men had been three days without water, and the camel flesh they had eaten had not improved matters.

* *Moyia lil atshan.*

(Water for the thirsty.)

While the struggle was still in progress, Hasseena, who with Elias had followed us up, ran to me saying that the dervishes were returning, and, looking in the direction of "E," I saw about a hundred and fifty men advancing at a rapid pace. I raised the alarm, and Ismail gave the call to arms; but few heard his voice in the din. Those few fired a few shots, but it was now too late; in a moment the dervishes were upon us, friend and foe one struggling mass. Above the noise could be heard the voice of the dervish leader reminding his men of some orders they had received, and to "secure their men alive." Even in that moment it flashed upon me that we had been led into an ambush, else why the reference to "our master's orders" given by their leader? Elias, Hasseena, and I ran towards "F" to take cover; it was no use my using my fowling-piece on that struggling mass, as I should have struck friend and foe. Just as we reached the base of the hillock, Elias was captured, and the five or six dervishes who had pursued us occupied themselves with examining the contents of the bag he was carrying—my three hundred dollars, jewellery, etc. They gave a mere glance towards me, and then moved off.

Pushing a few stones together, I laid out my cartridges, reloaded my revolvers, and prepared to die fighting. Ismail, the leader of our caravan, had by some means managed to get clear of the mass, and, reaching my camel, mounted it and rode off, riding hard to the right of "F." Seeing Hasseena and me, he called to us to try and secure camels and follow him up. Hasseena on this ran down the hillock; I had not noticed her disappearance from the immediate vicinity of the hillock, as I was too much occupied hurriedly making my diminutive zareeba of stones. Glancing over the stones later, I was astonished to see her walking at the head of the dervishes who had secured Elias, they following in Indian file. Hasseena called out that I was given quarter, and that I was to stand up unarmed. This I refused to do, and as they kept advancing, I kept my gun pointed at them from between the stones. Hasseena again called out, saying that they had orders not to hurt me, in evidence of which they fired their rifles into the air, and then laid them on the sand.

By this time I could see that our men were bound, and grouped together on the plain; I left my cover, descended the hillock, and advanced to the dervishes, when I was saluted with yells and cries of "El Kaffir, El Kaffir" ("the unbeliever"). One, maybe more fanatical than the rest, after vituperating me, made a motion as if to strike at my head with his sword. Looking him in the eyes, I asked, "Is this the word of honour (meaning quarter) of your Prophet and master; you liar, you son of a dog? strike, unclean thing!" While, as is only to be expected, I was at that moment trembling with fear and excitement, I had lived too long in the East to forget that a bold front and fearless manner command respect, if not fear. My words and manner had the desired effect, for one, turning to my would-be assailant, asked, "What are you doing? Have you forgotten our master's orders?" This was the second time something had been said about "orders." I put a few questions to my captors, but they declined to reply to them, saying that I could speak to the Emirs Hamza and Farag, and they hurried me towards them. The Emir, whom later I knew to be Farag, asked my name, and what I wanted in his country; then, turning to his followers without waiting for a reply, called out, "This is the Pasha our master Wad en Nejoumi sent us to capture; thanks be to God we have taken him unhurt." The latter remark was made as a reproof to the man who had threatened to strike me, as the incident had been reported, and also as a warning to the others.

Taking me apart from the others, he continued, "I see you are thirsty;" and, calling up one of his men, told him to pour some water over some hard dry bread, and, handing it to me, said smilingly, "Eat—it is not good for you to drink." I divined his meaning. Had our men not made that mad rush for the water, we might have had a very different tale to tell, and who knows if, had we won the day and reached Sheikh Saleh, the history of the Soudan for the past twelve years might not have read differently? *Mine* would have done so.

CHAPTER III
IN THE HANDS OF THE DERVISHES

I was handed over to two men, who were held responsible for my well-being; Hasseena and Elias were placed together in the charge of others, and we were ordered to seat ourselves a little distance away. The dervishes had with them military tents which must have been taken at Khartoum, and one was soon pitched. Here the Emirs and principal men met to hold a conference and inquiry. Darb es Safai and others were taken up one by one, and the question put to them direct, "Where are the rifles and the cartridges?" for no case had, of course, been brought on with us to the wells. They denied any knowledge of them; then replied Farag, "We will find them for you, and show you how they are used." My turn came, and in reply to the usual question, I said that I knew nothing at all about them; questioned still further, I admitted that I had seen a number of boxes, but I could not pretend to know what was inside of them. Asked then as to where they were, I said I could not tell—in the desert somewhere; they had been thrown away, as the camels, being tired and thirsty, could not carry them any longer. Still interrogated, I replied that the guide who had brought us here was the first killed in the firing, and that I did not think any one else of our caravan could find their way back to the place where the boxes were left.

At this, rapid glances were passed from one to the other. Asked if I was sure he was killed, I could only reply that my clerk had told me so, that I had seen him fall, and indicated the place. Farag sent off a man in that direction after whispering some instructions to him, and during the few minutes he was away perfect silence reigned in the tent, with the exception of the click, click of the beads of the *Sibha* (rosary). When he returned, he whispered his reply to Farag. Two of the Alighat Arabs who had joined us at Wadi Halfa were next brought up and questioned; they did not give direct replies; they were taken aside, but not far enough away to prevent my overhearing part of what went on, when, as a result of promises and then threats, I gathered that they undertook to lead the dervishes to the spot where the cases had been left in the desert. It is quite certain, from the questions put by the dervishes, that they were ignorant of the precise spot where the baggage had been left, and it in a measure confirmed the death of Hassan; but I have always had a suspicion that the man shammed death and got away, to present himself later on to Nejoumi. He might easily have mingled with the dervishes and not been seen by us.

The sun had now set; the conference ended, and orders were given by Farag for all to march back by the route we had come, the Alighat Arabs, with Amin between them, leading. We marched for only an hour or so, for our camels, being tired and not having been watered, gave trouble. A halt was called for the night, and what water the dervishes had was partly distributed. By sunrise the next day we were on the march again, twenty-five men, well mounted, having been sent on in advance with the guides. All Saleh's men, wounded and sound, were compelled to walk, the dervishes and their wounded riding on camels.

In the afternoon we reached the spot where we had left the four men in charge of the baggage, to find them with their hands bound behind them. The advance party had reached them about ten o'clock in the morning, and had doubtless found them asleep, as no shots had been fired. The men were not to be blamed in any way, and it really mattered but little whether they were asleep or awake when taken, with the odds against them. I had, on starting for the wells, left them the little water I had saved; had they not had this, they could not have slept.

In the same way that Saleh's men had forgotten everything in that mad rush for the water, so did the dervishes break loose, forget all about their prisoners, and rush on the pile of cases. The ground was soon littered with rifles, packets of ammunition, sugar, clothing, food, and the hundred and one articles to be found in a trading caravan, for the cases and bales of the Arabs who had joined us at Wadi Halfa contained only merchandise. My mind was soon made up; running towards the other prisoners with my hunting-knife, I thought that at all events the thongs of a few might be cut, and making for the camels and scattering in different directions, a few might have got clear. It was a mad idea, but it was something. Before any part of my half-formed plan could be put into execution, the guards were down on us. I was taken to the Emir, Said Wad Farag, but I excused myself, saying that, being a medical man, I had gone to see if I could attend to any of the wounded. Complimenting me on my thought for the others, he recommended me to think of myself, appropriated the knife the guards had found in my hand, and told me he would let me know when to use it, warning me at the same time not to attempt to speak to any of the other prisoners.

When the excitement over the loot had cooled down a little, a camel was killed in honour of the occasion, and my servant Hasseena was ordered to prepare some of the dishes. I was invited to eat with the Emirs. Our first dish was the raw liver of the camel, covered with salt and shetta—a sort of red pepper. I had seen this dish being eaten, but had never partaken of it myself before. I had two reasons for eating it now: first, I was hungry and thirsty; secondly, one of the first signs of fear is a disinclination, I might say inability, to swallow food, and fear of my captors was the last thing I intended to exhibit. After the meal, my clothes were taken from me, as they looked upon them as the dress of a kaffir, and I was turned out into the night-air with my singlet, drawers, and socks as my complete wardrobe. My turban and Baghdad Kofiyeh were also taken, so that I was bareheaded into the bargain.

When the dervishes had finished their food, and before they lay down for the night, the Emir Farag sent for all the loot to be collected and brought before his tent, when it would later on be distributed according to the rules of the Beit-el-Mal (Treasury). This institution and its working will be described later. Only a part of the loot was collected, for the men, knowing from experience the extraordinary manner in which loot "shrank" in bulk and numbers when placed in the hands of the Emirs to be distributed according to rule, concealed in the sand or beneath their jibbehs, whatever could be hidden there. The pipes and tobacco found in the baggage were burned, as their use was prohibited by the Mahdi. Amongst my things was found my letter-wallet, and this was handed to the Emirs, who afterwards sent for me and demanded to know the contents of the letters. I replied that they were only business documents, receipts for goods, and such like, but that if the wallet was handed to me, I would translate each document. Being satisfied with this answer, Farag kept the wallet. Complaining of my clothing having been taken, he allowed me to have my flannel shirt, and gave me a piece of rag as head-dress. In this guise, I lay down in the sand to doze and wake the whole night through, conscious yet unconscious, with the incidents of the last eighteen days chasing each other through my brain.

The camp was astir long before sunrise, and by sunrise we were on the move east towards El Kab, which we reached about three o'clock in the afternoon. The "wells," at the part we arrived at, are upon ascending ground; but the name "well" in this instance is a misnomer. They are shallow basins scooped out with the hands or any rough implement, the water being found about three feet below the surface, shrubs indicating where to scoop. The camels were watered and left to graze on the scanty herbage. Another camel was killed to celebrate the capture of the caravan, and again I was invited to take food with the Emirs. I was asked only the most commonplace questions, but I could not get any reply to those I put, except that Abdel Rahman Wad en Nejoumi would tell me all I wished to know. While still with the Emirs, Farag called up his followers again, and after congratulating them upon the capture of the "English Pasha" and the caravan (though the Emir knew very well who I was, from old days at Korti), he harangued them on the advisability of obeying to the letter the orders of the Mahdi transmitted to the Khaleefa, and by the Khaleefa to him, winding up his oration with threats of punishment and imprisonment to any of the faithful who robbed the Beit-el-Mal by concealing any of the loot, after which he ordered every one to be searched again. I had many opportunities later of seeing evidences of what the Emirs most relied upon, in regard to the handing over of any loot—an exhortation to their followers, and an appeal to their religious scruples—or threats of punishment and imprisonment. Both went together, and were administered in the order I have given them, and there was seldom an occasion when a search did not follow the appeal to their honesty, and when punishment did not follow the search for concealed loot.

Wad Farag dismissed me for the night, but I had hardly lain down when two dervishes stole up, and asked me to describe all the baggage I had with me. I said that a list would be found in my wallet, which, if they would bring to me, would allow of me giving them the required information. One left me, for the purpose, I imagine, of asking the Emir for the wallet, but returned shortly saying that I should *have* to remember, and that the list I then gave would be compared with the list in the wallet. There was no list in the wallet, but there were one or two letters I wished to extract. I have thought since that, had I exhibited less anxiety to get hold of the wallet itself, I might have induced them to hand over these letters under one pretext or another. I soon discovered from their questions that the dervishes were spying one upon the other, for they asked me directly what were the contents of the bag taken from Elias my clerk. I told them three hundred dollars, gold and silver jewellery, and some jewellery which my servant Hasseena had asked Elias to carry for her. Hasseena was sent for to describe her jewellery. The information evidently gave these men huge satisfaction, and taking Hasseena with them, they sent her back with cooking utensils, food and firewood, and ordered her to prepare food for me. Having had my food with the Emirs but a little time before, I was at a loss to understand the meaning of this, but learned later on that it was to prevent any one else approaching her for information. Whether these two men were, as they said, in charge of the Beit-el-Mal, or whether, having seen any of the money or jewellery, they wanted to get their share of it, I cannot say, but, in the light of subsequent events, I should be inclined to believe the latter.

When the food was ready, I invited my guards to eat it. I was hoping that a full meal, especially as their fatigue was very evident, would induce them to sleep, and feigning drowsiness myself, moved off a few yards, and scooped out a sand bed. I was prepared to risk anything for liberty; we were in the neighbourhood of the wells, and might travel for days without being out of reach of water. Explaining my plans to Hasseena, I told her, under the pretence of collecting firewood, to try and get up to Amin and Elias, cut their thongs with the large knife we had had to cut up the meat sent us for food, and tell them to creep towards a small tree which I had noticed during daylight, and await me there. Some camels with their feet fastened by ropes were grazing there, and I believed that we might get away unobserved, and get some hours' start. But the guards of the prisoners were not asleep; they were very much awake, searching the prisoners for any valuables, an operation which was carried out by each relief of guards, so that the sun rose with us still in the hands of the dervishes.

THE KHALEEFA'S EUNUCHS AT ATTENTION.

It was just after sunrise that we moved off again; my guardian must have been impressed with my importance, for he saddled the camel for me himself, and brought me a gourd of camel's milk. During this day's journey, the Emir Mohammad Hamza, of the Jaalin tribe, who was commanding a section of the dervishes, rode up to me and inquired about my health—the usual form of salutation. He told me not to be afraid of any harm coming to me, and then rode off again. That evening we arrived at a small encampment of dervishes close to some wells, when I was taken before another Emir whom I was told was Makin en Nur, and who, from the deference paid him by the others, was doubtless the chief. He, too, put a few questions to me of the same commonplace nature as the others, and waved his hand for me to be removed. On being sent for again, I was accused of being a Government spy, and asked what I had to say for myself. I replied, "I have told you the truth; what do you want me to do now? tell you a lie, and say I *am* a spy? If I do so you will kill me for saying I am one, and if I say again I am *not*, you will not believe me, and kill me just the same. I am not afraid of you; do as you please." When he questioned me again, I said, "I refuse to answer any more questions." My manner of speaking to them caused no little surprise, as it was doubtless different to what they had expected, and to what they had formerly experienced from captives.

A young dervish was called in, and told to conduct me to a spot removed from the other prisoners. As we walked along, the youth said, "God is just; God is bounteous; please God to-morrow our eyes shall be gladdened by seeing a white Kaffir yoked with a shayba to a black one." This shayba is the forked limb of a tree; the fork is placed on the neck pressing against the larynx, the stem projecting before the wearer; the right wrist is then tightly bound to the stem with thongs of fresh hide, which soon dry and "bite" the flesh, and the ends of the fork drawn as closely together as possible, and fastened with a cross-piece. It is a cruel instrument of torture, for the arm must be kept extended to its utmost; to attempt to relieve the tension means pressure on the larynx; but when yoked to another man he throws pressure on you, and you on him. A prod in the ribs under the arm of either victim, with sword or rifle, affords endless amusement to their tormentors in the victims' gapes and grimaces as they gasp for breath; but the captor's cup of happiness is filled when an extra hard prod knocks one man off his feet, and the poor wretches are only helped up again when they are almost choking.

Irritated beyond endurance by the youth's jibes and jests, and hoping to put an end to everything at once, I threw my weight and strength into one blow—and I was a powerful man then—and felled him senseless. Taking his rifle, I strode back to the tent, almost foaming with rage, and entered; my eyes must have been blazing; I glared from one to the other, wondering whether to fire the one shot and then start "clubbing" until I was cut down. Hamza was the first to speak, and jumping up, held up his hand, saying, "Istanna" (wait). I hurriedly related what had occurred, and said what I intended to do. Hamza came to me, saying, "La, la, la (no, no, no), there must be a mistake. You are not to be put in a shayba; our orders are to deliver you alive and well." Then turning to the others, he continued, "Hand this man over to me; I shall deliver him alive and well to Wad en Nejoumi; I hold myself responsible for him." Some demur was made, when, lowering the rifle, I placed the butt on the ground, rested my chin on the muzzle, and addressing myself to all, said that unless I was left in Hamza's charge I should press the trigger—on which my great toe was then resting. Hamza again pressed his point, and said, "If you do not agree, and this man does any harm to himself, I declare myself free of blame and responsibility. I have heard of him; he will do as he says." The effect of the words was magical. "Take him away—keep him; do what you wish with him; never let him come near us again—never. Never let him look upon us with his eyes."*

> * The Soudanese, indeed all Easterns, have a great horror of the "Evil Eye;" and the grey and grey-blue eyes of Europeans in anger, or even in a fixed stare, as I learned later, strike fear, if not terror, into the hearts of most.

Hamza, turning to me, said, "You must know now that our master, Wad en Nejoumi, knew of your coming, and sent us to conduct you to him. His orders were that you should be treated well; he wishes to speak to you. I will give you security until Dongola, where he is waiting for you. I do not know what he will do with you; maybe he will kill you—I cannot say; but, for myself, I promise you will arrive in Dongola alive. If anything happens to you, the Emir Wad en Nejoumi will kill me. Will you promise that you will leave yourself in my hands, will not try to kill yourself, or attempt to escape?" I gave my promise, upon which Hamza said, "Leave this man to me."

The conversation which took place between us was of much longer duration than the above would appear to indicate, but I cannot pretend to remember *all* that was said after the twelve years' interval; the above is the gist of it. I handed Hamza the rifle, and he, taking me by the hand in the Bedawi manner, led me out of the tent, and towards his section of the dervishes. On the way, in a few hurried whispers, he gave me to understand that he was really still a friend of the Government, and that I might trust implicitly in him. On reaching his people, he called four men to attend to me, and sending for Hasseena, told her to prepare such food as I was accustomed to. Hasseena came in rags; her clothes, like mine, had been taken from her. He ordered one of her dresses to be returned, and on my showing him how the skin had been burned off my back and shoulders with the sun, he ordered that I, too, should be supplied with more clothing.

CHAPTER IV
ARRIVAL IN DONGOLA

Instead of our starting off the next morning at sunrise, a sort of "fantasia" was held. This consisted of men riding up and down the camp with mimic combats between individuals—a sort of circus display. Stricter watch was placed over me, and my guards warned against allowing me to hold conversation with any one. At sunset we were off again, and the following day halted in the desert, El Ordeh (Dongola) being then, I was told, a few hours' distant. We rested probably a couple of hours, and marched until evening, but had not yet sighted Dongola. A final search was made for concealed loot, and a piece of my leather bag having been discovered on one of the men, he was flogged, and, offering to confess, confessed that he had found the bag empty on the ground. His clothing, and that of his section was searched, and resulted in the discovery of seventeen of my Turkish dollars; a further application of the courbag resulted in the discovery of the remainder of the three hundred dollars, and a third one, of the greater part of the jewellery. The flogging and searching delayed us, and instead of travelling that night, we only got away in the morning, arriving within sight of Dongola at noon, when men were sent in to report our arrival.

While awaiting the return of the messengers, discipline—what there was of it—was relaxed, and the camp given over to jubilations. The attentions bestowed upon me were not pleasant; both by words and actions I was given to understand what the men hoped and expected would be my fate. A respite was granted, when the man who had received the floggings was brought to me so that I might certify that all the things discovered on him and his companions were extracted from my cash-bag, and that all the articles had been recovered. He seemed none the worse for his experiences, and the matter was explained to me. When the Ansar are flogged, upon an expedition, for a theft which, as the Emirs know, every one would commit, so many stripes are ordered to be given; these are given with the courbag (rhinoceros-hide whip) on the fleshy part of the back, and over the clothing.

He forgave me, and blamed the sugar for his discovery. The sugar-loaves, which were part of the goods of the Arabs who had joined the caravan at Wadi Halfa, had been broken up and distributed. At the wells some of the men had been noticed dipping pieces in the water and munching them, and none of the sugar having been handed in when the loot was collected, the first search was instituted, and this resulted in the discovery of other hidden loot. I do not happen to know who might be the "father of sugar," but I trust that the curses and imprecations showered on his head by my dervish friend may not reach him.

Hasseena was brought to be searched, and stripped naked; she cleverly dropped my seal in the sand, and pressed it in with her foot. I had asked her to get this seal from Elias, as, with this in their possession, the dervishes might have written, through my clerk, whatever letters they chose, and sealing them with my seal, have made them appear authentic. Hasseena was again questioned as to who I was, and persisted in saying that I was a merchant and not a Government official, and while she was being threatened with the courbag, which in this instance would have been applied as the cat-o'-nine-tails is at home, the Emir Hamza came forward as a witness in my favour. Hamza was another who, friendly as he was to the "Government," had been driven into the ranks of the dervishes. After the final search, a move was made towards Dongola, opposite which town we arrived between two and three o'clock in the afternoon. Before the town we descried a grand parade of troops taking place, and as we halted a band struck up; from the sound which reached us, the band must have been composed of bugles and trumpets of all shapes, sizes, and pitch, with just as varied an assortment of drums. In the medley they played could be heard snatches of the so-called Khedivial hymn.

When the prisoners had been ranged up in such a manner as to make their exhibit most effective, and when I, as the prisoner of the occasion, had been placed in the midst of the Emirs, a signal was given, on which the horsemen of the paraded army charged down upon us in their much-lauded and over-rated exhibition of horsemanship. This exhibition consists of individual and collective charges right on to the opposing line of onlookers, a sudden pulling up of the horse which throws it on to its haunches, a meaningless shaking of swords and spears over one's head, a swerve to the left or right, the direction being dominated by the half-broken jaw for which the sudden pulling up with the brutal ring-bit with which the horses are ridden (?) is responsible; another charge, and so on until the rider is tired or the horse jibs. This is the usual programme, but it is occasionally varied by accidents to horses and riders and onlookers, as, for example, the affair of

Khaleefa Ali Wad Helu, who, some few days before the battle of Omdurman, gave an inspiriting exhibition to the faithful in front of the Mahdi's tomb, in order to instruct them how to charge the British lines, and spoiled the whole thing by being thrown, breaking his wrist, laming the horse, and nearly killing half a dozen of his most ardent admirers who were in the front rank. This is not fiction.

THE KHALEEFA'S TENDER MERCIES.

The parade and exhibition, called El Arrdah, given in celebration of our capture, lasted more than an hour, when a move was made towards Dongola, and on arrival at the town, Wad Hamza and Wad Farag led me to the gateway of Nejoumi's enclosure. We were kept waiting at the entrance for some time, and it was as much as my guards could do to protect me from the rabble; the people were in a most excited state, and my position was not rendered any the more comfortable by my understanding the language. I was prodded with spears and swords, and maybe for a quarter of an hour—it may have been more, it may have been less—I was subjected to as severe an ordeal for patience as ever man was put to. Many of those in the rabble knew me from pre-abandonment days, but the cringing supplicants of former days were now my bitterest foes and tormentors. Curses and imprecations are such common accompaniments in ordinary disputes in the East—disputes over the most trivial matters—that little new could assail my ears in a country where a child just learning to babble may be heard, in childish innocence, to lisp to its mother, "Il la'an abook," or a much shorter expression which, owing to the large number now understanding Arabic, I cannot here use, but both of which expressions are in constant use. It was the suggestive actions—some of beheading, some of mutilations, others of a description which I may not even hint at, which nearly drove me to exasperation; they did so actually, but I controlled myself, and did not allow my exasperation to exhibit itself in any way, either by word or deed.

On entering the enclosure, I was shown to a small room, on the floor of which three people were sitting; one rose, and, taking my hand, said, "El Hamdu lillah," "Bis-Salaamtuk" (thanks be to God for your safety). I was told to sit down. The three scrutinized me, and I returned their gaze. For some moments nothing was said, and I was determined not to be the first to break the silence. Presently food was brought in, and I was told to partake of it. As with the first meal with the Emirs, I set to with a will, and continued eating after the others had finished, taking not the slightest notice of my hosts. I was acting a part, I admit, for indifferent as I might have appeared to all taking place around me, I was at the same time "all eyes and ears."

When I had finished, the one who had first spoken to me, and whom I had guessed was Nejoumi, "introduced" himself to me. He prefaced the series of questions he put to me by saying, "Do not be afraid; I hope it will be my pleasure to receive you into the true religion, and we shall be good friends." Nejoumi assured me that I should soon get accustomed to my new mode of life, and would in the end bless him for having saved me. He then told me that he knew perfectly well who I was, and, not being a "Government man," my life was safe at his hands, but my property, having been found in a caravan of enemies, must be confiscated. I did not follow his reasoning, nor was I allowed to, for he sent me off to the house of the Amin Beit-el-Mal (storekeeper or director of the

Beit-el-Mal), with instructions that I should be well attended to. Hasseena was sent into the hareem of the same house.

Early the next morning Nejoumi sent for me, and upon arriving at his enclosure, I saw that he had a number of Sheikh Saleh's men under examination. I learned later that some had admitted that I was once in Government employ, and had fought against the Mahdi, but that now I was a merchant only. There were, of course, numbers in the town who remembered me in connection with the expedition, and in order to curry favour, they were not averse to credit me with exploits and prowess which, if related to and believed in by the British authorities, would have placed me upon an unearned pedestal. In this instance they were related in the hope that I should be placed on the now well-known "angareeb," which in a few seconds would be drawn away, leaving me suspended by the neck. When my turn for interrogation came, my letter-wallet was handed to Nejoumi; he had, no doubt, had the contents examined the night before. His first question was, "Which are the Government papers?" I declared that there were none, and that all the papers were business ones. He then inquired, "Are there no papers from the friends of the Government?"—to which I answered, "There may be; I am a merchant; I buy gum, hides— anything from the Soudan, and sell them again to any one else who will buy them from me. It is 'khullo zai baadoo' (all the same) to me who the people are—friends or enemies of the Government— provided they pay me. I gave good money for what I bought, and wanted good money for what I sold." Nejoumi then told me that he had had the letters translated by a girl educated in the "Kanneesa" (church) of Khartoum. General Stephenson's letter had been translated as a "firman" appointing me the "Pasha" of the Western Soudan, with orders to wage war on the dervishes, for which purpose I had been provided with money, rifles, and ammunition, and about forty or fifty men as my personal bodyguard.

At first I was dumfounded; then, serious as my position was, I could not restrain myself from bursting out laughing. I protested that the translation was false, and asked to be shown the document. I was not shown it. To a man whom I surmised was the Kadi, I said, "If the letter is a 'firman,' then it should be written in Arabic, as the Soudanese did not read or understand English." This remark appealed to Nejoumi, who said that he did not believe the translation himself, *as it was quite different from the news he had received from Hassib-el-Gabou.* I made inquiries about this black female convert to Christianity, and learned that she knew not a single word of English, but few of Italian, and, like the remainder of such converts so-called, went to the mission for what she could get out of it. I have forgotten her name, but hope to discover it before completing my notes, when I shall give it. It would be interesting to learn how much Christian money had been wasted on the education of this supposed convert, married then to a Danagli, and a shining light amongst the most fanatical of the women, who, with their songs and dances, fanned the flame of fanaticism amongst the men.

More of Saleh's men were brought in and questioned—I questioned with them. In the end, I admitted that General Stephenson's letter asked me, if I was passing Sheikh Saleh's district, to tell him that arms and ammunition were awaiting him at Wadi Halfa; but that I had nothing to do with the sale of them, was proved by my arriving after they had been taken over, and my papers would show that I had not sold them to him, and that I was not going to collect the money for them, as they believed. The remainder of that conference is only a haze to me now, but I remember that later the same day I was told that Nejoumi, pressed by the other Emirs, had, in order to elicit the truth by frightening the others, ordered the execution of fourteen of the Arabs who had joined us at Wadi Halfa. Emin, my guide, for some reason or another which I never discovered, was ordered to be executed at the same time, and was first to be beheaded. My surmises upon this incident had better be left to my next chapter.

On the following morning, the Amin Beit-el-Mal ordered me to get ready to attend a "fantasia" which Wad en Nejoumi had arranged, and at which he had ordered me to be present; but, being his prisoner, I must appear as one, for which purpose a light ring and chain was placed on my neck, and a light chain fastened to my ankles. On arrival at Nejoumi's place, I found the Kadi trying to persuade Darb es Safai and about twelve or thirteen of Saleh's men to become Mahdists. Darb es Safai was their spokesman. They scorned the exhortations of the Kadi, and heaped on his head whatever insults they could. Nejoumi was present, and to him Darb es Safai said, "We have ridden behind our master, Sheikh Saleh, and we refuse to follow you on foot as slaves; we have come here to die—let us die." Being told that if they persisted in their stubbornness they would be killed, Darb es Safai repeated, "We have come to die—let us die." I was then removed to a small mud hut, told to sit down, and here hundreds of the populace came to see me, flinging at me all the abuse their rich language is capable of, striving with each other to excel in virulence. Darb es Safai and the others had been marched off a short distance, and set to dig a shallow trench; when this was finished, they were ordered to kneel at its edge, and their hands were tied behind them; this action is practically the declaration of the death sentence. Es Safai asked to be beheaded last, as he wished to see how his men could die. Only one jumped to his feet when a few heads had rolled into the trench, when Es Safai called out, "Kneel down. Do you not see these cowards are looking at us?" This was the "fantasia" I was to have assisted at, but, by some misunderstanding, I was spared the horrible spectacle.

When the executions were over, my chains were removed, and I was again taken before Nejoumi, and questioned as to what property I had in the caravan, and also if I had any slaves. I said I might not possess slaves, but had two servants—Elias, my clerk, and Hasseena, who was a freed slave, and now my female servant. Elias had been cross-examined, but had evidently, in his fright, contradicted himself time after time. First he said he was my clerk, then he was the servant of some Ali Abou Gordi of the Alighat tribe, then trading in the Soudan. Nejoumi told me that, if Elias's last tale was true, he could not be returned to me, as he must be an enemy. I did my best for Elias, telling Nejoumi that he was a good clerk and good writer, and that he might be very useful to him in writing letters. Hasseena was brought in and protested that she was my slave, not my servant; that I had bought her, but, as slaves were not allowed by the Government, I had had to give her a *shehaada* (certificate) declaring her free. Nejoumi made a present of her to one of the men present, and on this Hasseena squatted on the ground and refused to budge. She screamed to Nejoumi that he might, if he chose, marry her himself, but said that whoever her husband might be, he would die the same night, since she knew how to poison people secretly. She knew nothing whatever about poisons, but this remark probably was the reason for her being sent to the Khaleefa, as she might be useful. She was sent back as "property" to the Beit-el-Mal.

My ordeal was not yet over; other chiefs came in, and the conference opened soon developed into a heated, if not acrimonious, discussion and dispute. I did not know Soudani sufficiently to follow all that was said, besides which three or four were speaking rapidly at the same time; but I gathered that Nejoumi wished to keep me by him, as he believed that I might be made useful in signing letters which my clerk would have to write. The others, believing the girl's translation of the letter, were for despatching me to the next world, and sending my head as a gruesome present to the commandant at Wadi Halfa, accompanied by the supposed "firman." It is not a pleasant experience to sit down and hear your fate being discussed, conscious that the sentence will be carried out immediately. No criminal ever scanned the face of a jury on its return to court as I did those of my savage captors, with ears strained to catch every familiar word; and, difficult as it is after all these years to attempt to give a real analysis of one's feelings then, I can remember gloating over the thought that, if death were the sentence, I would spring at the throat of the first Emir I could reach, with my nails buried in and tearing at the flesh, until a blow would finish all, and so rob the fanatical horde outside of the pleasure of seeing a hated "Turk" publicly executed. That the recollection is no imaginary one may be guessed from the fact that, when I asked about Gabou's "health" at Assouan after my release, one part of that conjured scene sprang up, and doubtless would have been acted, had Gabou been alive.

Nejoumi only partly won his point—I was to be sent to the Khaleefa. Seven men were sent for, and Hasseena and I placed in their charge. Nejoumi gave me some clothing, and also a hundred dollars from the three hundred taken from me, and we were ordered off that night.

CHAPTER V
THE REAL HISTORY OF THE CAPTURE

(Extracts.)

"He (Nejoumi) captured in the Oasis of Selima a large part if not the whole of the rifles. This was mainly owing to the imprudence of an enterprising German merchant named Charles Neufeld, who had accompanied the convoy, and, desirous of obtaining a supply of water, had descended to the Oasis, where he was captured by the enemy."

". . . Most of them were killed, and a few, including Neufeld, were taken captive to Dongola; there they were beheaded, with the exception of Neufeld, who was sent to Omdurman, where he arrived on March 1, 1887."

March 21, 1887.—"Sixty Kabbabish have arrived, sent by their chief to take over arms and money."

May 15, 1887.—"Mr. Neufeld is reported to have diverged from caravan of Kabbabishes to Sheikh Saleh to Bakah Wells, and to have been taken prisoner by the dervishes, as well as a few Kabbabish letters are said to have been captured; none from this office were entrusted to him" (Blue Book No. 2, 1888—Nos. 50 and 90).

"Neufeld was now free. His release was owing to one of the Emirs representing to Abdullah Khalifa the great service Neufeld had been in enabling arms and ammunition to be taken from the Kabbabishes at the time Neufeld was captured" (Letter to Mrs. Neufeld from War Office. Cairo, 10.3.90).

It would be as well to give at once the real history of my capture as regards the circumstances and the arrangements made to effect it. I received the details first from Ahmed Nur Ed Din, who, some months after my capture, came to Omdurman on his own initiative to try and effect my escape. His version was confirmed and amplified by my intended companion Hogal, who again fell into the hands of the dervishes in 1897, and was imprisoned with me until we were finally released a few months ago.

The treachery of Gabou has also been confirmed by Moussa Daoud Kanaga, who has just arrived from the Soudan to meet me, he having heard of my release and arrival at Cairo. Moussa was one of the Soudan merchants with whom I had had many dealings in former days, and believing he could do something towards effecting my escape, he, after many attempts to reach me, finally succeeded in doing so in September, 1889.

Instead of wearying my readers with snatches from one narrative and the other, I will try, combining all, to make one clear and connected story, having for this purpose deleted from the last chapter remarks and questions put to me by Nejoumi at Dongola in order to introduce them here.

The guide I had engaged for the journey, Hassib-el-Gabou, belonged to the Dar Hamad section of the Kabbabish tribe which was settled in and around Dongola. Gabou was employed as a spy by the military authorities on the frontier, but there is not the slightest doubt that he was at the same time in the pay of Wad Nejoumi. He related to each side just sufficient to keep himself in constant good grace and pay, and failing authentic news of any description, he was able to fall back upon his intimate local knowledge, his double dealings, his knowledge of the people and language, and a fund of plausibility which at the present day would not pass current for five minutes.

Between the Dar Hamad section, and the section acknowledging Saleh Bey Wad Salem as their head, there were a number of old outstanding jealousies which had not been settled; what they were all about I cannot pretend to say, but one of the principal was, whether Sheikh Saleh or the head of the Dar Hamads should be considered the senior. It may not have been forgotten by those who have taken an interest in Soudan affairs, that the existence of these tribal jealousies and disputes between divided tribes was taken full advantage of by the Mahdi and Khaleefa, in very much the same way as a political agent runs one section of a party against another, and gains *his* point, at the cost and discomfiture of the others who, for the time being, were unconsciously playing his game for him. Sheikh Saleh's party were the real Bedawi (men of the desert), and, therefore, more reliable than the Dar Hamads, who had the "belladi" (town) taint or stigma attached to them.

Gabou's first plan was, according to his lights, to act loyal to his section of the tribe, and so to arrange matters that the arms intended for his rivals, Sheikh Saleh's section, should fall into the hands of his people; with those arms turned against the dervishes, he might see his section come to the front as *the* support of the

Government, and maybe be in possession of the coveted title of Bey and a Nishan (decoration), if his plans succeeded. I have no doubt that, had his first plan succeeded, he would have been prepared with a plausible tale, and gaining any slight advantage over the dervishes would certainly have atoned for his defections. His plan as originally conceived was as follows:—First, he wrote to his own sheikh giving him full details of the arms and ammunition awaiting Saleh's caravan, and there is every reason to believe that the letters sent by General Stephenson to Sheikh Saleh in the first instance, were delayed by Gabou until his plans were complete. The guide Hassan, whom I believed had been engaged at the last moment, had been engaged some time before, and fully instructed in the part he had to play. Gabou had promised his people that after Sheikh Saleh's caravan left El Selima Wells, they would be led towards the Wadi el Kab instead of El Agia Wells, so that even had we filled our water-skins at leisure at Selima, we should only have been provided with four, instead of eight days' water, and two days on the desert without water has its discomforts. When a Bedawi will travel two or three days without water and not murmur, it can be better imagined than described what Gabou's promise to hand us over "thirsty" meant; it meant precisely what actually did occur—the madness of thirst approaching—the lips glued together, the tongue swollen and sore in vain attempts to excite the salivary glands—the muscles of the throat contracted, and the palate feeling like a piece of sandstone, the nostrils choked with fine sand, and the eyes reddened and starting, with the eyelids seeming to crack at every movement. Only those who have experienced what we did during those last days on our journey to Wadi el Kab, can fill in the missing details in the history of Esau selling his birthright for a mess of pottage.

The Dar Hamads, on receiving Gabou's news, made their preparations; arms buried in the ground to conceal them from the dervishes were unearthed, but the very evident activity of the people excited the suspicions of Wad Nejoumi. Believing that a revolt was intended, he prepared to meet it; but, having his spies about, bits of the real truth leaked out. Gabou was put to the test; either written messages or messengers were sent to him by Nejoumi, asking about Saleh's caravan and the purposes for which they had gone to Wadi Halfa. When Gabou saw that his first scheme had miscarried, rather than the caravan should fall into the hands of his rivals, he preferred to reveal to Nejoumi the plot he had planned for the benefit of his own people. It was on this account that he had, as related, tried at one time to get me to abandon the projected journey; and, as can be understood, there were many reasons for his sending word to Nejoumi saying I was to accompany the caravan. His keeping back of Ismail, the leader, day after day, was only to allow of his messages reaching Nejoumi in time for him to make complete preparations for intercepting us.

Hogal arrived at Wadi Halfa the very evening of our departure, and sent over his message. Gabou met him and gave him his confidence. He told Hogal the means he had used to try and get me to abandon the journey, but that he dared not give me the real reasons, as he knew I should report the matter, and his head would then be in danger; he had done the best he could by letting Nejoumi know who and what I was. Still dexterously playing his cards, and to keep Hogal quiet, he said that he knew that the English were going away; they certainly would not take him with them, and as he and Hogal had their family ties in the Soudan, unless he worked with Nejoumi, his "good word" would be of no avail to his family and friends when the dervishes came down to occupy the abandoned towns.

I trust that my readers are now beginning to see the light through this dark conspiracy, and that I am making the narrative sufficiently intelligible and clear without constantly requesting you to turn back to earlier pages.

Gabou, playing a double part himself, and being naturally suspicious of every one in consequence, thought that I might have divined his treachery when the camels did not overtake us, and might change our route in consequence; these suspicions he communicated to Nejoumi. Had he not done this, I might have forgiven him—for it was every one for himself in those days. There was not the least necessity for him to warn Nejoumi that we might change our route on discovering that the guide was leading us in the wrong direction, for had Nejoumi's men *not* found us, Gabou would not have been blamed.

Nejoumi, on receiving the news, despatched a large number of dervishes under Wad Bessir to Umbellila, opposite Abou Gussi, and another under Osman Azrak to El Kab opposite to El Ordeh (Dongola), and Said Mohammad Wad Farag, Mohammad Hamza, Makin en Nur and Wad Umar to the various wells in the Wadi el Kab, the latter having orders to keep the Dar Hamads in check. I am giving this list of now famous names from recollections of what I was told at Dongola and Omdurman, not for the purpose of thereby investing with a halo of barbaric romance an incident which was nothing more nor less than a bit of highway robbery, but more with the idea, that should any of those named be still living, and eventually come into the hands of the Government, they might be questioned as to this affair, and their account compared with the series of contradictory passages which head the present chapter.

Wad Farag sent a flying party to Selima Wells, led by a slave of Wad Eysawee, named Hassib Allah. It was Hassib Allah who had fired the shot we heard on the day of our arrival at Selima. When taken before Wad Nejoumi at Dongola, one of the questions put me was, "Did you see any one, or hear a shot fired the day you reached Selima," to which I answered "Yes," as regards the latter part of the question, thereby making an everlasting friend of Hassib Allah, as a reward had been promised to whoever should first sight us and hurry back to the main body with the news; he had fired the shot, so that the question might be put. Even in this you may gauge the amount of faith or confidence the Ansar had in the word of their Emirs, and the amount of credence a European might give to their tales when they lied to, and deceived each other with such charming impartiality.

After despatching Hassib, Wad Farag divided his party, sending one to the district between Wadi el Kab and the Nile, and the second, commanded by himself, he led to the desert to intercept us. The Alighat Arab sent out as a scout, who did not return, must have either been captured by Farag, or what is more likely, as he was sent out by Hassan, was an emissary of Hassan's to Wad Farag or any of the other dervishes to give them the news, as Hassan must have been aware of our position and the proximity of the dervishes. The tracks we had picked up on the road, when the embers of the caravan's fires were found still hot, were the remains of the fires of Hassib's men, who had kept within touch of us the whole time, only losing touch on the day following the disappearance of the Alighats.

On reaching the broken ground leading to El Kab, my guide Amin and the two others had been allowed to pass unchallenged intentionally, as the dervish plan was to form themselves into three parties, which were to rush us from three sides at the same moment. It was in direct disobedience of orders that the first shots were fired at us, but it was probably done by some one to gain the promised reward for sighting us, and it ended, as already related, in a general fusilade. The camels loaded with filled water-skins were left behind purposely, but their being left was a happy thought at the moment of Farag's men. When they retired, it was only to join the other section which was to have rushed us from the left; the section to rush us in the rear being a little further out in the desert than the plan shows.

Our leader Ismail I never saw or heard of again; he may have succeeded in escaping altogether, only to be killed when the virtual extermination of the tribe took place and Sheikh Saleh, standing on his sheepskin, fell fighting to the last.

This account of the capture of the caravan, and the explanations given, though not agreeing in essentials with the accounts given officially, may be accepted as being as nearly correct in every detail as it is possible for memory to give them, and the occasion was one of those in life where even twelve years' sufferings are not sufficient to obliterate the incidents from the mind.

I feel some little confidence in offering to the world my version of the circumstances attending my departure from Wadi Halfa for Kordofan, the date upon which I really did leave Egypt—as unfortunate a date for me as it evidently has been to some of my biographers,—and the actual circumstances attending my capture, as I happened to be present on the various occasions spoken of, and I do not think it will be asking too much if I request that the same amount of credence be given to my own story as has been given to that of others referred to in my introduction, and in the extracts which head the present chapter.

It now remains, before closing this chapter, to deal with Dufa'allah Hogal and his part in the affair. In my first letter from Omdurman, which letter was written for me by dictation of the Khaleefa, I am made to say that I blamed Hogal for his deceit, but at the same time thanked him for his deceit, as it had led me to grace. This was a clever invention of the Emir's at Dongola, or the Khaleefa himself, to get Hogal into trouble with the Government, and draw away suspicion from Hassan and Gabou. This letter was received by one of my clerks at Assouan, who fortunately retained a copy before forwarding it on to Cairo; a translation of it will be given later.

Hogal is not to be blamed for keeping his own counsel after Gabou had given him his confidence. He had nothing to gain by telling the authorities the truth, and he had everything to lose if he did. The Khaleefa's spies were everywhere in the Government and out of it, just as the Government spies were amongst the Mahdists, and there can be no doubt but that they were paid by both sides—

and who is to blame them? Hogal's family ties and relations were in the Soudan, and there was no use in his raising a question over a dead man. I may have something to say about guides and spies later on, but it will not be with the idea of calling any of them to justice. The only justice they knew of was that contained in "Possession is nine points of the law," or "Might conquers right," and it suited their natures admirably to play a double game, rendered so easy for them with a Khaleefa who, having made up his mind to do a certain thing, ever kept that object in view, and worked for its accomplishment, whilst on the other hand was a Government which in their opinion did not seem to know its own mind from one day to another as to what should be done with the Soudan and its subjects resident there.

CHAPTER VI
DONGOLA TO OMDURMAN

During the early part of the night of April 27, the Amin Beit-el-Mal told me to prepare for my journey to Omdurman, as Wad Nejoumi had sent for me. There was little preparation I could make, except to beg some sesame oil to rub over my face, shoulders, back, and feet. The woollen shirt and clothing I had been allowed had not been sufficient to protect me against the burning rays of the sun, and the skin was peeling away from my face, shoulders and back, while my feet were blistered and cut. My stockings had been worn through in a day's tramping through the sand. Taken to Nejoumi's enclosure, Nejoumi and I sat together talking for a considerable time. He told me that he had wished to keep me by him for the purposes of "akhbar" (information, or news), but that the other Emirs had insisted upon my being killed at once, or sent to the Khaleefa with the supposed "firman" appointing me "The Pasha of the Western Soudan," to be dealt with by the Khaleefa at Omdurman. Nejoumi said he had written asking that I should be sent back to him. He put to me many questions about the Government, the fortifications of Cairo and Alexandria, Assouan, Korosko and Wadi Halfa, and in particular he was anxious to know all about the British army and "Ingleterra." The advance up the Nile for the relief of Gordon had evidently given him a very poor opinion of our means of transport, at least as regards rapidity of movement, for when I told him of the distance between Alexandria and England, and assured him that steamers could bring in a large army in a week's time, he smiled and said, "I am not a child, to tell me a tale like that." He may or may not have gone to his grave believing that I was romancing, when I described to him what an ocean-going steamer was like, and did my best to give him some idea of the proportions of a Nile Dahabieh compared with an ocean-going steamer and a man-of-war.

SHEIKH ED DIN'S EUNUCH IN HIS MASTER'S
MARRIAGE-JIBBEH.

I left him firmly impressed with the idea, and this impression was
only intensified months later when a number of his chief men were
ordered back to Omdurman and thrown into prison with me, that
had Nejoumi had any one in whom he could repose his confidence
and absolute trust in such a delicate matter, he would have sent in
his submission to the Government, and laying hands upon the
Emirs sent by the Khaleefa to spy upon him—for he was then
under suspicion—would have led his army as "friendlies" to Wadi
Halfa, and have asked assistance to enable him to turn the tables on

the Khaleefa. What further leads me to make such a bold assertion or statement is that the Emirs, or chief men, referred to already as having been thrown into prison with me at Omdurman, gave me, as their fellow-captive, first their sympathy, and then their complete confidence. I learned from them the fate of those of Saleh's caravan whom I had left alive at Dongola. They had, they told me, been executed in batches of varying numbers at intervals of some days, Elias my clerk being the last to be executed, and he not being executed until about two months after my departure from Dongola. Nejoumi, for reasons which will be at once seen, kept him alive to the last, and then doubtless only gave the order for his execution when, despairing of my being sent back to him, he gave way to the importunities of the other Emirs anxious to see the last of Saleh's people executed.

From what they confided to me, there could not be the slightest doubt that a conviction of the imposture of the Mahdi's successor was growing and spreading amongst the Mahdists; but the system of espionage instituted by the Khaleefa nipped in the bud any outward show of it. There can be also no doubt that these confidants of Nejoumi had, in some way, compromised themselves when speaking in the presence of some of the Khaleefa's agents, and that Nejoumi himself had only not been ordered back with them because of his popularity and the Khaleefa's fear and jealousy of him. There was no one whom Nejoumi, or, for the matter of that, any one—not even excepting the Khaleefa himself, might implicitly trust in the Soudan. The man to whom you gave your innermost confidences might be friend or foe, and as all changed face as rapidly and constantly as circumstances dictated, it would be safe to say that no one in the Soudan for a single moment trusted any one else.

Whatever Nejoumi's convictions may have been in the earlier days of the Mahdist movement, it is certain that they underwent a great change. Indeed, his advance against the Egyptian Army at Toski, when he was killed, was, as I was told by some of his people imprisoned with me after their return, only undertaken when he was goaded to it by the reproaches of the Khaleefa, accusing him of cowardice and treachery, accompanied with threats of recalling him to Omdurman—and Nejoumi knew well what this implied.

In the last chapter I remarked that I would later offer some surmises as to the reason why my guide Amin was the first to be executed at Dongola, and it would be well to insert them here, while speaking of my fellow-prisoners from Nejoumi's army.

Though they could not be positive on the point, they were certain that Amin's two or three passages-at-arms with the guide Hassan had been related to the assembled Emirs at Dongola immediately after our arrival, and Amin was in consequence ordered to be at once executed. I expressed my suspicions as to the actual death of Hassan at El Kab, and in face of what I was told, I cannot help but believe that his falling from the camel was an arranged affair, and that he came with the caravan to Dongola, and gave evidence against Amin. Following up this suspicion or supposition, it is very probable that he originated the "cock-and-bull" story related to the military authorities, detailing the supposed incidents of the capture of Saleh's caravan and myself. It will not have been forgotten that the published official and semi-official records report my capture at two different places a hundred and fifty miles apart, or, in other words, a minimum of five days' journey, and at different dates,—in one instance announcing my arrival at Omdurman as a captive one month before the caravan which I was supposed to have betrayed—or been the cause of the capture of through "imprudence"—had even started from Wadi Halfa.

In the early morning of April 28, I and Hasseena were taken outside the town to where the guards and camels were awaiting us, and setting off on our journey, travelled through Hannak, Debbeh, Abou Gussi, and Ambukol. The incidents connected with our appearance at these places are not of sufficient interest to warrant my detaining my readers with them. From Ambukol we struck into the desert, making for the Nile at Gebel Roiyan, enduring the inevitable discomforts and privations of such a journey. On arrival at the village near Gebel Roiyan, we took possession of what we believed to be a deserted house, and, after taking a little food, lay down to sleep. During the night a wretched old woman crept into my room, and commenced that peculiar wailing known to those who have been in the East. She was, she said, "El umm Khashm-el-Mus" (the mother of Khashm-el-Mus—but the expression may be taken to imply merely that she was one of Khashm-el-Mus's family or relatives), whom Gordon had sent with gunboats to Metemmeh to accompany Sir Charles Wilson on his voyage to Khartoum. Her sons, the whole of her family (or tribe), had been killed by the Khaleefa's order, and, as far as she knew, she was the only one left. Taking no notice of my guards, who had come in, attracted by the wailing and talking, she cursed the Mahdi, and every thing and every one connected with him. The wailings of the poor creature, her pinched, sunken cheeks, her glistening eyes, her skinny, hooked fingers, her vehement curses on the Mahdi and

Khaleefa, and the faint glow from the charcoal embers which only served to outline the form of the old woman as some horrid spectre as she stood up and prophesied my death, completely unnerved me. If there was one night in my life upon which I required a few hours' rest it was on this—the last, as I knew, before my entering Omdurman. But no sleep came to my eyes that night. Soon after the woman left, a sound of dull thuds, a shriek, a moan, and then silence told its own tale. She had been battered to death with curses on the Mahdi on her lips.

The night was one long, horrible, wakening nightmare, but all was real and not a fantasy of the brain. How I longed for the dawn! and how impatiently I waited for it! For the first time I had fears for my reason. The sensation I felt was as if a cord had been slipped round my brain, and was gradually but surely tightening. But enough of this; it is not necessary to interlard my experiences with painful mental sensations, real as they were.

It was with some little difficulty that I shuffled my way to the camels next morning, to mount and get away on our last stage of the journey to Omdurman. We reached the town at noon, on Thursday, May 5, and passed in almost unnoticed until we reached the market-place, when the news having spread like wildfire, we were soon surrounded by thousands of people, and it was with the greatest difficulty we fought our way to the open praying-ground adjoining the burial-place of the Mahdi. (The tomb had not then been built.) Here I was placed in the shade of the rukooba. (The rukooba is a light structure of poles supporting a roof of matting and palm branches, in the shade of which the people rest during the heat of the day.) Two of my guards went off to deliver Wad Nejoumi's despatches to the Khaleefa, and also to announce my arrival.

Shortly afterwards, Nur Angara, Slatin, Mohammad Taher, and the chief Kadi, with others, came to question me. Slatin addressed a few words to me in English, but not understanding him, I asked him to speak in German, upon which he said in an undertone, "Be polite; tell them you have come to join the Mahdieh in order to embrace the Mahdi's religion; do not address me." Nur Angara, who put the majority of the questions, asked, "Why have you come to Omdurman?" I hesitated a little before replying, but did not hesitate long enough to allow my European blood to cool sufficiently to reply "politely" to the imperious black confronting me. I told him, "Because I could not help myself; when I left Wadi Halfa it was to go and trade and not fight, but your people have taken me prisoner, and sent me here; why do you ask me that question?" Slatin at this moved behind the other Emirs, and I believe made some attempt to make me understand that I should speak differently to them. My helplessness was galling to me; there was not a man there whom, pulled down as I was, I could not with sheer strength have crushed the life out of.

I was questioned about the number of troops at Wadi Halfa and Cairo, the fortifications, etc., but neither places would have recognized the fortresses I invented for the occasion, and the numbers of troops with which I invested them. When told that news had been received from Wad Nejoumi that the British troops were leaving, I admitted the truth of this, but said that they could all be brought back to Wadi Halfa in four days. All the questions, or nearly all, were in connection with the army and the movement of the troops, and this will be understood when it is remembered that, by some, I was believed to be "Pasha," and all Pashas in the Soudan were military leaders.

I have been shown a statement to the effect that my readiness to talk "made a bad impression," but this remark was not, at the time of writing, sufficiently explanatory—and yet it may have been. Other captives had grovelled at the feet of their captors; I did not, hence probably the "bad impression" created; and while the world may blame me for being so injudicious as to treat my powerful captors with such scant courtesy, it can hardly be expected that I, even had I not passed six years in close connection with the British Army on the field of battle, and in times of comparative peace, should in a moment forget and lose my manhood, and cover with servile kisses the hands of a savage black—and one of the murderers of Gordon to boot. I thank God, now that I am restored to "life," that my first appearance as the Khaleefa's captive "made a bad impression," for even in this I choose to accept an evidence that I was not what I have in some instances been represented as being.

On the Emirs and others leaving me, some dervishes advanced, stripped me of the jibbeh and clothes given me by Nejoumi, replacing them with a soldier's old jersey and cotton drawers. My feet were next fettered, and a ring, with a long heavy chain attached, was fastened round my neck. During that evening— indeed, during the whole night, crowds came to look at me, while the ombeyeh (war-trumpet made from a hollowed tusk) was sounded the whole night through. A woman, a sort of Mahdist amazon, walked and danced up and down in front of me, singing and gesticulating, but I could not catch the full meaning of her words. Noticing Hasseena sobbing violently a few yards away, I called to her, and asked what was the matter with her. She told me that the ombeyeh was calling up the followers of the prophet to come and witness my execution, and that the woman, in her rude rhyme, was describing my death agonies, and my subsequent tortures in hell as an unbeliever. One of my guards told me that what Hasseena had related was true, and I had curiosity enough to ask him the details of an execution; these having been described to me, I refused food and drink. I was determined to deprive the fanatics of one looked-for element connected with my execution—but I may not enter into details.

At dawn the following morning, a dervish came to me, and crossing my right hand over the left at the wrists, palms downward, proceeded to bind them together with a rope made of palm fibre. When the ropes had, with a bit of wood used as a tourniquet, been drawn well into the flesh, water was poured over them. The agony as the ropes swelled was excruciating; they "bit" into the flesh, and even now I cannot look at the scars on my hands without a shudder, and almost experiencing again the same sensations as those of twelve years ago.

With the perspiration rolling off me with the pain I was enduring, and no longer able to conceal that I was suffering, I was led forth to be the sport of the rabble. Made to stand up in the open space, bareheaded, with thousands around me, I believed the moment for my decapitation had come, and muttering a short prayer, I knelt down and bent my head, but was at once pulled to my feet again; the populace wanted their sport out of me first. Dervishes rushed at me prodding with spears and swords, and while this was going on, two men, one on each side of me, with the mouths of their ombeyehs placed against my ears, blew their loudest blasts. One powerful man in particular, with a large spear, gave me the idea that it was he who had been told to give the final thrust, and when he had made a number of feints, I tried in successive ones to meet the thrust. One of the men guarding me, taking the chain attached to the ring round my neck, pulled me back each time, much to the delight of the assembled people.

The ropes with which I was bound had now done their work; the swollen skin gave way, and the horrible tension was removed as the ropes sank into the flesh. If I had exhibited any feeling of pain before, I was now as indifferent to it as I was to the multitude around me. A messenger of the Khaleefa, Ali Gulla, asked me,

"Have you heard the ombeyehs?"—a bit of the Khaleefa's supposed pleasantry, when it was by his orders that the mouths of the instruments had been placed against my ears. On nodding my reply, Gulla continued, "The Khaleefa has sent me to tell you that he has decided to behead you," to which I replied, "Go back to your Khaleefa, and tell him that neither he nor fifty Khaleefas may so much as remove a hair from my head without God's permission. If God's will it is, then my head shall be cut off, but it will not be because the Khaleefa wills it." He went to the Khaleefa with this message, and returned saying, "The Khaleefa has changed his mind; your head is not to be cut off; you are to be crucified as was your prophet Aisse en Nebbi" (Jesus the Prophet); after saying which, he told my guards to take me back to the rukooba while preparations were made.

By this time, what with the fatigue and privations on the journey, my head almost splitting as the result of the ombeyeh's blasts, the agony caused by the ropes binding my wrists, and the torture of scores of small irritating and stinging flies attacking the raw flesh of my hands, and the sun beating down on my bare head, I was about to faint. An hour later, I was ordered off to the place of crucifixion; being heavily chained, I was unable to walk, so had to be placed upon a donkey, on which I was held up by two men. On coming to a halt, instead of the crucifix I had expected, I found a set of gallows. I was lifted from the donkey and placed close to the "angareeb," with the noose dangling just over my head. Pain and faintness at once left me. A few minutes more would end all, and I had made up my mind that that horde should respect me even in my death. I tried to mount the angareeb, but my chains prevented me. A tall black (the chief Kadi of the Khaleefa), placing his hand on my arm, said, "The Khaleefa is gratified at your courage, and, to show this, offers you the choice of the manner of your death." I replied, "Go back to your Khaleefa, and tell him that he may please himself as to what form my death comes in, only if he wishes to do me a favour, be quick about it; the sun burns my brain." To which the Kadi replied, "You will be dead in a few minutes; what will you die as, as a Muslim or a Kaffir?" I was growing desperate, and answered at the top of my voice, "Ed Deen mush hiddm terrayer nahaarda ou Bookra" (Religion is not a dress to be put on to-day and thrown off to-morrow).

My reply, and the manner in which I gave it, I was gratified to see, made him angry. While we were still talking, a man on horseback made his way through the crowd to us, and spoke to the Kadi, who, turning to me, said, "Be happy, there is no death for you; the Khaleefa, in his great mercy, has pardoned you." To which I asked, "Why? Have I asked for his pardon?" for I did not believe for a moment that such was actually the case. I was at once bundled on to the donkey, however, and taken back to the rukooba. Some one had reported to the Khaleefa about the state of my hands, and a man was sent at once with orders to have the ropes removed. Food in abundance was sent me, but this I gave to the ombeyeh men who had escorted me back to the rukooba, and I could even then smile at one of the men who complained that he could not enjoy the food, as his lips—great thick black ones they were, too—were as raw with blowing the ombeyeh all night as my hands were with the ropes.

WRITING UNDER DIFFICULTIES.

On the following day I was taken before the Kadis, with whom was the Khaleefa and Slatin. I was asked, "Why have you come to Omdurman?" to which I gave the same reply as I had given to Nur Angara. The letter of General Stephenson was exhibited to me, and I was asked, "Is this your firman?" to which I replied that it was no firman, but a letter from a friend about business, and that it had nothing to do with the Government. Slatin was told to translate it, but, fortunately, did not translate it all. On his being asked his opinion of me, he told the Khaleefa that from the papers found in my wallet, I appeared to be a German and not an Englishman, but that I had the permission of the English Government to go to Kordofan on merchant's business. He also said that Sheikh Saleh's name was mentioned, but only in connection with business of no consequence. I was then asked if I wished to send any message to my family. Naturally I did, and pen and paper being given me, I commenced a letter in German to my manager at Assouan; but, after a few lines had been written, the Khaleefa said the letter had better be written in Arabic. The letter, when finished, was handed to me to sign; but, not knowing the contents, I scrawled under the signature, as a flourish, "All lies," or something to this effect.

The letter was sent down by one of the Khaleefa's spies, and was delivered to the Commandant at Assouan. The word "Railway" appearing as part of the address, it was sent to Mankarious Effendi, the stationmaster, who, after taking a copy of it for reference, returned it to the commandant, with the address of my manager. Mankarious Effendi, having heard of my recent arrival in Cairo, has come to me with the original copy of the letter taken in June, 1887. The following is a literal translation of it:—

"In the name of the most merciful God, and prayers be unto our Lord Mohammad and his submissive adherents.

"From the servant of his lord Abdallah el Muslimani the Prussian whose former name was Charles Neufeld, to my manager Möller the Prussian in the Railway Assouan.

"I inform you that after departing from you I have come to the Soudan with the men of Saleh Fadlallah Salem el Kabbashi, who were carrying with them the arms and ammunition and other articles sent to Saleh by the Government.

"On our march from Wadi Halfa, notwithstanding our precautions and care for the things in our charge, we arrived at the so-called Selima Wells, where we took sufficient water, and proceeded on our journey. Suddenly we were met by *six* of the adherents in the desert; they attacked us, and we fought against them. Our number was fifty-five men. At the same time, a number of men from Abdel Rahman Nejoumi came up; they reinforced the six men and fought us, and in the space of half an hour we were subdued by them. Some were killed, and the rest were captured with all the baggage we had. Myself, my servant Elias and my maidservant Hasseena were among the captives. All of us were taken to Abdel Rahman Nejoumi at Ordeh, and by him sent to the Khalifat el Mahdi, peace be unto him, at Omdurman. On our arrival at Omdurman, we were taken to his presence, where we were found guilty and sentenced to immediate death; but the Khalifat el Mahdi, peace be unto him, had mercy upon us, and proposed unto us to take the true religion, and we accepted El Islam, and pronounced the two creeds in his presence: 'I testify (bear witness) that there is none but God, and Mohammad is his prophet'; and then, 'I believe in God and his Prophet Mohammad, upon whom God has prayed and greeted; and in the Mahdi, praise, peace be upon him and upon his Khaleefa.' I further requested the Mahdi to grant me the 'bai'a' (oath of allegiance) which he was pleased to grant me, and thereupon shook hands with me. He then named me Abdallah, after embracing the true religion. Therefore I was pardoned by the Khalifat-el-Mahdi from the execution which I have deserved. He pardoned me because he is gracious, and for the sake of the religion of Mohammad which I now adhere to. So I thought it well to inform you all about these events, and I inform you further that Dufa'allah Hogal, although he deceived me, I cannot sufficiently thank him, because his deceiving me has resulted in the great mercy and good which has come to me. Saleh Fadlallah Salem is deserting and hiding in the desert, for fear of his life. All that I have informed you is pure truth. I am still living, thanks be to God for this and my health. 17th Shaaban, 1304 (May 10, 1887)."

It is only now, November 25, 1898, that Mankarious has placed me in possession of the real details. My manager, who when he returned to Egypt a few weeks ago, on hearing of my release, denied ever having received any communication from me, on August 6, 1887, addressed a letter to my father, written on my own business paper, saying that he had received the above letter, had had it translated, and communicated to the *Egyptian Gazette*, which paper published the letter in its issue of August.

Slatin I saw but once again during my long captivity, and then it was only in the distance on one occasion when he called at the prison to give some orders to the head-gaoler. The Khaleefa I saw twice again, on occasions to be referred to later.

After signing the letter, I was taken back to the rukooba, where, about sunset, a man carrying a long chain came to me and said he had orders to remove my fetters. Passing the chain through one of the anklets and round one of the posts, he took a short pole, and used this as a lever to force the anklets open. Whilst still engaged in removing the chains, the chief Kadi came in, and ordered the anklets to be hammered back again, and the ends cold welded.

I remained in the rukooba for the night, and the following morning was placed upon a donkey and taken to the prison. I was told that, to save my life, Slatin had suggested this course being taken, using as an argument that I could there be converted to the Mohammedan religion, and devote all my time to my instructors.

CHAPTER VII
THROWN INTO PRISON

On entering the prison I found myself in the company of about a hundred poor wretches, Soudanese and Egyptians, and all chained. I was taken at once to an anvil sunk in the ground until the striking surface was almost level with it; first one foot and then the other had to be placed on the anvil, while more anklets with chains connected, were fitted to me. I had now three sets of shackles, and another ring and chain was fastened to my neck. During my twelve years in chains, and amongst the hundreds who came directly under my observation, I never saw, as has been illustrated in some papers, any prisoner with chains from the neck connected with the wrists or ankles. All prisoners were shackled in the manner as shown in my photograph; the chain from the neck was allowed to hang loose over the shoulder.

The shackling completed, I was taken to a room measuring about thirty feet each way, but having a pillar about four feet wide to support the roof, thus reducing the actual space to about twenty-six feet between each face of the pillar and the walls. I was assigned a place at the wall furthest from the door, and between two men—in chains—dying of small-pox. There were about thirty other prisoners in the room, some lying down ill, to whom not the slightest attention had been paid for days, as sickening visible evidences proved. Near the roof were a few small apertures presumably for ventilation, but the only air which could come into the place was through the doorway when it was opened. The stench in the room was sickening—overpowering. I had little hopes of surviving more than a few days in such a hole, and must have swooned off soon after entering, for I remember little or nothing until roused after the sun had set, when in the dim light I could see what appeared to be an endless stream of prisoners coming through the door, and no sooner was the door closed when a terrific din and uproar ensued. Mingled with the clanking of chains, the groans of the sick, the moans of the dying, and their half-uttered prayers to Allah to relieve them of their sufferings, were the most fearful imprecations and curses as the prisoners fought and struggled for a place near the walls or the pillar, against which they could rest their backs; no sleep was to be had; this had to be snatched during the day, when allowed out into the zareeba.

It is out of the question to try to describe my first night; it is a confused horrible dream to me.

On the opening of the cell door next morning, I swooned again, and was carried into the open air to come round, and I had no sooner partially done so, when I was carried back, in order, as I was told, "to get accustomed to the place." My first three days passed in fever and delirium; my legs were swelling with the weight of the chains and anklets; my earliest clear recollection was on what I knew later to be the fourth day, when an Egyptian, Hassan Gammal, was sent to attend to me. Later on, the same day, my servant Hasseena was sent to me to prepare food and bathe my legs. Until now I had eaten nothing, and I have no recollection of even taking a drink of water. Hasseena, on my being sent into prison, had been sent into the Khaleefa's hareem; but, on her telling the women and eunuchs that she was with child, she was promptly turned out. The money I had brought with me, and which had been taken from me on my arrival, and sent to the Beit-el-Mal, was given to Hasseena with which to purchase my food. On her entering the prison enclosure, Idris-es-Saier, the head-gaoler, relieved her of the money, saying he would take care of it, and shackling her with a light chain, sent her into his hareem.

I now received permission to sit outside during the day, and also to converse with the other prisoners. On my first entering the prison I had been warned, under threats of the lash, not to speak to any one, and the other prisoners, under the same threat, had been warned not to speak to me. They, as may be guessed, were most anxious to talk to me, and get some news from the outer world, but they were most guarded in their inquiries. There were many prisoners in the place, who, to curry favour with the gaoler or the Khaleefa, would have reported anything in the way of a complaint against their treatment—a wish on the part of any one to escape, or an expressed hope that the Government would soon send troops to release us. Knowing that the Government had, for the time being, abandoned all thoughts of re-conquering the Soudan, I told my fellow-captives, when they spoke to me about a probable advance of the combined armies, that they must have patience until the hot weather passed. Had I told them what I knew, their despair could not have been concealed, and the truth would soon have reached the Khaleefa's ears. A number of the prisoners were old soldiers of the Egyptian army, who had been taken at the fall of Khartoum and elsewhere, and they waited day after day, week after week, and year after year, still hoping that the Government for whom they had fought would send troops to release them; but, with the greater number, their release came only with death—at the gallows, at the Khaleefa's shambles, or by disease and starvation.

Imprisoned at one time with me was Mahmoud Wad Said, the Sheikh of the Dabaanieh tribe, who for years had kept the Abyssinians in check on the Egyptian frontier in the Eastern Soudan. At one time he was powerful, rich in cattle, slaves, and lands, but had been taken prisoner early in the Mahdist movement. When he had been imprisoned about three years and four months, he became paralyzed, and his release was ordered by the Khaleefa, who had so far relented as to allow of his dying with his family, then at Omdurman, patiently waiting for his promised release. By their careful nursing and attention, the old man recovered, only, when the Khaleefa heard of it, to be thrown into prison again, where he passed another thirteen months, at the end of which time he was once more released, on condition that he would collect the remnants of his tribe, and attack his old enemies the Abyssinians, whom the Khaleefa was then fighting with. A few months later I heard that Mahmoud was dead, one report saying that he had died of a broken heart, and the other that he had been "removed" by order of the Khaleefa, for failing to bring together again a tribe, which the Khaleefa himself had almost exterminated.

Another of my companions in adversity was Ajjab Abou Jinn, of the Hammadah tribe; he fought with the Government troops at Sennar, and, when defeated by the dervishes, he retired to his country with his men until, on the fall of Sennar, he was attacked and defeated, his property confiscated, and he taken prisoner to Omdurman, his wife being sent into the Khaleefa's hareem. After spending four years in prison, he was considered sufficiently "educated," and released, and in a few months was allowed to return to his own country, when he set about making preparations to attack the dervishes, and tried all means to get into communication with the Government. Many of his people came to see me in prison, in the hopes of learning news from me of a forward movement.

Shereef.   Zeigheir.   Zeigheir's father.

A GROUP OF PRISONERS.

The three sons of Awad el Kerim, Pasha of the Shukrieh tribe, were also in prison with me; their father had died in prison shortly before my arrival. After keeping the three brothers—Abdalla, Mohammad, and Ali—for nineteen months, the Khaleefa promised to release them on condition that their tribe came to Omdurman and tendered their submission, which they did; but, coming unprovided with food, the tribe in the four or five months they were kept waiting at Omdurman, was decimated by disease and starvation, and then, and then only, the Khaleefa kept his promise, and released their chiefs.

A man whom I almost struck up a real friendship with, was Sheikh Hamad-el-Nil, a well-known religious teacher from the Blue Nile. Having great influence over a large number of people, the Khaleefa, fearing he might obtain a following, ordered him to Omdurman. Here a difficulty arose as to what charge could be brought against him in order to condemn him to imprisonment. Sheikh Hamad had taken neither one side nor the other— Government nor Mahdieh, and had devoted his whole time to a strict preaching of the Quoran, as he had done for years. No Kadi dare condemn him on any charge made, suborn "witnesses" as the Khaleefa would. But the Khaleefa was determined to effect his condemnation by some means, more especially as Sheikh Hamad was rich, and the Beit-el-Mal was short of funds. Men were sent to the Sheikh's house with orders to conceal some tobacco in the ground—others were sent to discover it, and tobacco being forbidden by the Mahdi, Sheikh Hamad, in spite of all protestations, was sentenced by the Kadi to imprisonment and the confiscation of his property. His health broke down after about eighteen months' privations, and he was released; but recovering as did Mahmoud, he was again imprisoned, and died a few weeks later. Of all those in the prison, Sheikh Hamad was the only one who dared say openly to those whom he trusted that both Mahdi and Khaleefa were impostors. Two of my first four years were spent mainly with the Sheikh learning to read and write Arabic, discussing the tenets of the Christian and Mohammedan religions, and telling him of our social life and customs in Europe.

There was one arrival at the prison which I was rather pleased to see—Ahmed Abd-el-Maajid, of Berber, a great supporter of the Mahdi and Khaleefa, and one of the bitterest enemies of Christians and Europeans. He was, for the Soudan, well educated, and he was also rich, and had much influence, but his vanity got the better of him. He gave evidence of his wealth in the richness of his dress and luxurious living, and this had been reported to the Khaleefa, but as yet Maajid had not accepted any of the Khaleefa's pressing invitations to pay him a visit to Omdurman. Maajid made up his mind to marry another wife—a young and pretty one; preparations for the marriage ceremonies, and the feastings which accompany it, were made on a large and lavish scale. The Mahdi had fixed ten dollars as the sum to be paid to the parents of the virgin upon her marriage; but Maajid paid one thousand, and this scouting of the Mahdi's orders coming to the ears of the Khaleefa, he sent off a party to Berber with instructions to bring Maajid and his bride back with them. This party arrived at Berber while the festivities were still going on, and Maajid could not refuse the Khaleefa's invitation this time. When he arrived at Omdurman, he was, with his bride, who was reputed to be the most beautiful woman ever seen in the Soudan, hurried before the Khaleefa and the Kadi. The latter, having his brief ready, accused Maajid of having broken the rules as laid down by the Mahdi, and also of having detained moneys which should have been sent to the Beit-el-Mal, as was proved by his having so much money when the coffers of the Beit-el-Mal were empty. His property was confiscated and sent to the Beit-el-Mal; his bride was taken possession of by the Khaleefa, and Maajid himself sent to prison, where he spent six months, mainly occupied in cursing the face of his bride, as it was this that had brought him to grief. At the end of the six months, he was released and sent back to Berber "educated," with a strong recommendation from the Khaleefa not to be so ostentatious with his wealth in future. The Khaleefa kept Maajid's money—and also his bride. It was this same Maajid, who, after Slatin's escape, ferreted out the people in Berber who had assisted Slatin's guides, and had them sent to the White Nile, where those who did not die on the journey there died later.

Those I have mentioned above were what I might call the better class of prisoners, with whom I mainly associated during my first two years in prison; the remainder were slaves, thieves, ordinary criminals, debtors, murderers, etc.

When I had recovered a little from my fever, I was placed upon a camel, and paraded past the huts, rukoobas, and zareebas, which at that time constituted the town of Omdurman. A number of Hadendowas had come in to tender their submission to the Khaleefa; and he had seized the occasion to exhibit me to the "faithful" as the great Pasha sent to conquer from him the Western Soudan, and to impress the Hadendowas. A halt was made at the hut of the Emir Said Mohammad Taher, a relative of the Mahdi, who, after relating his version of the death of Hicks Pasha, and the destruction of his army, both of which events had, according to him, been brought about through the agency of angels sent by the Prophet for the purpose, gave me a long lecture on Mahdieh, at the end of which he asked me my opinion of it. I told him that if he wished for a few lessons himself on religion, and as to how the God I prayed to dealt with His faithful, and the means His teachers in Europe employed for converting people and making them religious, I should be pleased to give him a few. The reply angered him, and another batch of prisoners were, by his orders, told off to lecture me the whole day long on Mahdieh. While quite ready to talk to them about the Mohammedan religion as propounded in the Quoran, I would not believe in the mission of the Mahdi or his new religion. When Taher asked what progress I had made in my "education," he was told that I would make none in Mahdieh, but was ready to become a Mohammedan. I knew perfectly well what an out-and-out acceptance of Mahdieh meant—my release, but only to be put in charge of some troops, and, as I had fought with the British against the Mahdists, I had no wish to be caught in the dervish ranks, fighting against them, or be found dead on the field, after the fight, in the garb of a dervish, and pierced by a British bullet.

Taher was not pleased, and reported my insubordination to the Khaleefa. It was probably on my fifteenth day that, accompanied by the Hadendowas, who had come in to make their submission, I was taken by steamer to Khartoum, in order that I might be "impressed" with the power of the Khaleefa and the truth of Mahdieh. We were first taken to Gordon's old palace, where Khaleel Hassanein, acting as the Mahdist governor of the town, and at the same time director of the arsenal, received us, and gave us food. We were taken through the rooms, then dismantled, and shown at the head of the stairs what we were told were the bloodstains of Gordon. After this, we were placed on donkeys, and taken round the fortifications, while our "instructors" in Mahdieh, pointing to the skeletons and dried bodies lying about, gave us word pictures in advance of how the fortifications of Wadi Halfa and Cairo would look after the Khaleefa, assisted by the angels, had attacked them. It was a melancholy journey for me; and I am not ashamed to say that as my thoughts flew back to that day at Kirbekan, when, full of hopes, we pictured to ourselves the rescue of Gordon, fortifications and skeletons grew dimmed and blurred, and finally were lost to view, as a hot tear fell upon the back of my hand.

Taken back to prison, I became worse; the weight of the chains and anklets dragging on me as I rode, and the chafing of the skin, set up an irritation, and the filth and dirt of the prison soon contributed to the formation of large ulcers. It was while lying down in the shade one morning, unable to move, at the time of the great Bairam feast, that two camel men rode into the prison enclosure, and, making one of the camels kneel down near me, ordered me at once to mount, as the Khaleefa had sent for me. The other prisoners crowded round and bade me good-bye, Mahmoud Wad Said telling me to pull myself together, and to act as I did "when they tried to burst your head with the ombeyehs." There was a grand parade of the troops that day, and no one but believed that I was to be executed in front of them.

The two men could tell us nothing but that the Khaleefa had sent for me, and, living or dead, they were bound to take me. I was lifted on to the camel, and taken off to the parade-ground outside the town. The long, swinging stride of the camel communicated its motions to my chains, and by the time I reached the Khaleefa, I was in a fainting condition, with the ulcers broken, and their contents streaming down the flank of the camel. The Khaleefa, noticing this, asked one of the Emirs what had happened; although close to him, he would not address a word directly to me, though I could hear what he said, and he could hear my reply. When he heard the reason, he gave orders that the chains were to be removed that night, and a lighter set fitted. The Khaleefa was surrounded by his Emirs and bodyguard, and ranged on the plain in front of us was his great army of horse and camel men, and foot-soldiers. I should have been marched past the whole army, but before reaching the horsemen, the Khaleefa said to the Emir Ali Wad Saad, "Tell Abdalla (myself) that he has only seen a quarter of the army, and let him be brought for the parade to-morrow."

The prisoners were astonished to see me return alive that evening, and still more astonished at the orders given to Idris-es-Saier to remove my chains at once, and put on a lighter set. For once, the Khaleefa's orders could not be carried out; the legs having swollen so much, the anklets almost buried in flesh, could not be brought near enough to the face of the anvil to allow of their being struck at, and the following day I again attended parade in pretty much the same state of collapse as the first. The Khaleefa was furious at this; he had no wish to parade before his troops, as an evidence of his power, a man who had to be held up on his camel. My gaoler was sent to, and asked why he had disobeyed orders. He gave as reasons, first, that he had no lighter chains, and secondly, that my legs were so swollen that he was unable to get at the anklets. The Khaleefa replied that they were to be removed that night, and they were, but it was a terrible ordeal for me. Before leaving the parade-ground, he sent to me Said Gumaa's donkey and Slatin's horse, telling me that I might ride either of them back to town, as their motion would be better for me than the camel, but I elected to remain on the camel.

I had done my best to get near Slatin, to have a few words with him, but he was hardly for a moment near the Khaleefa's side, galloping from one part of the army to another with his orders. Ali Wad Saad, on the part of the Khaleefa, asked me what I thought of the army; to which I replied, "You have numbers, but not training"—a reply which gave little satisfaction to the Khaleefa, who could overhear it without having to wait for Saad to repeat it to him. This was the last time upon which I saw the Khaleefa, but I live in hopes of seeing him once again.

CHAPTER VIII
PRISON LIFE

My first spell in prison was one of four years. After nine months the rings and chains were removed from my neck, but the fetters I wore continuously—with the exception of thirteen days—during the whole of my captivity. A day-to-day record of my experiences is out of the question, besides being unnecessary, even were it possible to give them. I must content myself with a general description of the life passed there, and give an idea of the day's routine.

When I reached Omdurman, the prison proper consisted of the common cell already mentioned ("Umm Hagar"—the house of stone), surrounded by a large zareeba of thorn trees and branches, and standing about six feet high. There were thirty guardians, each armed with a "courbag" (rhinoceros-hide whip) with which to keep their charges in order. There were no sanitary arrangements, not even of the most primitive description. All prisoners had to be fed by their friends or relatives; if they had neither they starved to death, as the prisoners, charitable as they were to each other in the matter of food, had barely enough to eat to keep body and soul together, for the best, and greater part of the food sent in, was eaten by the guardians.

At sunrise each morning the door of the common cell was opened, and the prisoners were allowed to shuffle down to the banks of the Nile, a few yards distant, for their ablutions and for water for drinking. After this, we assembled for the first prayer of the day, in which all had to join. When not working, we had to read the Mahdi's "ratib," a description of prayer-book, containing extracts from the Quoran with interpolations of the Mahdi. All the faithful were ordered to learn this "ratib" off by heart,* and for this purpose each one had either to purchase a copy or write one out. At noon the second prayer was held, followed by another mid-time between noon and sunset, and a fourth at sunset. We should have repeated the night prayer when the night had set in, but as we were driven into the "Umm Hagar" at sunset, the time which should have been given to this prayer was fully taken up with brawls, fights, and those comprehensive curses of the Arabs, commencing with the second person's father, going back for generations, and including all the female ancestors.

* The "Ratib" occupied about three-quarters of an hour in recitation, and, by the Mahdi's orders had to be repeated daily by every one after the morning and afternoon prayer; it ranked in importance with the five obligatory daily prayers ordained by the Quoran. It was also looked upon as a sort of talisman, and it was given out, after such fights as Toski, Ginniss, and the Atbara, that those killed were those who had either not learned the Ratib or had not a copy with them. The book was carried in a small leather case suspended from the neck. A number of copies were printed on the old Government press, but it was considered more meritorious to write out a copy rather than to purchase one, and the Mahdi had hoped that this Ratib would eventually become a sort of Quoran accompanied by its volumes of "traditions," hence his anxiety that every one should learn to write.

LEARNING THE MAHDI'S RATIB.

It has been found impossible, even in the most guarded and disguised language, to insert here a real word-picture of a night in the Saier. The scenes of bestiality and filthiness, the means employed for bringing the most powerful man to his knees with a single blow, the nameless crimes committed night after night, and year after year, may not be recorded in print. At times, and sometimes for weeks in succession, from 250 to 280 prisoners were driven into that small room; we were packed in; there was scarcely room to move our arms; "jibbehs" swarmed with insects and parasites which in themselves made sleep an impossibility and life a misery. As the heat grew more oppressive, and the atmosphere—always vile with the ever-present stench of the place—grew closer with the perspiring bodies, and with other causes, all semblance of human beings was lost. Filth was thrown from one side of the room to the other by any one who could move his hand for the purpose of doing so, and as soon as this disgusting element was introduced, the mass, in its efforts to avoid being struck with it, swayed from side to side, fought, bit, and struggled as far as their packed-in condition would allow of, and kicked with their bars and chains the shins of those next them, until the scene became one that only a Dante might describe. Any prisoner who went down on such a night never got up again alive; his cries would not be heard above the pandemonium of clanking chains and bars, imprecations and cursings, and for any one to attempt to bend down to assist, if he did hear, only meant his going under also. In the morning, when we were allowed to stream out, five and six bodies would be found on the ground with the life crushed and trampled out of them.

Occasionally, when the uproar was greater than usual, the guards would open the door, and, standing in the doorway, lash at the heads of the prisoners with their hide whips. Always when this occurred death claimed its five or six victims, crushed and trampled to death. I wish I might say that I had drawn upon my imagination for what is given above; I can but assure you that it gives but the very faintest idea of what really occurred.

Until we had been set to make bricks and build a wall round our prison, our life, in comparison with what it was later, was I might say endurable. By baksheeshing the guards, we were allowed to go down to the river during the day almost as often as we pleased; and these excursions, taken presumably for the purpose of ablution and drinking, gave us many opportunities of conversing with the townspeople. This life I enjoyed but for a few months. A large number of prisoners succeeded in escaping. Consequently the digging of a well for infiltration water to supply the prisoners, and the building of a wall round the prison were ordered by the Khaleefa to be completed as rapidly as possible.

The prisoners who escaped were mainly slaves, and as most slaves were chained to prevent their running away from their owners—hundreds going about the town fettered—they had little difficulty in effecting their escape from prison, and also from Omdurman. On being allowed to go to the river to wash, they would wade down the bank until they came opposite some large crowd of people, and coming on the bank, their chains would excite no suspicion, for, as I have already said, hundreds similarly fettered were going about the town. Making their way to the nearest blacksmith, he would remove their chains in a few moments for the sake of obtaining the iron, which was valuable to him.

We were not at that time altogether without news; papers published in Egypt were constantly arriving, brought by the Khaleefa's spies, who passed regularly backwards and forwards between Omdurman and Cairo, keeping up communications between the Khaleefa and some of the more fanatical Mohammedans resident at the capital. Since my return I have inquired as to an incident which happened on the frontier in connection with the army some years ago. I shall only relate what we heard, and as given out by the Khaleefa and his Emirs. All the English officers, according to the report received, had been dismissed, and had left with the Sirdar. The English soldiers had also been removed from Egypt; so the Khaleefa was jubilant, and looked forward to the near future when the Egyptian troops would attempt to attack him, and when not a man of them was to be left alive. I was to have been a witness of the great battles when the angels of Allah were to fight with the believers, and assist the Ansar to utterly exterminate the Turks. While this was still the topic of conversation, another messenger arrived to say that the trouble had been arranged; the English officers and troops were not leaving, and as the Khaleefa's hopes fell, ours rose.

Of all the people whom the Mahdi himself appointed to posts, two, and, I believe, two only, retained their positions up to the time of the taking of Omdurman. One was Khaleel Hassanein, the director of the arsenal, and the other Idris es Saier, the gaoler. Idris—for he is still living—is a man of the Gawaamah tribe, a tribe that the first missionary will have some little trouble with, unless he is prepared to revise one of the Ten Commandments out of the Pentateuch altogether, as the following story connected with my gaoler's first appearance in the world may indicate. Idris's mother had a sister who, tired of single blessedness, proposed to, and was accepted by, a swain of the tribe who was a constant visitor to their hut. Idris's mother had also the intention of proposing to the same man, and having told her sister this, the sister popped the question first, was accepted, and then Idris's mother upbraided her after the manner of her tribe, which evidently consisted more of actions than of words. When the happy swain put in his next appearance, Idris's mother, with Idris in her arms, asked him how he dare go against the custom of her section of the tribe, and accept in marriage a girl who had had no children, while she had already had two! "Saier" in the Gawaamah language means "custom" and "customary," and Idris was named Idris es Saier when, in after years, a satisfactory explanation could not be found for his not boasting a father. Idris's mother afterwards married and ruled, with her legitimate son, Saier's family. When appointed as gaoler by the Mahdi, his prison was called "El-Beit-es-Saier" (the house of Saier), which later was contracted to "Saier," and the name eventually replaced the proper word for prison, all prisons being called the "Saier," and the head-gaoler, "Saier."

Idris had been a famous robber and thief, and he was never tired of relating his exploits, and then winding up by pointing out what Mahdieh had done for him, for by his conversion he was now the honoured guardian of all thieves, robbers, and murderers, and there is little doubt but that he had a sneaking regard for all such, as a link between himself and his earlier days.

He was superstitious to a degree, and although the Mahdi and Khaleefa had strictly forbidden fortune-telling and the writing of talismans, Idris followed the example of the Khaleefa himself, and regularly consulted the fortune-tellers, most of his ill-gotten gains going to them in fees. He had had made twenty-five to thirty boards of hard wood, about eighteen to twenty inches square, and on these he had written daily, a Sourah from the Quoran. The ink with which the Sourahs were written was a mixture of wood-soot—or lamp-black, when that could be obtained—gum arabic, some perfume, and water. As soon as the writing was finished, Idris would, after carefully washing his hands, take a small vessel holding about two teacups of water, and carefully wash off the writing, allowing the water to drip back into the vessel; not a drop was to be spilled on the ground, otherwise the writing would have to be done over again, for the name Allah, and many of His attributes, were then in the solution. Having washed the board clean, caught every drop of water, and then drunk it, he would come to us, and deliver himself of the following harangue, and as we heard it two or three times a week for years, I have an almost verbatim recollection of it.

"I am a born thief and robber; my people killed many on the roads, and robbed them of their property; I drank as no one else could, and I did everything possible against rule and religion. The

Mahdi then came and taught me to pray and leave other people's property alone." (This last always raised a bitter smile from his hearers, as he used to torture us to deliver up for "the Khaleefa" any small coin or article of value we might come into possession of.) "How I have to thank the Mahdi for having made me a good, holy, and new man, and he will at the Day of Judgment be my witness, and take me with his ansars to heaven. Think what I have been, and see what I am now! I have been worse than any of you. If you stole anything, you stole when you were with the Government, and you only did what the Government and every one else did, you had authority to do so. I was worse than you, I had no authority. God has pardoned me, and will also pardon you if you repent and give to the Beit-el-Mal what you have taken from the poor, for there are many poor now in the town crying for food, and there is no money in the Beit-el-Mal to purchase any. I have given all my money in charity, and my wives and children are crying for food. I have no boats to bring me merchandise, and I have no land to cultivate to grow dourra" (Sorghum, a grain in the Soudan, which takes the place of our wheat). "I am a prisoner as you are, and the pay I get is not sufficient to feed my family. Yesterday there was no dourra in my house to feed my children, they had to lie down hungry, and I thank God for His grace in supporting me through these trials for which I shall be rewarded in the next world. I am going to see my starving children now, and then I shall pray to God, and ask him to release you if you repent, and turn the Khaleefa's heart to you. The Khaleefa knows everything you do, and sees you all the day, for 'El Nebbi Khiddr' is his eyes and ears, and El Nebbi Khiddr not only sees and hears what you are doing and saying, but sees what your thoughts are."

After this, all but myself used to rise and kiss his hands; I never did so. At the end of the first harangue he gave in my presence, and at the end of his harangues for weeks later, he would continue:— "And now you man from the bad world, you understand Arabic well. The Khaleefa has told me to instruct you in the true religion; your fellow-prisoners will tell you how Hicks Pasha was, with all his army, killed by the angels; not a single shot was fired, or a spear thrown, by the Ansar; the spears flew from their hands, and, guided by the angels, pierced the breasts of the unbelievers, and burned up their bodies. God is great. You will soon learn that you are mistaken, and that all your world is wrong; there is no religion but that of the Mahdi. How happy you should be to have lived in his time and entered into the company of the Ansar. God now loves you; it is He who has brought you to us, and with the Khaleefa's blessing you will yet be numbered with the Ansar, and you will fight against the unbelievers and Turks as other converts have done. You have a strong mind, and the Khaleefa therefore has not a bad opinion of you. Thank him for his mercy that he did not kill you. Be converted, and I shall be pleased and proud of you, and be as your father. You others, you have seen the Mahdi and the Khaleefa and their dealings; tell him of them. You Hamad el Nil, you are a learned man, and know more of religion than I do; make Abdalla know who God is, and who is His prophet."

IDRIS-ES-SAIER.

At the end of my first lecture, Abou Jinn asked me how much money I had. I inquired why. He replied, "Do you not understand? The Saier wants some money from you." I told him of the money Hasseena had, and which the Saier was taking care of, on which he smiled and told me that the Saier would not take the money himself, but he would compel me to *give* it to him for his "starving children." A few days later I was sent for to hear the Saier hold forth again, and on this occasion he finished up by saying that some of us must have done something wrong. The Nebbi Khiddr had reported it to the Khaleefa, who had in consequence ordered him to add more chains to our feet, but that we were to submit to this without bad feelings against the Khaleefa and him. If we repented, the Nebbi Khiddr would report it, and the Khaleefa, as he was full of grace, would soon order the chains to be removed again. All the principal prisoners, with the exception of myself, were then marched to the anvil, and had their chains hammered on. I was spared, as, after the first lecture, I had, on Abou Jinn's advice, sent word to the Saier to take fifteen of my dollars for his "starving children." We prisoners held a conference, and it was decided to present more moneys. It took us two days to scrape together the requisite sum—about fifty dollars—to which I added seventeen of mine. This had the happy result of not only removing the extra chains of the prisoners, but Hasseena's also. The Saier called us together, gave us a homily on repentance and good behaviour, and told us to continue in the same path, as it was evidently looked upon with approval by the Nebbi Khiddr.*

> * The Nebbi Khiddr is a mythical character in Islam. Sects are divided as to whether he is a prophet or not. His name does not appear in the Quoran. By some of the old writers he is made the companion of Noah, Abraham, and Moses. Having drunk of the waters of the Fountain of Life, he is believed by some to be ever present at one of the holy places. His exact whereabouts and his attributes have never been defined. The Mahdi killed two birds with one stone by appropriating this unclaimed prophet to himself; first, his supposed presence made Omdurman a holy place, as the Nebbi only appeared at holy places, and then, by investing him with the powers as related by Idris es Saier, he was able to impress the more ignorant of his followers of his—the Khaleefa's—omniscience and omnipresence through the Nebbi Khiddr's agency. The Mahdi laying claim to this prophet and attributing to him the powers he did, raised in the minds of Hamad-el-Nil and others their first suspicions as to the Mahdi and his mission.

But this Nebbi Khiddr was never satisfied for long with our conduct. Every month he had something to report to the "Khaleefa," and just as regularly we were given extra chains, until a few dollars, entrusted to Idris for the poor, had sent him to the Khaleefa with a favourable report. All these ill-gotten moneys, as I have said, went to soothsayers, fortune-tellers, and talisman writers, in whose absolute power the Saier was, though part went in baksheesh to the servants and counsellors of the Khaleefa, whom the Saier had to keep in funds in order to retain his place.

The Saier knew very well that not a single one of us believed in this Nebbi Khiddr business, but as on the outside of the circle of the principal prisoners—and they were the only ones from whom money could be squeezed—were always gathered a number of the ignorant and, therefore, more fanatical of the Khaleefa's adherents, he had invented this tale, which he gave year after year without the slightest variation in words, in order to hoodwink them and prevent any tales reaching the Khaleefa as to the sums "presented" by the prisoners.

CHAPTER IX
MY FIRST CHANCE OF ESCAPE

It was during my first months in prison that Ahmed Nur ed Din of the Kabbabish succeeded in getting into prison, in the hope of effecting my escape. I had for some years had dealings with Nur ed Din in connection with the Intelligence Department, and also the caravan trade. When I left Wadi Halfa with Saleh's caravan, Nur ed Din was then at Saleh's camp with messages to him from the Government. On his return to Wadi Halfa, he heard of what had happened, and coming at once to Omdurman, he sent a message by my servant that he had come for me. All his applications to get into the prison being refused by the guards, and fearing to make an application to Idris es Saier or the Mehkemmeh, he arranged with a friend to have a petty quarrel in the market-place; his friend hurried him before the Kadi, and Nur ed Din was ordered into prison. On seeing me walk towards him as he entered, as I did not know then that he came as a prisoner, he gave me a "hooss," the Soudan equivalent for our "ssh" (silence), and walked off in another direction. Later in the day, and when we were being marshalled to be driven into the common cell, he came next to me, and whispered, "I have come for you; be careful; keep your eyes open; try and obtain permission to sleep outside the Umm Hagar." Two weeks elapsed before we had another opportunity of exchanging a few words, but in the interval Nur ed Din was ingratiating himself with the prisoners who associated with me, and gradually allowing his curiosity to speak to the "white kaffir" to be evident. It was necessary for him to act in this cautious manner in order to avert suspicion, and another week passed after his introduction to our little circle, before he dare seize an opportunity to consult me about his health and numerous ailments—which was his explanation when questioned about our long conversation together.

It was a strange story he had to tell. On meeting Gabou, Gabou at once commenced to talk to him about some double dealings which he proposed with both dervishes and Government. Nur ed Din was suspicious, and did not fall in with the proposals; this then left Gabou at the mercy of Nur ed Din, and the former picked a quarrel, during which Nur ed Din accused Gabou of the betrayal of the caravan to Saleh. Others of the Kabbabish were already looking askance at Gabou, and wondering whether, if the truth once came out, they too would not be punished as conspirators. Gabou was, they believed, then engaged upon some plot which would render them harmless as regards himself should they make a report against him to the Government, and in self-preservation they held a conference with Nur ed Din. It was proposed that some one, for the honour of the tribe, should try and effect my release or escape from Omdurman, while, as will have been seen, there was also the element of self-interest in the matter. There was now a feud between Gabou and Nur ed Din, and the latter volunteered to undertake the risk of the journey to Omdurman.

His plan, when he saw that there was not the slightest hope of my being released from prison, was a desperate one, and we ran every chance of being killed in the attempt to escape, but this risk I was quite willing to take. I knew Nur ed Din would make no mistakes. It was not as if he was actuated by avarice in assisting me; but being engaged in a death-feud, he sought every means to be the one left alive, and he knew that if he could conduct me to Wadi Halfa, Gabou would soon decorate a scaffold or be shot out of hand.

Nur ed Din, through the services of one of his party, a boy whom he had brought with him, and who came into the prison daily as Nur ed Din's food servant, first arranged for relays of camels, then for the purchase of rifles and ammunition, which were buried in the desert a short distance from Omdurman. These preparations being complete, six of the ten men at his first relay station were sent for to cut a hole through the wall of the prison nearest the Nile, and this they were to do on the night we sent a message to them or gave a signal, one of the men being always near the bank, close to the selected part of the wall. Final instructions were given on hearing that the camels were ready and well provided with water. After creeping through the aperture, we were to make our way to the river, dragging an old fishing-net behind us; rags were to be bound round the chains to deaden their rattling; this part of the scheme was to hide my chains, and prevent their clanging being heard. On passing the last of the huts, we were to leave the river, and, mounting the camels, we were to travel as fast as the camels would go, twelve hours direct west, where we would pick up the first relay. We had sent the boy out with a message to our people to procure three revolvers and ammunition. Nur ed Din and I were to take one each for use in case necessity arose before we could reach the buried rifles; the other one of the men was to take, and, if our flight was at once discovered, he was to fire towards a boat which had been taken to the opposite bank, and swear that we had escaped by its means. This would put our pursuers on the wrong scent for some time. One revolver and seventeen cartridges only could be found then, and Nur ed Din decided on waiting a few days until others could be obtained.

Whilst these were being searched for, Nur ed Din became feverish, and to my horror I saw all the symptoms of typhus fever developing. This fever had been named Umm Sabbah (seven), as it invariably carried off its victims in seven days. It may be guessed how anxiously and carefully I nursed Nur ed Din, and how Hasseena was kept busy the whole day brewing from tamarinds, dates, and roots, cooling draughts to allay his fever. He might have recovered, had he not kept himself excited over the fear of losing his vengeance on Gabou, but he gradually sank and died.

I was locked up in the Umm Hagar on the night of his death, and the fever was then taking hold of me; two days later I was senseless, and of course helpless. Hasseena, with two boys, used to carry me about from shade to shade as the sun travelled, but my neck-chain dragged, and sometimes tripped one or the other up, and then it was that orders were given to remove it. Hasseena had been told that the best remedy for me was a description of vegetable marrow soaked in salt water; the water was drunk and the marrow eaten as the patient recovered. The purgative properties of this medicine might suit Soudan constitutions, and it evidently suited mine at the time, but I should warn any of my readers, should they be so unfortunate as to contract this fever, against attempting the remedy. When the decoction has acted sufficiently, the mouth is crammed with butter, which to the throat, at this stage of the "cure," feels like boiling oil, and you experience all the sensations of internal scalding. The next operation is to briskly rub the whole body, and then anoint it with butter or oil—butter by preference. The patient has nothing to say about his treatment—he is helpless; every bit of strength and will has left him, and when he has been rolled up in old camel-cloths and "sweated," weakness hardly expresses the condition he has arrived at. It was on the thirteenth day of my attack that I reached the final stage of my treatment, and then I fell asleep, waking some hours later with a clear head and all my faculties about me, though I was then but a living skeleton.

The Khaleefa, hearing of my condition, thought it a favourable opportunity for me to receive a few more lessons in Mahdieh, and my period of convalescence was much prolonged owing to the worry and annoyance which these teachers of Mahdieh were to me.

Kadi Hanafi, one of Slatin's old Kadis, then imprisoned with me owing to his open avowal that the justice and the sentences given by the Mehkemmeh (religious courts) were against the teachings of the Quoran, told me that it was a mistake on my part so openly to defy the Khaleefa, and that it would be more "politique" to submit as had Slatin, who had now his house, wives, slaves, horses and donkeys, and cultivated land outside the city. But in my then condition, a little procession, for which my dead body would be the reason, was much more to my liking, and I did not care in what shape death came, provided that it did come.

Hanafi used up all his arguments in trying to persuade me to become a good Muslim. Dilating on the power of the Khaleefa and my impotence, he pointed to my chains, then weighing about forty pounds, and said that the Khaleefa would certainly torture me with them until I submitted to become a good Muslim. To this last argument I replied that if I did say I would be converted, the Khaleefa, as soon as he heard of it, would make me proclaim my conversion publicly, and just as certainly behead me immediately afterwards, to prevent my slipping back into Christianity. Hanafi believed that the Khaleefa would still let me live after embracing the Mohammedan faith in the hope of my accepting the Mahdieh; he failed though to convert me, and the Khaleefa, hearing of the result, and not believing that Hanafi had done all that he might have done with his arguments, for this and other reasons sent him later as a convict to Gebel Ragaf, near Lado, the convict station of the Soudan.

By the time I had gained sufficient strength to attempt the flight, the men engaged had lost heart, and there was no one to lead them. Nur ed Din was dead, and as they only came into the thing for the money they were to receive, and the dollars were not then forthcoming, they decided not to run any risk, disbanded the camel-posts, and scattered to their various homes.

How many hundreds of times have I regretted since that I did not take Nur ed Din's advice and escape at the time, leaving him behind. As he said, there was no reason to be afraid that he would lose his head, as his being so ill and also his being left behind would prevent suspicion being directed towards him. During my twelve years' captivity, this, my first chance of escape, risky and desperate as it was, was the only one which had in it a real element of success, for my conductor in saving me was to save himself.

As is customary in all oriental prisons, the prisoners in the Saier had either to purchase their own food, or their friends and relatives had to send it into the prison for them; failing money, friends and relatives, the prisoners starved to death. I have already said that the best and greater part of the food sent to the prison gates was appropriated by the gaolers, that is to say, after Idris es Saier had seen to the wants of his "starving children" and numerous household first. Idris, even during the worst period of the famine, did not lose flesh; he was always the same tall, stout, flat-nosed black, both when I first saw him on May 10, 1887, and when I last saw him in September, 1898. Nor was Idris quite so bad as he had been painted; he would often—when the Nebbi Khiddr tale had had the desired effect in repentance, or when he was in a good humour after a bout of marrissa drinking—go out of his way to do his prisoners small kindnesses, such as the removal of extra chains, and giving permission to sleep in the open; but the Nebbi Khiddr institution left him so much at the mercy of the Khaleefa's immediate attendants, that his periods of good humour were, in consequence, of very short duration. Some day, if I return to the Soudan, or Idris pays a visit to civilization, I may learn from him whom I have to thank for a few of the unnecessary hardships inflicted upon me.

It might be asked why we, knowing that the guards would purloin the greater part of the food sent in, did not arrange for a larger quantity to be sent. There are two reasons, and the first is the least of the two: the guards knew very well what was the minimum amount of food to keep us alive, and just that quantity of food would be allowed to pass the portals of the Saier. The second reason was, that the sight of more or better food being brought to a prisoner proved one of two things: either the prisoner himself had received some money, or his friends had, and the following day the time-worn Nebbi Khiddr tale, properly translated, meant chains until more dollars were forthcoming. Under such circumstances, the unlucky offender against Saier politics would be called upon by the other mulcted prisoners to make good the money they had been bled of, for the Saier was most impartial in the matter of chains, and, certain of always getting the proper victim in the end, invariably loaded a dozen or so with extra chains, and ordered all into the Umm Hagar. An attenuated and burned chicken, or pigeon, cost a few dollars in repentance, and also the wearing of extra chains and the horrors of the Umm Hagar for nights, for it was advisable to keep Idris waiting some days for an evidence of repentance, so that he should believe, and the Khaleefa's attendants believe also, that some little difficulty had been experienced in collecting the few dollars you had to pay.

Our usual food was "Asseeda," the Soudan dourra (sorghum), roughly pounded moist, and mixed into a thick paste, feeling and tasting to the palate like sawdust. It was not a very nourishing dish, but it was a heavy one, and stayed the pangs and gnawings of hunger. A flavour might be imparted by allowing a quantity to stand for a day or two until fermentation set in. Occasionally, but only occasionally, a sauce made from the pounded seed of the Baamia hybiscus, and called "Mulakh," could be obtained, and this, with the fermented asseeda, made a veritable banquet. Friends in the town sent us, when they could either afford or obtain it, a little wheaten bread, a bit of cheese or butter, or a few pinches of coffee.

CATARINA.

Amongst the many captives in Omdurman who did so much for me stands out prominently Father Ohrwalder, the old Greek lady, Catarina—who was a ministering angel alike to prisoners and captives—Mr. Tramba and his wife Victoria, Nahoum Abbajee, and Youssef Jebaalee. Surely the recording angel has placed to the right side of the account the little deceptions practised by Father Ohrwalder to gain access to the prison, when the few piastres of baksheesh he could afford were not sufficient to satisfy the rapacity of the guards, in order to bring me some little dainty, when, God knows, he was bringing me the lion's share of what he was in absolute need of himself. At one time he would present himself at the gates as being "Iyyan Khaalas" (sick unto death), and, of course, wished to see me once again before his dissolution. At another time it would be that he had heard *I* was dying, then, of course, he wished to see *me*; and the changes would be rung by his coming in on the pretext of wishing to see some other prisoner. With bowed head and bent back, exaggerating the weak state he was then in, he would crawl towards me, dragging one foot after the other, and, reaching me, would sit down on the ground and sway his body to and fro—a little pantomime which allowed of his surreptitiously passing to me the dainties he had brought in the old leather bag slung from his left shoulder. Time after time he was turned away from the gates, and this, too, after having paid the baksheesh; but his persistence secured his seeing me every one or two months during my first three years in prison, and the scraps of news he brought from the outside world—news to both of us, though a year or two old—gave me something to think of and turn over in my brain until his next visit. Death, as I told Father Ohrwalder, I did not fear, but my great fear was insanity.

Often and often, when allowed to sleep in the open air at night-time, instead of experiencing all the horrors of a night in the common cell, the cool night-air would send me off into a sound sleep, from which I would start up from some confused dream of old days, and, looking up to the sky, would wonder to myself, half awake and half asleep, which was the dream and which the reality, the old loved scenes, or the prison of es-Saier at Omdurman. I would for some moments be afraid to look round at the men chained on each side of me, and when I mustered up courage to do so, and felt the weight of my irons and the heavy chain across my legs, which bound our gang of fifty or sixty together, I would speculate on how long it would be before the slender thread holding me between reason and insanity snapped under the strain.

That my reason did not give way during my first period of imprisonment I have but to thank Father Ohrwalder and the friends mentioned. Each one of them risked his or her comparative freedom, if not life, to help me. Even during the worst nights in the Umm Hagar, when Hell itself might be defied to match such a scene, when Madness and Death stalked hand-in-hand amongst the struggling mass, and when, jammed in tight with a number of the more fanatical prisoners, I fought and struggled, bit and kicked, as did they for bare life, the thought of having friends in adversity, suffering almost as much as I did, kept that slender thread from snapping; but the mental strain caused me most violent headaches and periods of forgetfulness or loss of memory, which even now recur at times. But it was during the famine that the Christian— more than Christian—charity of my friends was put to the severest tests and never faltered. Food was at enormous prices, but, day after day, Catarina brought her scrap of dourra or wheaten bread; every day Youssef Jebaalee sent his loaves of bread, unmindful of how much the guards stole, provided that I got a mouthful.

All the food sent for the prisoners did not, of course, reach them; what little passed the gates of the Saier was fought for; those having longer chains, or bars, connecting their anklets stood the best chance in the race for food, as they were able to take longer strides. Had it been under other circumstances, the scenes enacted might have provided endless amusement for the onlookers, for they had in them all the elements but one of a sack-race and old country sports. Seeing thirty or forty living skeletons shuffling, leaping as far as their weight of chains and strength would allow, you knew, when one fell, that it was the weakness caused by starvation which had brought him down. There he would lie where he fell, given over to despair, whilst those who did reach any messenger with food, rather than resenting the stripes given by the guards with the courbash, would almost appear glad of the open wounds these caused, so that they might caress the wounds with their hands and lick the blood from their fingers. This picture is not *over-* but *under*drawn; but I have been advised to leave out minute details and other scenes, as unnecessarily harrowing.

We heard that cannibalism was being practised in the town, but none took place in the prison; in the Saier, when once the despair engendered by starvation and cruelty took hold of a prisoner, he would lie down and wait for death; food he would never refuse if offered, but if water without food was offered, it was refused. Day after day, for months, the bodies of eight or ten prisoners, who had died of starvation, would be thrown into the Nile, and thousands must have died in the Saier. The population of the prison was always kept up owing to the hourly arrivals of starving wretches committed there for trying to steal food in the market-place, and it was from such as these that the fighting for food in the prison emanated chiefly. It can be well imagined how the most civilized being might be driven to madness and desperation, when, as the result of his trying to steal a bit of food, maybe for himself, maybe for a dying child, he is committed to an oriental prison, and there, as he is taken to the anvil, the body of the last victim to starvation is dragged up to have the shackles knocked off only to be fitted on to him. Yet this happened not twice, not scores, but hundreds of times in the prison of es-Saier during that terrible famine.

After my servant Hasseena had been knocked down a number of times and the food she was bringing me had been devoured by the starving prisoners, we hit upon an expedient. Buying a gazelle skin, she had this hung from her waist, under her dress, and left dangling between her knees; the food for me was placed in this, but Hasseena always carried, as a blind or decoy, a little food in her hands. This would be pounced upon, when Hasseena, who had a healthy pair of lungs, as Wad Nejoumi discovered at his first interview with her, would raise the echoes with her screams. These gave her a clear path to me, and she waited for a favourable opportunity to drop the gazelle skin on the ground beside me.

It must not be thought from the foregoing that the prisoners had no feelings for each other, and for those worse off in the matter of food than themselves. There was more charity shown by those wild fanatics, and almost savages, than is often shown in more civilized places. Mahmoud Wad Said, so long as his little property held out, sold portions of it day after day, and had sent into the prison for his poorer fellow-prisoners, a large "geddahh" of asseeda and milk, night and morning, and this gave thirty to forty prisoners a meal each day; others divided with their less fortunate friends the little food they received. I have seen it stated that my charity to other prisoners created a very good impression; but, then, how could I, the only white and Christian in the prison—and, for the matter of that, the only avowed Christian in the Soudan—not strive to show just a little more self-denial and charity and kindness of heart than those "fanatics" showed me?*

> * On reading over the foregoing to Father
> Ohrwalder, and asking him if he knew of any
> others who had assisted me with food while in

prison, he first objected to my giving him any credit for what he had done, saying he had done but part of his duty towards me, and, in deference to his wishes, I have curtailed the account of his kindnesses towards me. He then expressed surprise that the name of Slatin did not figure amongst those of my benefactors, and it is only now that I hear from Father Ohrwalder of the risks Slatin ran in trying to help me. As can be well understood, this is hardly a subject on which, at the present time, I could approach Slatin, as it would practically be asking him how many dollars' worth of thanks were due to him.

On my arrival at Omdurman, it was believed by the Khaleefa, and others, that I was a brother of Slatin, and had started for Sheikh Saleh's country with the idea of organizing an expedition to attack the Khaleefa and effect Slatin's release; the latter, in consequence, was looked upon with more suspicion than ever, and bad as my position or condition was, his, in a measure, may have been worse. People in Omdurman—my servant and the prison barber in particular—gauging Slatin's position to a nicety, had little fear or compunction in blackmailing him, day after day, after his first contribution to my sustenance, for more money and food, and in each instance it was asked for in my name. Others doubtless did the same, and poor Slatin, as he was then, must have been robbed right and left, his robbers perfectly secure in the conviction that even, should he discover their trick, he would be powerless to punish them, for had he attempted to do so, he would have placed his head in a noose for disobeying the Khaleefa's orders, which were that he was never to speak to, or have any dealings with me. It is the least that I can do here to place the matter on record in connection with my experience, and leave Slatin to await the appearance of this in print to learn that my heartfelt thanks go out to him, while, at the same time, the world will better understand from the foregoing the difficulties of Slatin's position with the Khaleefa.

CHAPTER X
PRISON JUSTICE

What I have written previously concerning the Nebbi Khiddr history will, in the following notes of prison life, assist the reader in better understanding how such mutual and transparent deceptions might be practised by the Khaleefa and the gaolers as are related here. It will be remembered that the Khaleefa, following the example of the Mahdi, laid claim to the Nebbi Khiddr as his prophet or constant messenger—a sort of modern Mercury amongst the Soudanese; hence the mutual, but unacknowledged deceptions which might be practised by the Khaleefa and his followers one against the other, but with always this proviso: as the Khaleefa had the power of life and death, and his spoken word was absolute, no one dare, even by suggestion, imply that he had in any way deceived or hoodwinked Abdullahi, else the Nebbi Khiddr would not have rested content until his detractor had been shortened by a head.

When the many escapes from the Saier zareeba became of too common gossip to be any longer concealed, Abdullahi ordered a wall to be built in place of the thorn zareeba, and later, to obviate the necessity of the prisoners going to the Nile banks for drinking water and ablutions, a well was sunk to provide infiltration water for the purposes mentioned.* Until these works were ordered to be made, the prisoners were mainly employed in building mud-brick houses for the gaolers; and when these were finished we had to attend to certain of the household duties—the tending of children, sheep, goats, and the carrying of water from the Nile. Of all the tasks set the prisoners, the household duties were the most pleasant, or, at all events, the least distasteful. Most of the gaolers were able to keep up a large establishment on the proceeds of their baksheesh and ill-gotten gains, but with a multiplicity of wives or concubines a very natural result followed—household bickerings and squabbles, in which one wife or concubine was bound to come off worst; and this gave the wide-awake prisoner engaged upon household duties his chance. He would soon detect which concubine was being "put upon," or whom the women-folk were most jealous of, and in a few days' time, as a result of his attentions in carrying her pots and pans, and bringing her water as many times in the day as she wished, he would be bemoaning in her sympathetic ears the hard fate of both of them, and trying to persuade her that what she was enduring was far worse than his imprisonment and chains. The old truism that "pity is akin to love" obtains equally as well under the dusky hide of a Soudanese damsel as under the white skin of her European sister, and very soon the pair would be maturing plans for an escape and elopement. The main difficulty was the removal of the man's chains and a rapid flight to some distant village; but the Soudan ladies are not a whit behind in woman's resourcefulness face to face with apparent impossibilities. Failing to arrange for a regular flight, the woman would secure some place of hiding in Omdurman itself. She would undertake all the arrangements, and I never knew of a failure in their plans.

> * This well was named "Beer-el-Ummarra" (the well of the Emirs). When ordering its construction the Khaleefa instructed Idris es Saier to put all the important prisoners on the work, as the exercise would do them good. My gang consisted of Ibrahim Wad Adlan, Ajjab Abou Jinn, Mohammad Wad Bessir, Mohammad Abou Sinn, Abdalla Abou Sinn, Ali Wad-el-Hadd, Ahmed Abd-el-Maajid, Mahmoud Wad Said, Hassan Um Barak, and the Shereef Khaleel—the aristocracy, I might say, of the Soudan. We did little or no work ourselves, we paid the imprisoned slaves for doing it; but whenever Idris es Saier made his appearance he would find us all busy. When telling us of the Khaleefa's orders, Idris hinted that it might be advisable for us to subscribe amongst ourselves for paid labour, and he would take charge of the money. At Wad Adlan's advice, we said we rather liked the idea of having some work to do to keep us occupied, Adlan knowing that Idris would keep the money and make us work just the same, or else pay over again for another batch of slaves.

Each month a list of the prisoners in the Saier, and an account of their progress in "education" would be submitted to Abdullahi, with recommendations for the release of certain prisoners, and each month, coincident with the preparation of this list, some prisoner would be missing from his usual place that night and next morning—and for ever afterwards; and this is how Soudan romances were managed. Sheep and goats would stray unaccountably. As these accidents always happened about sunset, the concubine would set off with the chained prisoner to bring in the strayed animals at the precise moment when her lord and master was engaged upon his official duties and locking up the prisoners in the Umm Hagar. On his calling at his house, the temporary absence would excite little or no suspicion, but as the hours sped on suspicions were aroused, and if on the following morning or the same night the sheep and goats found their way back unaided, the gaoler's only way out of the difficulty was to present a favourable report of the conduct of the escaped prisoner, in the hope that his release would be ordered by the Khaleefa. To acknowledge that he had escaped while employed in tending his sheep and goats would be to place the gaoler's head or liberty in danger, and the eloping couple well knew this. No sooner was the release ordered, than the happy couple would present themselves before the Kadi, to be married right off—the Soudanese damsel in the possession of a husband, with no other wives or concubines to worry her in the house, and her husband free of his chains. True, he might divorce his wife the same day if he so chose, but then his and her object had been gained—they were both clear of the gaoler, whom they knew dare not trump up any case against them in the hope of one or the other being again committed to prison, for, once released by the Khaleefa's orders, a prisoner might only be recommitted on them. Moreover, if one of the two should relate what had actually occurred, the gaoler himself, having deceived the Khaleefa with his report of good conduct and "education," would certainly be sent to prison or to the gallows.

I was too important a prisoner to make my escape at all possible by such happy means as those above described. My only hope lay in trusty natives and swift camels which would outstrip my pursuers. I often envied my fellow-prisoners who exchanged the bonds of slavery for those of matrimony, for numbers of them came to see me after their "release," but I shudder to think what might have happened had I been released by the Khaleefa's orders, for, following the old adage that a drowning man clutches at a straw, I must have promised marriage to dozens of Soudan beauties (?) in the event of their doing anything towards wheedling their masters or the Khaleefa into releasing me, and it is quite certain that, on my release, I should have met at the prison-gates a clamouring crowd all claiming the honour.

But I should explain how it was that I came into direct contact with the hareems of the gaolers. Having studied physiology and medicine at Königsberg and Leipzig, I was often called upon by the natives in Upper Egypt, before the place was so well known to the travelling public as it is now, and in the absence of doctors, to attend them in cases of sickness or accident. My practice, being gratuitous, was a large one, and I soon became the "Hakeem Pasha" (principal medical officer). My reputation, if it did not precede me, at least accompanied me to Omdurman when I was captured, so that I was in constant requisition at the gaolers' hareems, paying "professional" visits ranging from cases in which the Khaleefa was soon to be presented with another subject, to the most trivial and sometimes imaginary complaints. So long as the women kept ailing, my life was rendered endurable, for I was able to sit down and chat with them for hours, waiting to see the result of concoctions made from, to me, unknown herbs and roots, of the properties of which I was ignorant; but the results were always satisfactory. The only medicine or chemical I came across of any value in the stores of the Beit-el-Mal was permanganate of potash, and I soon discovered that a Soudan constitution necessitated the application of this in crystals and not in liquid form. The effects, as may be imagined, were rapid, and, though my medical readers might be inclined to doubt the statement, the results were eminently satisfactory both to the patients and myself.

Occasionally I would be sent for to attend some one in the women's prison, which was situated a short distance from the Saier of Idris. The women's prison consisted of the common cell and a light zareeba, through which the curious might gaze on the women as they lay stretched on the ground during the day in the sun, undergoing their first period of imprisonment. The majority of the women prisoners were slaves locked up on some pretence or other to prevent their escaping. It might be that their master was arranging for some trading trip which would occupy him for weeks and, maybe, months. The simplest way of preventing his property from running away during his absence was to trump up some charge against her, and have her locked up, knowing that her release might not be obtained until he returned and requested it. As in the mean time she would have to be fed at his expense, and gave her services free to the household of one of the gaolers, he was equally sure that the gaoler would not be too anxious to secure her release.

Married women were sent to prison on all sorts of charges, ranging from suspected conjugal infidelity to the delivery of a curtain lecture. The women prisoners wore light chains connecting their anklets, but their lot was little better than that of the men. A charge of infidelity "not proven," as the Scotch have it, was followed by imprisonment and the application of three hundred stripes with the courbag, and when the woman had recovered from these, she would be sent into the house of one of the gaolers to be the maid-of-all-work for every one there; she would have to grind corn, attend to the children, carry water, and be driven as a slave night and day for weeks. A Mrs. Caudle or a termagant received from fifty to eighty lashes, and she too on recovery would be sent into one of the gaolers' hareems to work as hard as her possibly innocent and more severely punished companion in misery. A few weeks of such treatment sent the women back home completely cured of the faults for which they were sent to prison to be corrected, besides which the relation of their experiences acted as an effective deterrent on budding Mrs. Caudles and others.

The unloading of boats was the hardest work we were set to, and we were kept up to the mark by the ever-present lash; we might only be tired and ill when we could afford the luxury of paying for the complaint, for this labour was the most lucrative task our gaolers could set us to; we had either to work, or pay many times the equivalent of our labour. It was in connection with the unloading of boats, and this, too, when I was slowly recovering from my attack of typhus fever after the death of Ahmed Nur ed Din, that I received my first flogging. A young gaoler had pestered me for money, and as I had none to give him, he ordered me to slave at the unloading of the boats. The only way of exhibiting a real refusal was to sit down upon the ground, which I did, upon which the gaoler commenced to drag me towards the gateway of the Saier. On this I got upon my feet and knocked the gaoler off his. He ran to Idris es Saier, told his own tale, and Idris, approaching me, ordered me to get up—for I had again sat down—and assist in the unloading of the boats. I refused, and accused the gaoler of trying to extort monies from me. Upon this Idris struck me with his "safarog" (an instrument almost the exact counterpart of the Australian boomerang, and used by the Soudan tribes for precisely similar purposes); the blow he gave smashed the safarog and stunned me, and while only partly conscious I was turned over and condemned to receive there and then five hundred lashes.

Only sixty or seventy, I was told, were inflicted; the remainder were not given, as Idris, seeing that I was unconscious, believed that I was dead, and in consequence received a terrible fright. I was carried to my place in the cell, while Idris set about clearing himself with the other prisoners, and explaining that it was all the work of the young gaoler. Idris knew what it meant to him had I been flogged to death, and, believing that I would not recover, he, when I did recover, evidently made up his mind to pay out the gaoler who was responsible for his fright in the first place, and for his servility to the other prisoners at the moment when he thought there were good grounds for it.

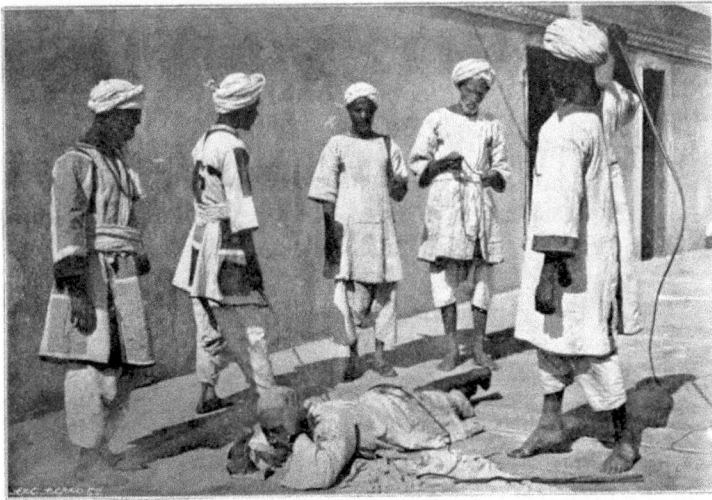

A FLOGGING BY ORDER OF THE KHALEEFA.

His opportunity came some little time later on, when the same gaoler invented another excuse for flogging me. I had bought from one of the gaolers a small mud hut, a few feet square, in the prison enclosure, and received permission from Idris es Saier to sleep in this at night instead of in the Umm Hagar. This young gaoler—and other gaolers as well—accepted baksheesh from prisoners to allow them to sleep in the open; and Idris, finding the contributions to his "starving children" falling off, suspected the reason, and lay in wait. Upon a night when a larger number than usual had been allowed to sleep outside the Umm Hagar, he suddenly made his appearance in the prison enclosure. There was nothing for our guardians to do but to pretend that the prisoners had been insubordinate, had refused to enter the Umm Hagar, and to lay about them with their whips. The young gaoler, not aware that I had paid the regulation baksheesh to Idris, made straight for my hut, dragged me out, and flogged me to the door of the common cell, a distance, maybe, of forty or fifty yards, but my thick jibbeh prevented the blows from telling with much effect as far as regards abrasion of the skin; nevertheless, their weight told on my diminished strength, and I again fell ill. The circumstance came to the ears of the Khaleefa through Idris, or the Nebbi Khiddr, and I had the huge satisfaction of seeing my tormentor dismissed from his lucrative post, subjected to the two hundred lashes he was sentenced to receive, and then sent as a prisoner in chains to work at the very same boats, which he had had me flogged for refusing to assist in unloading. This, at the present moment, is the only bit of real justice I can remember during my twelve years' captivity.

I have in a former chapter given a slight description of flogging as I saw it practised when first captured by the dervishes; but the flogging in the Saier was a very different matter. The maximum number of stripes ever ordered was a thousand, and this number was often actually given, but in every case the stripes were given over the clothing. The rules of flogging were generally as follows: the first two hundred on the back below the region of the lumbar vertebræ, the third and fourth hundred on the shoulders, and the fifth hundred on the breast. When the maximum number of one thousand lashes was ordered, they were always given on the same parts as those of the first two hundred, and this punishment was resorted to for the purpose of extorting confessions. After eighty or one hundred blows, the jibbeh was cut into shreds, and soon became saturated with the blood of the victim; and while the effect of the individual blows may not have been as great as those from the cat-o'-nine-tails, the number given made up in quantity for what might have been lacking in quality, as is evidenced by the large numbers who died under the castigation or as a result of it later.

On one occasion an old black soldier of the Egyptian Army, named Mohammad Ajjami, who was employed as a runner (a foot-galloper—if I may invent the expression—of the Khaleefa on field days), was sent to me while in the prison to be cured of the effects of a flogging. He had by some means incurred the displeasure of Sheikh ed Din, the son of the Khaleefa, and by him had been sentenced to receive a public flogging, after which he was to be sent to the Saier to be "educated." He was carried into the prison to me after his flogging. The fleshy part of his back was cut into ribbons, and the hip-bones were exposed. For six or eight weeks I was constantly employed bathing this man's wounds with a dilute solution of carbolic acid, the carbolic crystals being sent to me by Sheikh ed Din himself for the purpose, for his father, the Khaleefa, jealous of his authority, had censured his son, telling him, as he constantly told others, that "In Usbaiee shareeknee fee mulkee, anna ikktahoo."* Ajjami recovered, and often came to see me in prison to express his gratitude. Sheikh ed Din himself was so pleased at the man's recovery that he begged his father to release me, so that I might practise the healing art amongst his Ansar, and teach it to others; but the Khaleefa was obdurate, and refused, his reasons for refusing to release me being better left to be related later by some of my fellow-captives.

> * This expression was always used by the Khaleefa in any discussion. Holding up his forefinger, he said (translation of phrase): "Rather than this finger should be a partner in the governing of my realm, I should cut it off."

My third flogging was received under the following circumstances. Having from Idris es Saier received permission to remain in my mud hovel, instead of spending the nights in the Umm Hagar, and feeling secure in my comparative freedom and safe from the exactions of the other gaolers, as I had baksheeshed Idris well, I firmly refused to be bled any further. My particular guardian, not daring, after what had occurred to my former guardian, to order me into the Umm Hagar, went a step further, and refused to allow me to leave my mud hut at all for any purpose whatever. I insisted upon being allowed to go to the place of ablution—about one hundred yards distant—and being refused, set off, receiving at every step a blow from the courbag. Being heavily chained, I was helpless, and could not reach my tormentor, as he could skip away from my reach, which limited to the length of the bars connecting my feet, which bars were fifteen inches in length. It was on this occasion, night-time too, that Idris es Saier paid another surprise visit to the prison enclosure to see what number of "unauthorized" prisoners were sleeping outside the Umm Hagar, and, furious at the number he discovered, he ordered all outside, without exception, to be flogged.

I and fifteen to twenty others received a hundred and fifty lashes each—at least, I received this number; others repented by crying out after twenty or thirty blows. I alternately clenched my teeth and bit my lips to prevent a sound of pain escaping, often as I was asked, "Will you not cry out? Is your head and heart still like black iron?" and the more they reminded me of the courage I was exhibiting, the more reason I had for not giving way or breaking down. But the mental ordeal was far, far more terrible than the corporal punishment. There was I, a European, a Prussian, a man who had fought with the British troops in what transpired to be the "too late" expedition for the rescue of Gordon, now in the clutches of the tyrant and his myrmidons, whom we had hoped to rescue Gordon from; a white and a Christian—and the only professing Christian—chained and helpless, being flogged by a black, as much a captive and a slave as I was, and yet my superior and master. It is impossible for any one not having undergone a similar experience to appreciate the mental agonies I endured.

I may have been self-willed and strong-headed; I may, if you wish, have acted like a fool in my constant defiance of the Khaleefa and the tenets of the Mahdi; but now, looking back on those terrible times, I feel convinced that had poor Gordon lived, my actions would at least have met with his approbation, for the outward ceremony or observance of adherence to the Mohammedan faith was carried out on me under force, after the escape of Rossignoli. Death, in whatever form it came, would have come as a welcome visitor to me; but while doing all in my power to exasperate my captors to kill me, something—hope, courage, a clinging to life, pride in my race, or personal vanity in defying them to the end— restrained me from taking my own life, though Heaven knows that, if ever man had a good excuse for doing so, I had. But my conduct so impressed the Khaleefa that he told Wad Nejoumi, who asked for my release so that I might accompany him to Dongola to "open up trade," and told many others later, "Neufeld I will not release, but I will not kill him." Invariably, in speaking of me to others, as I was still unconverted, the Khaleefa omitted the name "Abdalla" which I had been given, and spoke of me as "Nofal"—the Arabic pronunciation of Neufeld.

CHAPTER XI
A SERIOUS DILEMMA

As I write, there lie before me three successive paragraphs culled from a recent edition of a London paper. These paragraphs were intended to be, and doubtless were, amusing to their readers, but they contain inaccuracies. I have ascertained that one misstatement owes its origin to a report drawn up in connection with the guide's account of the successful escape of Father Rossignoli. The facts connected with that flight, and my reported refusal to escape when the opportunity (?) offered, find their place later in my narrative. For the moment I shall content myself with but one of the paragraphs, and fill in the details which, while not detracting from the humorous element introduced, will show that the episode referred to had somewhat of a pathetic, if not tragic, vein in it. This may have been lost sight of owing to the tale being recorded in an office about two thousand miles away from the scene of action, and the inaccuracies may be accounted for by the fact that the tale was told by one of that large class in the East whose greatest glory it is, when one of them has by constant practice attained a certain standard of inventive faculty and plausibility, to prove to the world that the race of Haroun-el-Rashid's story-tellers is not yet extinct. There can be little doubt that the guide and Wakih Idris, and maybe others, would be much entertained, if not a little surprised, if told that the whole of their tales had apparently been believed in.

On my servant Hasseena being sent into the Khaleefa's hareem in May, 1887, she obtained her release, or dismissal, by declaring that she was with child; she was not. In November, 1888, she certainly was, and the fact could not be concealed. Hasseena, having been a slave, could not well be legally married, so that when dismissed from the Khaleefa's hareem, she was sent as my property to the hareem of Idris es Saier, where she had, in addition to buying and preparing my food, to perform the housework and run messages for the women of Idris's household.

Idris I knew had long coveted Hasseena, and her being with child appeared to him a favourable opportunity of securing her for himself, for under ordinary circumstances, the woman being a slave and the child being born in his hareem, he could lay claim to the paternity, when mother and child would become free, the mother ranking now as a wife. He talked the matter over with Hasseena, and then sent her to interview me. I submitted the case to my friends in prison, and they showed that Idris had misread, or misunderstood, Surah IV. of the Quoran, which only justified his position towards Hasseena in the event of my being a prisoner of war, and he having captured Hasseena on the field. Things became still more complicated by Hasseena admitting to me that there were doubts in her own mind as to the child's paternity. Hasseena was of a light copper colour; Idris was as black as the ace of spades. It would only be reasonable to expect that the child when born would exhibit in the colour of its skin an evidence of its paternity, and it was precisely on this account that Hasseena wished to defer making any declaration until the event came off. If she elected to declare Idris the father, and the child at birth gave the lie to her statement, her life would be in danger; but before continuing the narrative, and detailing the complications which Hasseena's condition and her uncertainty on a vital point gave rise to—it might be well to refer briefly to one of the moral code of laws instituted by the Mahdi, as this will help the reader to a better understanding of the quandary we were placed in.

While a man, having already the regulation quota of four legal wives, might crowd his hareem with as many female slaves and concubines as he could support or keep in order, a woman was restricted to the one husband or master. All breakings of our seventh commandment were, if proved, followed by flogging in the case of unmarried women and slaves, and by the stoning to death of married women; but, in the latter case, *the sentence could not be given, nor the punishment inflicted, unless the woman confessed.* Very few stonings to death took place, and these were in the earlier days of Mahdieh, when religious fanaticism held sway.

The flogging has already been described. When a stoning to death was to take place, a hole was dug in the ground, and the woman buried to her neck in it. The crowd stood facing the victim, about fifteen to twenty yards distant, and on a given signal the stoning commenced; but it is only right to say that the Soudanese themselves hated and feared taking part in such an execution. None of the stones thrown had, singly, the force or weight to cause stunning or death, and the horrid spectacle was presented of what appeared to be a trunkless head, slightly jerking backwards and forwards and from side to side to avoid the stones being hurled at it, and this ordeal continued for an hour or more. Sometimes a relative or friend, under pretence of losing his temper in upbraiding or cursing the woman, smashed in her head with one of the small axes usually carried by the Soudanese, thus putting her at once out of her torture and misery. Shortly before sunset, the relatives and friends would come out to take away the body and give it decent burial, for the soul had fled, purified with the woman's blood, to the next world.

Knowing what would be the result of a confession, it will be wondered that any woman ever did confess; the number who did so is, admittedly, small. In one of the three cases of stoning to death I know of, the confession was extorted by torture, and the poor woman preferred the horrible but certain death by the time the sun set, to the lingering death she was enduring from day to day. Thousands of women were charged with the breaking of this particular rule or commandment of the Mahdi, but almost all the charges were made by other women—and this, too, out of sheer jealousy, not from any feeling of outraged morality.

I may now proceed with the narration of the quandary Hasseena had placed us in, herself included. I had been kept chained and closely confined for nineteen months, and was under Idris es Saier's particular supervision; Hasseena, during the same period, had been a servant in his hareem, and also in his entire charge. If I claimed the paternity of the child, the probabilities were that Idris would get into trouble with the Khaleefa; if Idris claimed it, his head might be in danger, for decapitation or hanging was the punishment ordered for the male offender, and in all cases Hasseena was liable to flogging or stoning to death. Again, if I claimed the paternity of the child, and there were reasonable grounds after its birth to believe that the paternity should be looked for in some other direction, and I knew that it should be; then, while Idris would clear himself to the Khaleefa, I should have been punished for lying to him, and Hasseena would be in the same predicament as before.

I had inquiries made outside as to Hasseena's movements when marketing, and as to those whom she associated with, or went to see; being satisfied, as a result of the inquiries, that the expected arrival would be a shade lighter in colour than its mother, I, acting on the advice of my prison friends, claimed the child as mine, thus leaving Idris to get out of the thing as best he could. There was, as above indicated, a risk in my claiming the paternity, but it was worth while running it. The Khaleefa, so my friends told me, would now certainly release me from prison, as my wife and child would be a guarantee for my good behaviour if released, and also guarantee me against any escape, for to try and escape with a woman and baby made success very problematical, while the woman would certainly hinder me in any attempt to escape, when it could only result in the death of herself and child. It was for this reason—to hinder escape—that the Khaleefa kept his captives well supplied with wives, and showed his displeasure very plainly if the expected results did not follow. But my claiming the paternity did not please Idris, as it deprived him of all chance of securing Hasseena for himself, and also left him at the mercy of the Khaleefa for his neglect of duty in allowing Hasseena to come near me, so he empanelled a jury of Soudanese matrons to inquire into the affair.

At the time when Hasseena startled our little world with her interesting condition, Omdurman was, and had been for some months, almost depleted of its male population; the rumours of an expedition (Stanley's, to rescue Emin) had resulted in a considerable force being sent to Equatoria. The army to attack Abyssinia had been in the field for months, so also had the army which Wad Nejoumi was to lead a few months later to its destruction at Toski.

A number of the ladies empanelled for the jury ought not, unless they belonged to the Gawaamah tribe, to have been eligible for election, and others, under the circumstances, should have avoided publicity; but here was an opportunity for them, and they were not going to miss it. They came together to save themselves—not Hasseena or Idris—hence the extraordinary verdict they gave: to the effect that it was not only possible for a woman to be with child nineteen months—as Hasseena presumably was, but for twenty-four months, while some hotly contested for an extension of the time to years!

Idris had still another card to play; he averred that it was impossible for the child to be mine, and he now swore it was not his. Then Hasseena ought to be flogged and sent to prison; but as Idris would be entrusted with the flogging himself, it was to be understood that he was not going to damage his prospective property. It was now the turn of those whom I remarked ought not to have been eligible for election to the jury; the tales they told to account for their own interesting condition are worthy of the best traditions of the "Thousand and One Nights;" but, even if written, they would be less fit for translation and publication than the originals of the famous tales. Idris now appealed to the Kadi, who, after interviewing the jury, supported their contentions, and related the whole story to the Khaleefa, much to his amusement and the discomfiture of Idris; for, while graciously sending me his congratulations on the coming event, he ordered the unconditional release of Hasseena, who went to live in what might be called the "Christian" quarter of the town.

In January the girl-child was born, and named "Makkieh" (shackles), a name which appealed to the humorous side of the Khaleefa, who, being tickled at the idea of the name, in a fit of good-humour, sent word to me to ask if I would undertake the manufacture of gunpowder if he released me. I unfortunately replied that I did not understand the manufacturing of it, and this aroused his suspicions, which did not abate one jot when, shortly afterwards, a Bohemian baker, who had strayed from Halfa, was taken prisoner, and sent on to Omdurman as a captured spy. This man, whom I knew only by the name of Joseppi—though he had a string of other names, which I have forgotten—was a Bohemian by birth and a baker by trade. He was not of strong intellect, and what intellect he had, had maybe been impaired by a "music madness." From the rambling statements he made to me during his year's imprisonment, I gather that he had tramped Europe as a wandering musician, landing finally in Egypt, where he tramped from the Mediterranean to the frontier. It is quite evident that instead of coppers he received drinks in exchange for his strains, and this further added to his mental troubles, though the drunkenness he has been charged with was, in my opinion, more the result of circumstances and misfortune than a natural craving for ardent liquors.

On leaving Wadi Halfa, he had expected to find, as he had found in Europe and the part of Egypt he had tramped through, villages or towns within the day's tramp. He had not the slightest idea of what the desert was until he found himself in it. After some days of wandering, during which he eat pieces of his worn-out boots in lieu of other food, he struck the Nile, and, wandering along, ignorant of the direction he was taking, he came upon a party of dervishes, whom he tried to communicate with, and after, by gesticulations, showing them that he wanted bread or food, he commenced to "soothe the savage breast" with strains from his violin. They took him prisoner, destroyed his instrument, and sent him on to Omdurman as a spy. On arrival there, he was ushered into the presence of the Khaleefa, who was undecided as to whether he had a madman or an actor to deal with, for on dates being brought for Joseppi to eat, he threw them about, and then lay flat on his face. He was sent to prison and heavily chained; in the process of having his chains and bars fitted, he fainted away.

Gaoler.

Neufeld.

Gaoler.

Son of Fauzi Pasha.

Fauzi Pasha.

MEAL-TIME IN THE SAIER.

Joseppi was in my charge for about one year, and while being as harmless as a child, he caused me endless trouble. During the day he would remain perfectly quiet, but at night-time he would insist upon singing or humming. As his tunes had neither beginning nor end, and were composed of notes snatched from here and there, we soon tired of it, and Joseppi received a light flogging on one occasion for not "shutting his mouth" when requested to do so. I remonstrated with him after he had been flogged, and told him that he should not continue to hum after other prisoners had asked him to keep quiet. He ruminated over this, and thinking, maybe, at the moment that I was taking the part of the others against him, he went off to the Saier, and told him confidentially that I was a great and well-known general in Europe, and a few other things. Joseppi had an enormous appetite, and was always hungry; he caused me a great deal of trouble during the worst days of the famine, when food was so scarce, for after sharing my scanty meal, he would wander off and pester every group for a scrap of food. Eventually, we had to provide three bowls for him; just when our food came in, we handed him his bowls, and thus were allowed a few moments' peace. We had finished our meal before he had finished his food, so that our group, at least, was free of his importunities. He came to grief through eating pieces of camel-skin, which the gaolers used to sell to the poorer prisoners during the famine.

Fearing that he would die in the prison, I sent word to the "Christian" quarter, asking that the Khaleefa should be prayed to release Joseppi, which was done, and he found congenial employment for a time in the bakery of Youssef Sawar. Soon afterwards, he borrowed a few dollars here and there for the purpose of buying grain at El Fun; he started off dressed in a new jibbeh, carrying his dollars, and a well-stocked basket of provisions for his two days' journey. At the very moment when Wad Adlan was pleading with the Khaleefa to release me from prison, so that I could assist him in the work of the Beit-el-Mal, a deputation of the captives arrived at the door of the house to tell the Khaleefa that Joseppi must have escaped, as he should have been back in Omdurman some days ago. Turning to Wad Adlan, the Khaleefa said, "El boomi mahhgaad—Abdulla Neufeld ogud? Khallee ossbur." ("The fool did not stop—when he had the chance to escape. Will Neufeld? Let him wait a bit.") This was the second time the poor fellow had cost me my liberty. There is no doubt that the man was murdered for the sake of his food or money, for his remains were found later, on the road between Khartoum and El Fun.

CHAPTER XII
IBRAHIM WAD ADLAN

A favourable opportunity here presents itself for referring to that little-written-about, and, therefore, little-known strange character in Mahdieh—Ibrahim Wad Adlan, the Amin Beit-el-Mal. Maybe in no one else did he confide as he confided in me while we were fellow-prisoners, and maybe he did so only because he knew that I was an avowed enemy of Mahdieh, that I was at the time defying the Khaleefa to do his worst against me, and that my interests lay elsewhere than in the Soudan. There was also a lurking suspicion that I had been sent up as a Government emissary, and that the letter of General Stephenson was purposely couched in the language it was, so that, if it fell into the hands of the Khaleefa, he would be led to believe that I had started upon a trading expedition pure and simple. The friendship formed during the two or three months, which Adlan and I spent as fellow-prisoners, was to end in the not least interesting of my experiences, but it also ended in a tragedy.

Wad Adlan, prior to the Mahdist revolt, had been one of the principal and richest merchants in Kordofan. His business connections had taken him a number of times to Cairo and other parts of Egypt. For intelligence, and as a man of the world, he was far and away superior to all the "great" people who from time to time became my fellow-prisoners; I should be inclined to place him on a higher level than the best of the old Government officials; he read and wrote well, and, as will be seen later, he was not deficient in certain qualities which go far towards making a successful Oriental diplomatist. To the end he was loyal to the core to the old Government, but he was compelled to act a part—and well he acted it. Had there been one more Adlan in the Soudan—and many had the opportunity of being such—the rule of Abdullahi would have ended with the insurrection of Khaleefa Shereef. That insurrection just missed being successful, but it was through no fault of Adlan. Carefully and secretly he had paved the way to it, but his task ended when he had paved the way; it was for others to take the goal.

Adlan was the one man in the Soudan who had the courage of his opinions, and expressed them to Abdullahi; he was a man himself, acted as one, and despised heartily those who, in his opinion, were carrying their obedience to the confines of servility. Failing to induce Abdullahi to rule with some little semblance of justice and equity, as laid down in the Quoran, he set about to undermine his influence and power, but he had to carry out his work by subterfuge, and single-handed. There were, he told me, a number of people he would have wished to take into his confidence, but some he was afraid might betray him, and the others he could not trust with the little discretion they could boast of. He feared they might unwittingly let slip a few words prematurely, and then his and their tongues would be silenced for ever.

As the director of the Beit-el-Mal, his first care was to keep the treasury and granaries full to repletion. During the famine this was an impossibility, but some grain and money had to be procured from somewhere. The poor, and those who had come by their little stores honestly, Adlan never made a call upon; indeed, he was the protector of the poor and the Muslimanieh (captive Christians). It was Adlan's policy to create enemies of Abdullahi, so that was another reason for his protecting the poor, who were already bitter enemies of their savage ruler. On reporting to Abdullahi the depleted condition of the treasury and granaries—and Abdullahi was aware that the doors of the Beit-el-Mal and Adlan's house were besieged night and day by thousands of starving wretches—Adlan would be given a verbal order to search for grain and bring it into the Beit-el-Mal. This order he would put into immediate execution against Abdullahi's particular friends and adherents, for the whole of their stores were the proceeds of robbery, and the plundering and murdering of weaker tribes and people. To all remonstrances Adlan would reply that he was carrying out Abdullahi's orders, and every one knew that disobedience to these, or any attempt to evade them, meant summary execution. Occasionally some "strong" man would enter a mild protest to the Khaleefa himself, who would feign ignorance of having given any general orders to Adlan. Adlan would be summoned, but, questioned as to his actions in the presence of the complainant, he dare not reply that he had but obeyed the general orders given him; he would be obliged to answer in such a way that the "strong" man would believe that he had acted upon his own initiative. After the audience, the "strong" man would follow Adlan to the Beit-el-Mal, and demand the return of his grain and dollars; but Adlan had distributed all on the Khaleefa's orders—which the registers proved, as nothing might leave the Beit-el-Mal without his sanction. The "strong" man now was undecided as to whether Abdullahi was playing with him or not, but his safest plan was to intrigue against Adlan. In this he would be helped might and main by Yacoub, Abdullahi's brother, and the bitterest enemy of Adlan, for Yacoub, as the Emir of Emirs (prince of princes), was insane with jealousy at the hold which Adlan had on the masses. The respect and veneration paid to Adlan Yacoub considered himself entitled to by virtue of his position and rank.

It may, or may not, be the case that Abdullahi himself was growing jealous of Adlan. As Khaleefa, his power was so absolute that he could remove any dangerous person by a suggestive motion of the hand, so that when he sent Adlan into prison for a time, it was, in Adlan's opinion, only to appease his enemies, to prevent any wavering in their allegiance, and to stem the rapidly approaching tide of discontent. But Adlan's committal to the Saier left a clear field for his enemies to intrigue against him, and being kept informed of every charge made, and the Khaleefa's varying moods towards him, Adlan saw serious danger ahead.

Reports reached us that the Beit-el-Mal was in sore straits, and that the Khaleefa had already expressed his intention of reinstating Adlan if matters did not improve. Then it was that Adlan unbosomed himself to me practically unreservedly. Gradually, but surely, he gave me to understand that if ever he was reinstated he would do all in his power to secure my release, and he so often told me *not* to attempt flight, if I was released, that I saw clearly he meant to assist me in doing so. As the Beit-el-Mal went from bad to worse, Adlan's spirits rose, and he appealed to me to advise him what to do in the event of his being reinstated. He saw that for a time, at least, he should have to abandon his old policy, and he did not know in what direction he might turn to revive the fallen fortunes of the treasury and granary.

Trading had been permitted to a certain extent, so I suggested its extension, but Adlan at first would not hear of this. Abdullahi's purpose was to keep the Soudan as much a *terra incognita* as possible, and the further opening up of trade routes would defeat this object. My next suggestion was that the Beit-el-Mal should hand over to merchants gum, ivory, feathers, etc., at a fixed rate, to be bartered against specified articles required at Omdurman, which, being received into the Beit-el-Mal to be distributed from there, would allow of it making double profits on the transactions. At first he scouted the idea, for there was not a single man he could trust, and if he gave merchants any goods and they did not return with the proceeds of their barter, Adlan would be held responsible. It was then I suggested that he should only advance goods to people who had families in Omdurman, which would ensure their returning; but he foresaw that the Khaleefa would raise objections, as these people might give information to the Government. As a matter of fact, they did do so eventually, returning to Omdurman and giving to Abdullahi as incorrect information of the Government as they had given the Government concerning him and affairs in the Soudan.

In the end, I drove home my point by falling into figurative language, a means of argument as general and effective in the East now as it was in ancient days. "Adlan," I said, "you have been feeding Abdullahi on his own flesh; he is sick, but he is hungry; you have cut all the flesh from his bones; if you try to feed him on his bones, he will kill you, for he wants flesh to eat; you must cut flesh from some one else to feed him, and cover his bones again." Adlan then jumped at the idea of trading, and said that as soon as his release came—for he felt sure he would be released—he would ask the Khaleefa to release me so that I might assist him in the work. The first essential, though, he told me, was to abandon my present attitude towards Mahdieh, and offer to become a Muslim. I agreed to do so, and Adlan reported to the Saier, who in turn reported to the Kadi, that I was willing to embrace the faith. "What," said the Kadi, "Abdalla Nufell a Muslim? No, his heart is the old black one; he is not with us; he is deceiving; his brain (head) is still strong; he is a deceiver; tell him so from me." The Kadi had not forgotten my old discussions with him in the presence of others, where he perhaps had the worst of it, and would not forgive me. Failing my "conversion," he knew that I should have to suffer the tortures of the Saier, and he intended that I should suffer them. Soon after this, Adlan was released and reinstated in his old post; but he sent word that I must be patient, as he could not speak to the Khaleefa about me until he had got back fully into favour.

I should have mentioned before, that on the Khaleefa asking for designs for the proposed tomb of the Mahdi, Kadi Hanafi and others suggested that I should prepare designs in the hope they would be accepted, when I should have to be released to see to their execution. Remembering the old tombs of the Khaliffs at Cairo, I had little difficulty in drawing a rough sketch of one, which I had submitted to Abdullah, as being an entirely original design. I was told by the Saier to make a clay model, and spent some three weeks in making one about two feet high. Hundreds came to see it, until it was knocked to pieces by a presumed fanatic, who objected to a dog of an unbeliever designing the tomb of the holy man; but from what I learned later, it was only kicked to pieces after it had been copied. Adlan, knowing of this incident, sent me word to prepare designs for the mural decorations of the interior, and I spent some weeks over these; when they were finished, I sent them direct to the Khaleefa, who sent for Adlan, and told him to make inquiries as to how long the transfer of the designs to the walls would take, and how much the work would cost. I gave an estimate of sixty days for the completion of the work. Adlan said the cost would be nil, as he had the paint.

While these designs were being sketched out, I made preparations for flight as soon after my expected release as possible, and having paper and ink in comparative abundance, I was enabled to write letters surreptitiously. On October 12, 1888, I sent my servant to a Greek captive, asking him to write me a letter in Greek to my old friend, Mankarious Effendi, station-master at Assouan. The original letter is before me, and the following is a literal translation:—

"Mr. Neufeld has asked me to write this letter because he could not write it himself; you cannot know what a difficult position he is in; since he came here he was taken twice to the gallows, but was not hanged, and is still in chains, and subject to their mercy. He wants you to take over his business, and to act forthwith as his agent. He borrowed from the bearer a hundred medjedie (dollars), which refund to him, and give him something for his trouble, and try and send him back with two hundred pounds which he might buy his liberty for. This letter is to be kept secret, as there are people who carry all news here, so if the authorities got to know anything about it Mr. Neufeld will grow from bad to worse.

(Signed) "NIROGHOPOLO."

On November 10, 1888, hearing that another old acquaintance was in Omdurman, I got another Greek captive to write another letter to Mankarious Effendi. This letter also was delivered, and Mankarious Effendi hands it to me along with a number of other documents which he has carefully preserved. I again translate literally—

"MR. MANKARIOUS BEY,—

"I wish you will be kind, and have all my things made over to you by Mr. Möller (my manager), and I pray you to act as my wakeel (agent); also please try and send me some money which I may help myself with, say two hundred or three hundred pounds; this money will be for my own use. As I was in need, I have taken from the bearer a sum of a hundred medjedie, which you will refund him and something as well, because he has done me a favour, and his name is Akkar (the real name—Karrar, was doubtless purposely changed). The money you can give the bearer of this, please take a receipt for and keep it with you; write me a letter, and send it to Ahmad Abou Idris, or his brother Kabbassi, and mention the sum you have sent me; also give bearer any assistance he may want.

(Signed) "PROTHOMOS" (I am ready).

I had heard from people who had come to Omdurman of strange doings in connection with my business, and in order that my manager should understand that the letter was authentic, I also signed the letter, and used our cypher for payment of £200— "u.r.r."

While in a fever of excitement and anxiety over the despatch of these messengers, Adlan sent me a secret messenger to say that Sulieman Haroun, of the Ababdeh tribe, then living at Omdurman, was sending his son Mohammad Ali to Cairo. Divining that Adlan wished me to communicate with Sulieman, I sent out word that I wished to see him. In a few days' time he gained admittance to the prison to see me, and I at once set to business, and asked him if he would undertake the arrangements for my escape. This he agreed to do, but only on condition that I succeeded in getting outside the prison walls. So that he should have some confidence that I would assist also, I asked him to call and see Adlan, and I believe it was Adlan who advanced to Sulieman the two hundred dollars he brought me, and for which I gave a receipt for £100. I gave him a letter for his son to deliver to my manager at Assouan, enclosing a receipt for £100, and an order for payment of a further £200. On receiving the money, he was to buy goods, arrange for relays of camels on his return journey, and bring the goods to the Beit-el-Mal, where Adlan assured him he would find me. Mohammad Ali was to leave immediately, and return to Omdurman at the earliest possible moment.

MOUSSA DAOUD EL KANAGA.

Within a few days of the despatch of this messenger, Moussa Daoud-el-Kanaga, also of the Ababdeh tribe, and an old acquaintance of mine, came to see me, and I enlisted his services. I told him of the other arrangements I had made, and asked if he would go partners with Mohammad Ali in effecting my escape. To Kanaga I gave a letter telling my manager that I had drawn against him a draft for £200, and instructing him to honour it; but, in case of accidents, I instructed Kanaga to see Mankarious Effendi at Assouan, and, failing to find him, to make his way to Cairo, and hand the letter to the German Consul. Kanaga left Omdurman about December 30, 1888.

After my remarks anent the *reliable unreliability* of every one in the Soudan, the deceptions practised one against the other, and the absolute necessity for secrecy, it will naturally be wondered that I entrusted my secret to so many, if secret it could be called when so many knew of it. The explanation is simple. I *knew* the people I had to deal with, and have you noticed the seemingly insignificant fact that I *borrowed money from each of the people I employed?* Later in my narrative I will explain these peculiar transactions.

While these different messengers are on their journeys, being "held up" at one place or the other, and at others pretending that they were gradually working their way to Berber or Dongola for trade, I relate what is happening in Omdurman.

News filtered through that the "faithful" had won a great victory over the English at Suakin; but as the Saier filled with prisoners who were present at the fight, and who gave different versions to that ordained by Abdullahi—hence their imprisonment—we learned the truth. The "faithful" had received a severe defeat. Soon after this, the army sent against Abyssinia won its great victory over the forces led by King John, and the fortunes of the Beit-el-Mal took a turn for the better from the proceeds of the sale of slaves and the loot brought in. Adlan was coming into favour again, but Abdullahi was too much occupied in goading on Nejoumi to attack Egypt to give any attention to the decoration of the Mahdi's tomb or the extension of trade. He was still less inclined to give any attention to such matters, when the news arrived—and it arrived very soon,—that Nejoumi's army had been almost annihilated at Toski. My evil star was certainly in the ascendant, and was mounting higher and higher, for it was at this time that Joseppi received a flogging for his vocal exercises, and having a severe fit of mental aberration in consequence, he went off to the Saier, and told him that he knew I was a great military general, and that I was maturing plans for the overthrow of Abdullahi. I do not for a moment believe the poor fellow knew what he was saying, for he came back to share my scanty meal as usual.

Kanaga and Mohammad Ali we had calculated would reach Omdurman some time in December or the early days of January, and as the time for their return approached, Adlan evidently became more earnest in his entreaties for the work of decorating the Mahdi's tomb to be put in hand. My flight would have to take place as soon as possible after the return of my messengers, otherwise the desert relays would disperse, believing that the scheme had fallen through; so it was necessary that I should have been at work for some time before their arrival, that is to say, long enough for my guards to grow lax in watching my movements.

Day after day Adlan sent in to inquire, "Have you any news from the Khaleefa?" and each day the messenger took back my reply, "No; have you?" but my inquiry referred to news of the messengers. At last the joyful news came; the work was to be done, and two guards came to the Saier, and conducted me to the Mahdi's tomb. There I discovered that my clay model had been faithfully copied, with the exception that the builders had shaped the dome conically. Adlan came to me there, and congratulated me on this being my last day in makkiehs (chains). Telling me to remain at the tomb until his return, he went off to the Khaleefa to receive his order for my transfer to the Beit-el-Mal, and at the very moment he was receiving it, the deputation of the Muslimanieh put in its appearance to report the disappearance of Joseppi. I was hurried back to prison, and an extra makkieh fitted to me. How I cursed Joseppi, but I did not know then that the poor fellow had been murdered. It was not long after this when I saw Adlan brought into the prison, heavily weighted with chains, and taken to a hut some distance from all the others, the prisoners being forbidden to approach or speak to him.

During the night, on pretence of going to the place of ablution, I shuffled towards his hut, and when a few yards distant, lay on the ground and wriggled close up, stretching my chains to prevent their rattling and attracting the notice of the guards. Asking in a whisper, "What has happened?" he replied in a startled voice, "Imshee, imshee (go away, go away), do not speak to me; a big dog has me by the leg this time; go away, or he will get your leg." I tried again to learn what was the matter, but Adlan's entreaties for me to go away were so earnest that I wriggled off, and gained my hut without being discovered. Soon afterwards Adlan's slave boy, when walking past my hut, said, "Do not speak to my master; if you do, you will hear the ombeyeh." The whole night through the boy passed backwards and forwards between Adlan's hut and his house outside. Asked as to what he was doing, he gave the same reply each time I put a question to him, "Burning papers; do not speak to my master." I had learned from Adlan that he had been in communication with "friends," and understanding from him that, in the event of my ever returning to Egypt, I was to be his "friend at court" with the Government, I suspected that he was destroying all evidences which might be used against himself and others. That the Khaleefa himself had received word of some correspondence is evident from the rage he exhibited when Adlan's house was searched, and no incriminating documents found. Idris es Saier nearly lost his head over the matter, for the Khaleefa accused him of having assisted Adlan in disposing of the papers in some way.

On the morning of the third or fourth day of Adlan's imprisonment, we saw him led out of his hut bound, and taken to the anvil to have his chains struck off. We all knew what this meant—an execution, but most of us believed that the Khaleefa was only doing this to frighten Adlan, and impress him with this evidence of his power. We were not allowed to approach him, but Adlan called out, "This is my day; have no fear, any of you. I am a man. I shall say and do nothing a man need be ashamed of. Farewell." While extra chains were being fitted to my ankles, the ombeyehs were announcing the death of Adlan. The mourning for his death was general, but few if any knew the reasons which actuated the Khaleefa in ordering his execution. Maybe the fugitive Khaleefa himself only knows, but it is possible I can throw a little light on the matter. To coin a word, Adlan had been "Gordonized;" about the time of the anniversary of Gordon's death, Adlan met with his, and while waiting for that help which, as will be seen, started "too late."

CHAPTER XIII
THE TRUE HISTORY OF MY ATTEMPT TO ESCAPE

If I am wearying my readers with this long-drawn-out episode, which never seems to draw to a close, I may ask their forgiveness on the ground that weeks have been spent in collecting the links which were scattered between Europe and Omdurman, and without the links complete the tale might, and very reasonably so, have been disbelieved.

The messengers I despatched with the first letters quoted, arrived in Assouan some time in January or February, 1889, and delivered the letters to Mankarious Effendi, who at once wrote to my manager, as he had sold up my business, and left for Alexandria. Receiving no reply, Mankarious Effendi wrote to the German Consulate at Alexandria, who, on March 4, replied as follows:—

"Alexandria, March 4, 1889.

"MANKARIOUS EFFENDI RIZK, Assouan,—

"In reply to your letter of February 18 last, I am very sorry to inform you that the agent of Mr. Charles Neufeld, the Mahdi's captive in the Soudan, Mr. Möller has shown that he cannot help Mr. Neufeld in any way. It is rumoured here that the house established by Mr. Möller for Mr. Neufeld has refused payments for some months back, therefore Mr. Möller finds it quite impossible to send to Mr. Neufeld any sum unless he refuses many payments to numerous creditors who claim any amounts from Mr. Neufeld's house. Mr. Möller was called to this Consulate, and directed to give a full statement as to his proceedings in the said house, and how the latter stands, and on doing so, it was found that Mr. Möller has done nothing wrong, and we have therefore nothing to say against Mr. Möller.

"But as regards the £500 deposited in the Credit Lyonnais by Mr. Neufeld before his departure to the Soudan, Mr. Möller has shown receipts for over £400 paid to creditors, and the rest was spent as travelling expenses between here and Assouan, and for the establishment of the new house in Alexandria. Still Mr. Möller has asked Abd-el-Kader Bey, who came recently back from the Soudan, to advise him as to the way in which he could send him a sum of money. Abd-el-Kader Bey's advice, however, was that no money should be sent to Mr. Neufeld, because the latter cannot make use of money there. Abd-el-Kader Bey stated, further, that Mr. Neufeld was then in chains, and was only induced by his guards to ask for money. He was then very much threatened and ill-treated by them. This is all about the case now which I lay before your notice.

"(Signed) The German Consul,

"HELWIG."

At the same time, my manager, on my own letter-paper, sent the following:—

"Alexandria (undated).

"After salaams, etc., yours to hand and details notified. In reply, I inform you that I presented myself at the German Consulate, and found a letter from you addressed to the Consulate, stating therein that Mr. Neufeld had written to you to the effect that he claims £500 from me, although I had paid this sum to creditors who claimed sums from Mr. Neufeld. I have sent goods to Halfa and Assouan, the value of which I have not yet received. I inform you further that Nicola Lutfalla has sold the dahabieh, the horse, and the donkeys, and did not send me the price of same, though he sold these without any permission from me. Consequently I wrote to him to send me the account or the money, yet nothing of the kind was received from him.

"Will you kindly arrange to sell all the goods in charge of Nicola, because he wrote me saying that he was ill, and can neither buy nor sell; so kindly sell the things and forward the money in order to cover the claims (*i.e.* the sums advanced to me by my guides, and the money I had asked for).

"Please also have a complete list made by Nicola, showing all the things he sold, and let me have this list, making thereby the thing clear, otherwise I shall have to take measures through the Government.

"Regarding our two houses in Assouan, will you kindly let them for any rent, from which you will pay the taxes. Should they be vacant now, please look after them, and send people each week to keep them clean. They should always be kept locked. Should anything remain what cannot be sold, keep it for Mr. Neufeld, and any letter you write me, please address to Mr. Möller, Mr. Neufeld's agent in Alexandria, and oblige.

(Signed) "MÖLLER.

"N.B.—Ask Nicola for account as well."

While this correspondence was being conducted, another of my messengers arrived, and again Mankarious Effendi wrote to the Consulate, receiving the following in reply:—

"Alexandria, March 12, 1889.

"A previous letter, dated March 4, was sent you. On the same date a letter was received from you. You may be sure that what Mr. Wilhelm Möller says is quite true, that is that Mr. Neufeld is no longer a German subject nor *protégé*, because during his stay in Egypt Mr. Neufeld has never claimed the protection of Germany, where he was born. Thus he has lost his nationality. This is according to what we learn from the parties interested in Germany. Upon this, this Consulate can in no way look into the affairs of Mr. Neufeld nor protect his rights, except to punish Mr. Möller should he have done anything to be punished for, as we stated to you in our letter of March 4th. But the investigations made in our Consulate show clearly that Mr. Möller has done nothing wrong for which he ought to be punished.

"Should you, however, think it necessary, with reference to Mr. Neufeld's two letters, which are returned herewith, to have his business made over to you, this step should be taken before the Mixed Tribunals, if Mr. Möller refuses to make over to you Mr. Neufeld's business willingly.

"As regarding the testament made by Mr. Neufeld, which you sent to this consulate on October 23, 1887, this was first kept in this consulate, and then, when Mr. Neufeld's wife came here in September, 1888, she asked for it, as it had been reported that Mr. Neufeld was dead. This testament was then sent to the Governor of Alexandria as the one concerned, to which Mrs. Neufeld had to refer as a local subject. So the Governor opened the testament, and handed it to Mrs. Neufeld, who is still in possession of it. Mr. Möller has now removed his business to Cairo, where he intends to get married. Salaams.

(Signed) "The German Consul,

"HELWIG."

Mankarious would have entered an action to secure my property, but the argument had been used that the letters were not written by me, and that perhaps I did not know their real contents. He did not know, nor did the Consulate in a later incident know, that the small Latin characters written by me on these letters proved their genuineness, as they were the "cash code" I had used with my manager in business telegrams. Mankarious sent Mohammad Ali back to Omdurman with my discredited bill, and with verbal messages that he would do all in his power to raise monies for my escape. While he was making arrangements, Moussa Daoud-el-Kanaga, who had spent some time on the road ingratiating himself with the people whose assistance we should require in our flight, put in his appearance, and learning how matters stood, without confiding in Mankarious or Mohammad Ali, came on to Cairo, in the hope that he would be able to get the money on the strength of the letter that I had given him, for, as he admits, he wanted all the glory and all the profit for himself.

I continue the history from the sworn statement of Kanaga, taken before a lawyer and in the presence of witnesses who could vouch for the greater part of it. I admit I was myself a little incredulous, but Kanaga has since backed up his statement by producing two documents, the authenticity of which cannot for a moment be called into question, while two are actually recorded *in extenso* in the registers of the German Consulate. Kanaga, according to his statement, on arrival at Cairo, presented the letter addressed to my manager, at the German Consulate, delivering at the same time my verbal messages. By the German Consulate he was taken to the Austrian Consulate-General, who, after hearing his news, sent a consular official with him to the War Office, where he related his story.

It is quite evident that Count Wass, the Austrian Consul-General, believed that Kanaga would be assisted to start back immediately on the proposed expedition, for he entrusted him with an autograph letter dated Sunday, October 27, 1889, addressed to Slatin, asking Slatin to request the Khaleefa to reply to the message sent him by the Emperor of Austria concerning the Austrian Mission captives. Kanaga was put off time after time on the grounds that no reply had been received to the letter he had delivered. Losing patience, he returned to Assouan and made up a caravan on his own account, and, when all was ready, returned to Cairo to report that all arrangements were complete. He was again passed from one to the other, and on April 26, 1890, he presented himself for the last time at the German Consulate, and being told that there was "no reply," he demanded a certificate to the effect that he had delivered my letter, but had not received any monies in connection with it, when a signed and sealed certificate was given him.*

> * "Attestation. At the special request of Moussa Daoud-el-Abadi (Ababdeh), this is to certify that the above on October 22, 1889, brought to the Imperial Consulate a letter addressed to William Möller Assouan, and said to be from Charles Neufeld. This is to certify also that the said letter to Mr. Möller was sent to Mr. Neufeld's father, but up to the present no monies have been received in respect of it. Signed, Becker."

> The letter itself was copied into the Consular registers G. 48, p. 385, and the following is a translation of the contents:—

> "William Möller Assouan. Three days ago I sent to you Mohammad Ali with a letter and receipt for £100. Do not make any difficulties about payment, and give him as much money as possible according to the letter I have sent you. He is a sure man, and I hope he will be the go-between between me and you after this, and there shall be reward for it. I have agreed with him that he shall receive 25 per cent. of the amount you give him for his services. With the other man mentioned in his letter and mentioned here, you might act as

you like, but do not make any difficulties to him. I hope I shall be able to buy my liberty after his return, and then all expenses shall be rewarded. I have sent to you up to now." ... The Consulate omitted to register the names of the guides sent, and left the space blank. The certified copy of this letter also states that the letter contained certain Latin characters which were undecipherable; these, again, were my 'cash code' to my manager, proving the authenticity of the letters and guaranteeing the contents. On the back of the letter was written, 'Pay to Moussa Daoud-el-Kanaga the sum of £30 received. Dated December 5, 1888.'"

Kanaga concealed the Consular certificate and the letter for Slatin in his jibbeh, and set off for Omdurman. On nearing Berber he was met by a dervish patrol, taken prisoner, and hurried before the Mahdist Governor of the town. There he was confronted by two men who swore to having seen him conversing with myself and Wad Adlan. This Kanaga did not deny, but said that he had only spoken about trade, and that he had permission to trade. The Governor told him it would be better to tell the truth, for he had received the news from Omdurman of Wad Adlan having assisted him in arranging my escape, and had also received news from Cairo of his visits to the War Office and the Consulates, and knew that the goods he had with him were a blind to his real object in going to Omdurman. But, continued the Governor, Adlan has been killed, and Neufeld has more chains on him. No confession could be dragged out of Kanaga, so he was flogged and thrown into prison, the Governor confiscating his camels and property. After a short spell in prison, Kanaga was set free and told to return to his own people. To have sent him as a prisoner to Omdurman would have necessitated the Governor sending at the same time the confiscated camels and goods, and as the Governor wished to keep these for himself, the only way he could keep them was by "forgiving" Kanaga, and releasing him. Kanaga lost no time in making his way back to his people, but after this narrow escape, he made no further efforts to penetrate into the Soudan, and the relation of his experiences deterred every one else from attempting my escape.

In giving my narrative to the world—owing to the very evident attempts made in certain quarters to discredit me—I have felt it incumbent upon me not for my own sake, but for the sake of my mother, wife and child, and relatives, to produce as far as lies in my power reliable evidence that the slanders persistently circulated in the Press before and since my release are only what I have characterized them to be. Therefore none may cavil at the means I adopt for the attainment of this object provided those means are honest, however disagreeable the process may eventually turn out to be for others.

In reply to the charges of refusing to escape from the Soudan, I have, I venture to believe, brought together the links of the chain of evidence in my favour up to the present period of my narrative. Other evidences will be forthcoming in connection with incidents to be treated of later. The letters I have quoted are ample proof that from October, 1888, until April, 1890, my guides and myself were doing all in our power to effect my escape. Meanwhile, the Intelligence Department on March 10, 1890, are writing to my wife as follows:—

"Mohammad Effendi Rafai, late Sub-Lieutenant, 4th Battalion, 5th Regiment, who left Khartoum three months ago, states he knew Neufeld very well, and saw him at Omdurman only a few days before he left. Neufeld had been under surveillance until about five months prior to this, but was now free. His release was owing to one of the Emirs representing to Abdullah Khalifa the great service Neufeld had been in enabling arms and ammunition to be taken from the Kabbabish at the time Neufeld was captured. He now was employed as one of the Khalifa's mulazimeen, and received a small salary; the Khalifa gave him two wives, and treats him well. Neufeld has very little to complain of except want of funds, which renders living difficult, good food being very dear. He is frequently staying with Ibrahim Bey Fauzi, who has opened a small coffee-shop. It is untrue that the Khalifa ever threatened Neufeld's life; he was only threatened with imprisonment unless he turned Mussulman. Does not think it possible that Neufeld can receive any letters, etc., from outside. Neufeld does not occupy himself in business in any way. Has never heard Neufeld express any wish to go away, but does not think he would be able to do so even if he wished it, as every one knows him."

In September, 1888, it had been reported to my wife that, having made an attempt to escape, I had been recaptured, and taken back to Omdurman and executed. It was therefore very kind and considerate of the Intelligence Department to see the error rectified, but I venture to think that the sweets of the good news need not have been converted into gall and wormwood by telling her that I owed my release to my "assistance" in betraying the caravan of the loyal Sheikh Saleh into the hands of the dervishes. Even had there been any truth in such a statement, I think that an English lady might have been spared this unnecessary heart-pang. I thank God nightly—ay, hourly, that He has brought me alive from the hell I lived in, to rescue my wife from the hell she was thrown into with such reports as these.

It must not be imagined, from the foregoing, that there is the slightest intention on my part to cast aspersions on the War Office or the Consulates. I place plain simple facts before you, and these because at the time when I was anxiously awaiting the return of my messengers, picturing to myself the efforts my friends were making to ensure success—though, as has been seen, they were very differently occupied—reports were being circulated that I refused to escape, and my wife in consequence was the recipient of numberless letters of sympathy, in which some were "praying to the Almighty to turn the heart of your erring husband," while others were expressing the hope that the ties which bound her to me would soon be severed by my meeting my deserts at the hands of the Khaleefa's executioner! Those who prayed for me I thank; One who knew the truth, heard those prayers: those who condemned me I do not blame, and feel no resentment against; they merely believed what was communicated to the Press.

CHAPTER XIV
A PRISONER AT LARGE

The disappearance of Joseppi, followed by the death of Adlan, threw me into a state of almost abject despair; there appeared to be no hopes of my ever being released from the Saier, and after the replies given by Abdullahi to Wad Adlan and the Muslimanieh when they interceded for me, my friends outside evidently abandoned all hope also. But I was to have an interesting fellow-prisoner whose deceptions on Abdullahi and others were indirectly to lead to my release. It will take many generations of Gordon College teachers to uproot the firm belief of the Soudanese in "jinns" (spirits, sprites, and fairies) and in the supernatural powers claimed to be possessed by certain communities and individuals. Centuries of most transparent deceptions have not shaken their belief, so that it was no wonder the Mahdi found many imitators in the miracle-working line, and that these people found thousands of believers. The more these charlatans failed in their endeavours to produce powder from sand, lead from dust, and precious metals from the baser ones, the more credence was given to the next professing alchemist who came along. A man named Shwybo of the Fellati country (near Lake Chad), had driven a good trade in Omdurman by inducing people to give him large copper coins to be converted into silver dollars; he had offered his services to Wad Adlan, but as the Beit-el-Mal had been mulcted in some thousands of dollars already by people like him, Adlan refused to entertain any of his propositions.

On the death of Adlan, Shwybo offered his services to the Khaleefa, and the Beit-el-Mal. The Kadi was instructed to inquire into his pretensions; Shwybo professed to have power over the jinns who converted copper into silver; a number of his dupes presented themselves to the Kadi, and complained that Shwybo's jinns had not only not converted the coins given them to work upon, but had stolen the coins into the bargain. Shwybo pleaded that the action of the jinns was in consequence of the want of faith of the complainants, and to their curiosity in trying to see the jinns at work; the jinns would never work in the presence of strangers; no one but himself might be in the place where the converting of the metals was in progress. Shwybo was given about a hundred dollars' worth of copper coins, and incense, drugs, spices, etc., to a further value of nearly two hundred dollars, which were taken from the Beit-el-Mal, and charged to the account of the Kadi. The incense, drugs, and spices were to propitiate the angry jinns; but to ensure their not being disturbed at work, the Kadi said Shwybo had better carry out his experiments in the Saier where Idris would see he was not interfered with.

He was given a hut apart from the rest, where he set to at once with his incantations and incense burning. Idris and a number of the prisoners were invited to go and see the coins buried in the ground—the jinns having been propitiated. A quarter of an hour's incantation was given, Shwybo speaking a language which must have been as unintelligible to himself and his jinns as it was to us. A similar incantation had to be given each day until noon on the following Friday, as it was at this hour each week that the jinns finished off any work they had in hand. On the Friday, at noon, we were asked to go to Shwybo's hut, and on the earth being removed, sure enough the copper coins had disappeared, and silver dollars had replaced them! The next Friday only part of the coins had been converted, when Shwybo remembered that the jinns had not been fed, and must be hungry. They had delicate tastes; asseeda they would not eat, so they were liberally supplied with roast chickens, pigeons, white bread, milk, eggs, etc. We were not permitted to see them eat, but we were allowed to see the clean-picked bones and empty egg-shells! Something went wrong again, for on the following Friday it was discovered that none of the coins had been converted; evidently Shwybo had run through his stock of dollars.

Idris, at the request of the Kadi, asked me my opinion of the whole thing, as Shwybo wished to have another try. I replied that little children in my country would not be deceived by such trickery, and that if the Kadi wanted to spend his money on food, he had better buy food for the starving women and children, and not waste it on supposed jinns. Whether my reply, or the conviction that he had been duped angered him, I cannot say, but Shwybo received a severe flogging. Not a cry escaped his lips; he laughed at the Saier, telling him to strike harder. The flogging over, he told Idris that although his silver-working jinns had flown off, and through no fault of his, his gold-working jinns had come to his succour, and had interposed their bodies between his and the lash. Idris, as I have already pointed out, was the incarnation of superstition and credulity, and it was only necessary for Shwybo to tell him that his faithful gold jinns could convert lead into gold, to set Idris collecting dollars from the prisoners on the Nebbi Khiddr account. With these he set up a special laboratory for Shwybo in the house of Wad Farag, one of the gaolers—and a reputed son of Idris. Shwybo was provided with a number of small crucibles, two sets of Soudanese bellows, with a couple of slave boys to work them, a quantity of lead and a number of packets of drugs and powders from the Beit-el-Mal pharmacy. Farag was told to keep an eye on him, and see that he did not purloin any of the gold when it appeared.

When the first lot of lead was melted, Shwybo drew Farag's attention to its reddish colour, proving that the conversion was taking place; then Farag retired while Shwybo uttered another incantation; on being called in again, and the cover being removed from the crucible, a bright yellow mass was seen, from which strong fumes arose. Farag was told to cover up the crucible quickly, which he did, and left the room with Shwybo to allow of the jinns completing their work and cooling the metal. Farag went off to Idris and the Kadi, telling them that the conversion of the lead to gold had actually taken place; that he had seen the gold for himself. The Kadi was dubious, but as Idris only was employing Shwybo on this work, he declined to come into the prison to see the gold turned out. When it was believed that the work was complete, Idris, Farag, and Shwybo proceeded to the laboratory, and lo! the crucibles were found empty. Shwybo thereupon accused Farag of having stolen the block of gold, and a pretty row ensued; the prison and the prisoners were searched, and the gold not being found, Farag was flogged to make him disclose its hiding-place. Shwybo essayed a second attempt, but as Idris insisted upon remaining in the laboratory from beginning to end, the jinns refused to work, and then Shwybo was flogged. One would have thought that, after this, people would see that Shwybo was duping them, but he continued to collect money for conversion from the prisoners, and now and again was able to give to an earlier dupe one or two dollars he had received from a later one. Complaints were made against him though, and he received repeated floggings to make him discontinue his frauds, dying in the prison as a result.

It was while Shwybo was working away at his alchemistic frauds that Hassan Zecki, an old Egyptian doctor, and then in charge of the medical stores of the Beit-el-Mal, came into the Saier in connection with the drugs being purchased on Shwybo's account; Zecki had known me by name for some time, for I had in my practice as "medicine man" frequently sent him notes for the medicines I required, and not knowing the Arabic terms, I used the

Latin names for such drugs as I was acquainted with. From this, Zecki must have come to the conclusion that I was a qualified chemist, and as at that time his assistant, Said Abdel Wohatt was, and had been for some time, trying to extract saltpetre in Khartoum and the neighbourhood, Zecki questioned me as to its production in Europe, but I had to admit that I had only seen the crystals obtained in the laboratory when at the University, and had no experience of their production on a commercial scale. I told Zecki what little I knew of testing the crystals, and you may imagine my surprise when three days later I was summoned before Yacoub to explain the manufacture of saltpetre.

The new Amin Beit-el-Mal—El Nur El Garfawi—came to the Saier after sunset, and conducted me to Yacoub's house. One thinks rapidly under such circumstances, and by the time we reached Yacoub's house I had my tale thought out. I saw that if I declared that I could not do the work I should not be believed, and would be flogged and have extra irons placed on me for contumacy. To lead them on to believe that I could manufacture saltpetre meant my release from prison. After a long discussion with Yacoub, it was arranged that I was to construct three large tanks, about six feet long and four feet high, in which impregnated earth was to be mixed with water, and the solution drawn off and allowed to evaporate. Believing that I should be set to make these tanks or reservoirs, I suggested them, as their construction would necessitate the removal of my chains. The following morning I was called to the anvil, the rings holding the heavy iron bar were cut and forced open, and the heavy ankle-chain I was wearing was replaced by a piece of light awning chain taken from one of Gordon's steamers. I was thankful even for this relief, as it removed a dead weight of fifteen to twenty pounds of iron from my feet. Under an armed escort I was taken to the Nile, where I found awaiting me the Emirs Yacoub, Ahmed Fedeel—who is now causing trouble on the Blue Nile—Mohammad Hamad'na Allah—Zobheir Pasha's old Wakeel—and a party of thirty to forty workmen with materials for the tanks. Whenever Abdullahi gave an order, immediate execution of it followed.

I had existed in the vile-smelling Saier for nearly four years, and you can imagine how I enjoyed the two hours on the river reaching Halfeyeh. On arrival at this place, we were met by El Fiki Amin, a Fellati then in charge of the works. He did not disguise his displeasure at my being taken there, as he evidently considered it a slight upon himself. He was extracting the saltpetre from mounds, mixing the earth and water in pierced jars lined with fine matting, allowing the solution to filter through, and then boiling it down to obtain the crystals; his appliances were very primitive, but he was producing a very good quality of saltpetre in "needles." Yacoub ordered me to search the ground for any deposits, and, coming to a dark damp patch, I tasted the earth, and, believing saltpetre to be present, I mixed some of the earth with water, pouring off the solution into a small coffeepot, and setting it to boil. More solution was added as the water boiled away, and at the end of two hours I had a small deposit of a thin syrupy consistence; pouring this upon a burnt brick, the moisture was absorbed, leaving the crystals behind, and these on being placed on hot charcoal burned away. I next took some of the earth, dried it, and rubbing it fine, allowed it to fall in a thin stream on to the fire; the "sissing" and occasional coloured sparks convinced them that a valuable deposit had been discovered, and Hamad'na Allah was sent to Omdurman to inform the Khaleefa.

During his absence, the Fellati told Yacoub that the burning of the crystals was no proof that they were saltpetre; I was therefore told to produce a quantity to be submitted to Zecki and the Greek Perdikaki, the Khaleefa's gunpowder manufacturer. Hassan Zecki came to Halfeyeh to examine the crystals and declared them good; Perdikaki sent a Greek employed with him, but he not being able to give an opinion, took the crystals to Perdikaki, who sent me a message to the effect that they were useless, but that rather than I should be sent back to prison he would say they were good on condition I tried to produce further quantities in "needles," and not in grains. On Hassan Zecki presenting his report to the Khaleefa, and telling him that I should have some large pans sent out to me, he sent off a number of large copper boilers, and an officer's camp bath. The latter must have been taken from Khartoum or Hicks Pasha's army. The Fellati grew very sullen, and Yacoub, knowing that the Khaleefa was entirely dependent upon the Fellatis—the only people who seemed to understand the extraction of the saltpetre—rather than offend the man, asked me if I thought I could not find deposits elsewhere. I suggested looking further north, but this would not do. He wanted a place close to Omdurman—where I could be watched. I then suggested Khartoum, but the Khaleefa would not at first hear of my transfer there. What probably decided him was, that when I had been two weeks at Halfeyeh, Hasseena came to tell me Makkieh was dead, and the Khaleefa, hearing of the loss, and believing that there was now nothing to hold me in the Soudan, agreed to the transfer to

Khartoum, as there a better watch could be kept upon me. I was not sorry to leave Halfeyeh, for although the place offered every facility for my escape, I saw that I had a jealous and bitter enemy in the Fellati, who was then spying on my every movement. It was certain that he would frustrate any plans I might make for flight, and suspicion would have been aroused immediately if any of the guides came to me there.

Hamad'na Allah was made director of the Khartoum saltpetre works! Abdel Wohatt was his second, and I was to work under the orders of Wohatt. On arrival at Khartoum, January, 1891, I was also placed in charge of Khaleel Hassanein, the director of the arsenal, and all three had to answer for me with their lives. Wohatt was given the chapel of the Mission as a house to live in; I was given one of the priest's rooms opposite the arches. Windows, doors, every scrap of wood, metal, and ornaments had been taken from the place; it was almost a complete ruin, but the garden had been kept in excellent condition, its produce—dates, figs, oranges, limes, and vegetables—being sold on account of the Beit-el-Mal. Wohatt, when arranging his sleeping quarters, found the altar in his way, and made two or three ineffectual attempts to pull it down; failing, he utilized it as a resting-place for household rubbish, and here cocks crowed and hens hatched out their broods.

When we came to construct saturation tanks, it was proposed to take the material from the walls of the Mission, but I told Hamad'na Allah and Wohatt that as we had to live in the place, it would be far better to repair than further demolish; so the necessary materials were brought from outside by the fifty to sixty slaves sent over to assist us in making the tanks and carrying the earth from the mounds. While the construction of the tanks proceeded, we had to extract saltpetre in the boilers, etc., sent to us at Halfeyeh, and which had been brought with us; we produced maybe four to five pounds per diem on an average during a period of six months—the time we were occupied in building the tanks. Perdikaki made some gunpowder with our first consignment; it was a failure. The good fellow, though, mixed it with some powder from the old Government stock, and sent us another warning. My chief, Abdel Wohatt, was the son-in-law of Ali Khaater, the director of the Omdurman arsenal, to whom our saltpetre went in the first instance; Perdikaki telling him of the bad quality, Khaater, fearing for his son-in-law, mixed our next consignment with an equal quantity of saltpetre from the old Government stock in his stores, and thus it passed muster, although Perdikaki complained again that it was only half purified. However, the powder made with it would explode, though it did leave about 25 per cent. of ash. The Fellati, hearing of the success, came to Khartoum to examine our product, for the secret of producing pure crystals was believed to be in the hands of the Fellati only, and, as a matter of fact, in the Soudan, it is. Again he declared the crystals were useless for the purposes they were intended for; but as Abdel Wohatt had been a dispenser in the Egyptian Army, and as such was supposed to be a chemist, and I, as a medicine man, being similarly credited, we won the day. Fellati appealed to Perdikaki, but got no satisfaction in that quarter. But Perdikaki was not long to be troubled with the rival saltpetre makers; on the sixth anniversary of Gordon's death, some tins of powder in his factory exploded, killing him and those working with him.

Some time about June or July, 1891, our tanks were finished; in about two months' time we produced between five or six cwts. of crystals, and then stopped work on account of the rains. These crystals were mixed with an equal quantity of good crystals from the stores, and were sent to the powder factory. It must not be imagined that at this time the Khaleefa was actually short of powder or ingredients for its manufacture; there were, unknown to others in the town, very large stocks indeed, which Abdullah was keeping as a reserve, but he wished to add to that reserve as much as possible, and to expend only such powder and ammunition as was then and there produced.

On the death of Perdikaki, Hassan Hosna—a Circassian, and, I believe, formerly an officer in the old army—and Abdes Semmeer, formerly in the ordnance section of the old army at Kassala, were placed in charge of the powder factory. When our mixed product was used for the manufacture of gunpowder, strange things happened. After a few cartridges made from such powder had been fired, the barrel of the rifle was found coated with a thick white fouling; then an inquiry was held. The rifles were brought to us at Khartoum, and, pointing to the cleaning rods, I asked what these were intended for; on being told for cleaning the barrel, I asked whether it was not better to have a powder which left a white ash which might be seen to a powder which left a black ash which could not be seen. But, for once, my argument was of no use. Wohatt replied that perhaps we were working on bad beds, and suggested our being transferred somewhere else. Nothing was done at the time, and we worked on for some more months; but as large quantities of saltpetre came in from Darfur, and later, considerable quantities of good powder came from Upper Egypt and by the Suakin route, Khaater was able to store away our saltpetre, and supply the factory with powder and saltpetre from these sources.

The Upper Egypt and Suakin supplies were supposed to have been put to the reserve, so that when cartridges exploded in the breeches of the rifles, and destroyed the eyesight of a number of soldiers, our saltpetre came in for the blame again. Another inquiry was held, when we were told that the bullet did not leave the rifle, and that the breech-blocks blew open. This, we argued, could not be the fault of the powder, but of the rifle. Whatever the Khaleefa's opinion might have been, he sent off Wohatt to Alti on the Blue Nile, where, with a number of Fellatis working under him, he was able to send considerable quantities of "needle" saltpetre to Omdurman, while I continued at the Khartoum works to turn out as poor a quality of saltpetre as before. Abdel Wohatt is in Cairo now, and tells me that our precious production—about two tons of saltpetre—is still lying unused in the stores at Omdurman. Khaleel Hassanein and Ali Khaater are still alive, and would doubtless smile at the legend that I "manufactured powder for the Khaleefa to shoot English soldiers with," particularly when I forbade the use of wood ash in the saturation tanks, and this addition, they knew later, was the Fellati secret for the purification of the saltpetre.

While employed at the Mission-house in Khartoum, Father Ohrwalder came on three or four occasions to see me, the last occasion being, I believe, about a month before his escape. We would sit together talking of old times, commiserate each other on our hard lot, and guardedly, very guardedly, breathe a hope that, in some way and by some means, our release would come, but I have no recollection that we ever confided to each other any plans for escape. Father Ohrwalder knew that I had had letters written by some Greeks, but I do not think he knew of any of my plans. That we did not openly discuss such plans now appears to me strange— and yet it is not strange. Where all led for years a life of falsehood, in which deception of self had a no less part than that of others, suspicious of every one around us, trusting no one, what wonder that deceit became a second nature, and that truth, honour, and morality—that is to say, morality as preached in Europe—should have retired to vanishing point!

When I heard of Father Ohrwalder's escape, the conclusion I at once jumped to was that my guides, seeing the impossibility of effecting my escape from Khartoum, had come to some arrangement with him. How fervently I cursed them all, but I did not pray for their recapture. Even had I done so, it would have been useless. There was nothing, provided you had money with which to purchase camels and arrange a couple of relays in the desert, to prevent every one who wished to, escaping from Omdurman. Your guides had only to lead you away from any settlements; no pursuers could overtake you once you reached your first relay, fast as their camels might go, and you would travel at twice the speed the news of your flight could, besides having some hours' start of it. In the event of your coming across any straggler on the desert, a few dollars would silence his tongue, for the dollar is not more "almighty" in America than it was in the Soudan. Supposing the dollars did not appeal to him, and your bullet missed its mark, the chances were a thousand to one against his picking up your pursuers on the route you had come, for they would make to the settlements near the river, and waste their time in useless inquiries, while you were lengthening the distance between you.

CHAPTER XV
DIVORCED AND MARRIED

As if my troubles were not all-sufficient in themselves, Hasseena, in addition to the begging and other undesirable proclivities she had developed since the death of Makkieh, added that of thieving. She naturally devoted her talents in this direction to my friends, knowing that they would not, on my account, prosecute her. Numberless complaints came to me, and many a recommendation was made to get rid of her; but as she had been sent to me by the Khaleefa, I could not send her off without his sanction. The question also arose as to what excuse I might offer for divorcing her; to give the real reasons might end in her being stoned, mutilated, or imprisoned, and this I shrank from. I must admit, too, that, bad as she was then, I did not like the idea of throwing her over. Being in receipt of ten dollars a month, I sent word to my friends that I would save what I could to repay their losses, and do my best to break Hasseena of her bad habits. My friends warned me that if I was not careful I should find myself before the Kadi as Hasseena's partner in crime; and the Kadi, being no friend of mine, would certainly order me into prison again, which would put an end to all chances of escape.

In the end Hasseena had to go. Nahoum Abbajee, my greatest friend, gave a feast at his house to celebrate the marriage of his son Yousef. Hasseena was one of the invited guests. She stole all the spoons and cutlery before the feast commenced, and also a number of articles of dress belonging to other guests, all of which she sold in the bazaar. Nahoum could overlook her stealing his property, but to steal the property of guests under his roof was carrying matters too far. He sent word to me that I must get rid of her, and at once. Calling Hasseena to Khartoum, I was compelled to quarrel with her in such a way as to attract the attention of Hamad'na Allah, and on his asking me the reason for our constant squabbles, I told him that Hasseena was not acting as she should by me, and begged his intervention in obtaining through the Emir Yacoub the Khaleefa's permission to divorce her. Abdullahi was "gracious," permitted the divorce, and sent word that he would select another wife for me. This was just what I did not want. Always expecting the return of my guides, my not having a woman in the place lent probability to my having a whole night's start upon my pursuers, for my absence might not be discovered until sunrise the following morning, at which time we went to work, and some hours more would be lost—and gained—by Hamad'na Allah and others making a thorough search for me before daring to tell the Khaleefa that I was missing.

Returning my thanks to Abdullahi, I asked to be left in single blessedness for a time; but to this he replied that "his heart was heavy at the loss of my child; that no man might be happy without children, and he wished me to be happy; he also wished me to have all the comforts of life, which did not exist where woman was not; that if I did not take another wife, he would believe I was not content with my life in the Soudan under his protection." It was a long rigmarole of a message he sent, and it wound up by saying that as I had been ill for two months, he must send a wife to attend to me, and had selected for the purpose a daughter of Abd-el-Latif Terran.

This was making matters worse than ever, for this girl, although brought up in the Soudan, and speaking only Arabic, was a French subject, being the granddaughter of Dr. Terran, an old employé of the Government. She was only nominally Mohammedan, and lived in the "Christian quarter." When marriages took place in this quarter, the Mohammedan form of marriage was gone through, and then Father Ohrwalder performed the Christian religious ceremony surreptitiously later in the day. I spoke to him about the Khaleefa's intention, and as he knew I was already married, he advised me to try and get out of the proposed marriage by some means or another, as it would be considered binding. After casting about for excuses which I thought might appeal to the Khaleefa, I asked Hamad'na Allah to inform him that I thanked him for his selection of a wife, but as she was of European descent, had been brought up in a rich family where the ladies are waited upon and never do any work, she would be no use to me, as I required some one to nurse me, do the cooking and house work, and go to the bazaar to buy food, all of which she had had servants to do for her; I therefore begged to be allowed to select a wife of the country.

The latter part of my message evidently pleased the Khaleefa; it appeared to him as an earnest that I was "content," but again he undertook the selection of the woman. When Abdullahi told any woman she was to be the wife of any one, she dare no more refuse to accept than the one she was sent to dare refuse to receive her. Fearing that he might send me some one from his hareem, I asked Nahoum and other friends to find me a wife—sharp. My object was to get her into the place before Abdullahi sent his "present," whom, on arrival, I might send back on the plea that I was already married, and could not support two wives. Nahoum found me a wife, and sent me the following history of her.

UMM ES SHOLE AND TWO CHILDREN.

Umm es Shole (the mother of Shole—Shole being the name she had given her first child) was an Abyssinian brought up from childhood in a Greek family settled in Khartoum. On reaching womanhood, she was married to one of the sons of the family. On the fall of Khartoum, her husband, with seven male relatives, was butchered in the house in which they had taken refuge; Umm es

Shole, with her three children, was taken as "property" to the Beit-el-Mal, where she was handed over as a concubine to the Emir of the Gawaamah tribe. Refusing this man's embraces, he in revenge tortured her children to death, upon which Umm es Shole escaped to Omdurman. Through Abd-el-Kader, the uncle of the Mahdi, she had her case brought before Mohammad Ahmed, who, after listening to the details, gave her a written document declaring that, as she had been married to and borne children to a free man, she was a free woman, but to make certain that she might never be claimed as a slave, the document also declared that she was "ateekh" (freed) by him.

When Abdullahi succeeded the Mahdi, he ordered every woman without a husband, and every girl of a marriageable age, to be married at once. He was most particular that every one in the "Christian quarter" should be married. Umm es Shole married an old and decrepit Jew, whom she nursed until he died two years later. Returning to a woman relative of her husband's, she supported the old woman and herself by cooking, preparing food for feasts, sewing, and general housework.

This was the wife my friends had selected for me, and I accepted her thankfully; but when she was approached on the subject, she positively declined to be married again, and it was only upon her being told that I was ill, and might die, that she consented to the marriage. I had to appoint a "wakeel" (proxy, in this instance) to represent me at the marriage and the festivities; Nahoum prepared the feast at his house, the bride preparing the food and attending to the guests. At the conclusion of the few days' ceremonies and feastings, Umm es Shole was escorted to Khartoum—a married woman, and introduced for the first time to her husband. She set to at once with her household duties and attendance upon me, and during a long and weary five months nursed me back to life.

As can well be believed, Hasseena resented no less bitterly my projected marriage with Umm es Shole, or any one else, than she resented her divorce, and this she resented very bitterly indeed, for passing as the wife of a European and a presumed "General" to boot, gave her a certain social status in Omdurman, which she took advantage of when visiting in the various ways pointed out. On my saying to her, "You are divorced," which is the only formula necessary in Mohammedan countries in such a momentous domestic affair, she promptly replied that she was again pregnant. A few words on the subject of divorce in the Soudan—and the rules are practically identical with those laid down in the Quoranic law—will assist towards an appreciation of the fix this declaration of Hasseena placed me in.

If a woman, on being told "you are divorced," declared herself with child, the husband was compelled to keep her until its birth; if it was a son, the divorce was null and void; if a daughter, the husband had to support the wife during two years of nursing, and provide for the child until her seventh year, when he might, if he chose to do so, claim her as his daughter.

When a woman was divorced for the first time, she was not allowed to marry again without the consent of the husband; this was giving him a "first call" if he wanted her back, for divorce might be declared for less trivial things than incompatibility of temper. If the husband took her back, and divorced her a second time, the woman was free to marry, but if the husband again wanted her, he had to pay her a marriage dowry as at her first marriage. Should he divorce her a third time, and again want her back, he would have to arrange for her to be married to—and divorced from—some one else first, when she was free to return to him. All this may sound very immoral to people in Europe, but one cannot help but admire the simplicity of the proceedings; and consider the amount of domestic infelicity it prevented. There is no public examination of the parties concerned; no publication of interesting details in newspapers; some little thought is given to the woman who may have been the mother of your children, and should she have slipped in the path of virtue, you do not shout it from the housetops; the marriage was a private arrangement between you, so is the divorce, and the reasons for the latter are your affair and no one else's.

I have touched upon divorce in some detail, as many re-marriages under all the conditions given above occurred, and some family records became a hopeless tangle to all but those immediately concerned. When the new Soudan Government comes to settle up claims to properties, they will be confronted with a collection of "succession" puzzles to solve, for one woman might be the proud mother of the legitimate heirs of three or four different people, and being, as the widow and mother of the heritor, entitled to a fixed proportion of the properties, you may be quite sure that she will fight to the death for her sons' interests.

Hasseena ought not to have been in the interesting state she declared she was, for we had been separated for a much longer period than that ordained by law. I was obliged to tell her that if she empanelled a jury, after the example of Idris es Saier, all the explanations they might offer would not convince me that I held any more relationship to the child than I did to Makkieh, and there was nothing now to induce me to claim the paternity,—indeed just the reverse. However, if Hasseena was with child, I should be bound to keep her for at least two years, and if the Khaleefa sent on his present, I should have two households to support on ten dollars a month. When making my plans for escape, Hasseena was included; she was to have got away on the same dromedary as myself. When my guides returned, they would find me with two wives, and having made arrangements for one only, they might demur at taking the two. The probabilities were they would abandon the thing altogether, fearing that one or the other might betray them, which meant instant execution for them and imprisonment for me. If I kept Hasseena, she might steal from some stranger, as the houses of my friends were now closed to her, and then I should be sent back to the Saier; if I sent her away, she, knowing my guides and all my arrangements, would be the first to meet them on arrival in Omdurman, and would insist upon coming away with me under threats of disclosing the plot. It was a most awkward fix for me to be placed in; but after considering the whole matter most carefully, I decided upon sending Hasseena off, and trusting to luck for the rest. I had hoped she might get married to some one in Omdurman, and then I should not have been afraid of her. But Hasseena returned in February, 1892, some months after my marriage with Umm es Shole, carrying a little bundle of male humanity, who had only been three or four months less tardy in arrival than Makkieh.

Hasseena, doubtless, had for me the Soudan equivalent for what we understand as affection; she had saved my life when we were first captured; she had nursed me, as only a woman can nurse one, through my first attack of typhus fever, and had kept me from starvation during the famine. But while I could not forget all this, I could not forget also that she had become a source of great danger to me, and although my treatment of her in sending her away when I did, might to some appear harsh in the face of what she had done for me, it must not be forgotten that self-preservation is no less a law of nature in the Soudan than it is elsewhere. I supported Hasseena for nearly two years, when her child died. She then left Khartoum, where I was still a chained prisoner at large, and went utterly to the bad. I heard of her from time to time, and, on my release in September last, hearing that she was at Berber, I delayed there until I had hunted her out of the den of vice in which she was living, and provided for her elsewhere, only to receive a telegram a few weeks later to say that, hankering for the life which she had led for a few years back, she had run off to return to it.

It was this action of mine, which probably gave rise to the legend that I had brought her to Cairo with me, where my wife arrived, "only to be confronted with a black wife after all her years of mental anxiety and sufferings." Why facts should be so persistently misconstrued, I cannot understand. In making that last—and I do not say final—effort, to do something for the woman to whom, at one time, I owed so much, I feel I have nothing to be ashamed of. Those who think differently must remember that it takes one some little time to fall again into European ideas and thoughts after twelve years of chains and slavery amongst the people whom I was compelled to associate with; and no one in the Soudan was more out of the world than I was.

CHAPTER XVI
HOPE AND DESPAIR

While still a prisoner in the Saier, Mankarious Effendi, with Mohammad Fargoun and Selim Aly, engaged a man of the Ababdeh, Mohammad Ajjab, to make his way to Omdurman with a threefold object: he was to inquire if I was still alive; if so, to pay me a hundred dollars, and then to try and make arrangements for my escape. On arrival in Omdurman, Ajjab met two of his own people—Mohammad and Karrar Beshir—who recommended him, when he inquired about me, never to mention my name if he wished to keep his head on his shoulders. They could only tell him that I was still in prison, chained, and under sentence of death. Similar information and the same recommendation were given to him by people in the Muslimanieh quarter; but a Greek whom Ajjab knew only by his Mahdieh name of Abdallah, said that he would arrange for a meeting between him and my servant. Through Hasseena, Ajjab sent me word of the object of his coming to Omdurman. As the Greek offered to become my trustee, Ajjab handed him the hundred dollars, taking from him a receipt, and sending the receipt to me concealed in a piece of bread, to be countersigned. Ajjab was to return to Assouan, let my friends know how matters stood, and tell them that I would try and communicate with them, if I ever got released from prison, as escape from the prison was an impossibility. Ajjab returned to Assouan, and handed over the receipt; but the tale he had to tell put an end, for the time being, to any attempts to assist me further.

When Father Ohrwalder escaped, bringing with him the two sisters and negress, Mankarious set about immediately to find some reliable messenger willing to undertake the journey to Omdurman with a view of ascertaining if my escape was at all possible. He argued that if Father Ohrwalder could escape with three women as an encumbrance to his flight, there was nothing, provided I was at liberty, to prevent my escaping; but those who knew the Soudan— and it was only such he might employ—argued that if the remainder of the captives were not already killed, they would be found chained in the prison awaiting their execution. Months slipped away before he could find any one to undertake the journey, and then an old but wiry desert Arab, El Haj Ahmad Abou Hawanein, came to terms with him. Hawanein was given two camels, some money, and a quantity of goods to sell and barter on his way up.

Some time in June or July, 1894, Abou Kees, a man employed in the Mission gardens, came to me while I was working at the mounds of Khartoum, and whispered that a man who had news for me was hiding in the gardens, and that I was to try and effect a meeting with him. The man was Hawanein. Always suspicious of traps laid for me by the Khaleefa, I asked the man what he wanted. He replied that he had come from friends to help me. He had brought no letters, but by questioning him my suspicions disappeared, and I was soon deep in the discussion of plans for my escape. The camels he had brought with him were, he said, not up to the work of a rapid flight, and he suggested that he should return to Assouan, procure two good trotting camels, and also the couple of revolvers I asked for, as it was more than likely I should have to use them in getting clear of Khartoum.

Soon after Hawanein's departure, the guide Abdallah, who brought away Rossignoli, put in his appearance. Ahmed Wad-el-Feki, employed in Marquet's old garden, asked that I might be allowed to call and see a sick man at his house. On reaching the place, Feki introduced me to a young man, Abdallah, who, after a few words, asked me to meet him the following day, when he would bring me a letter. I met my "patient" again, when he handed me a bit of paper on which faint marks were discernible; these, he said, would come out clear upon heating the paper, and, as cauterization is one of the favourite remedies in the Soudan, some live charcoal was procured without exciting any suspicion. The words, which appeared, proved that the man was no spy, but had really come from the Egyptian War Office; however, before we had time to drop into a discussion of plans, some men employed in the place came near, and we had to adjourn to the following day, when I was again to meet my "patient." On this occasion we were left undisturbed, and fully discussed and settled upon our plans.

To escape along the western bank of the Nile was not to be thought of; this would necessitate our passing Omdurman, and to pass the town unobserved was very improbable. Abdallah, having left his camels and rifle at Berber, was to return there for them, and come up the eastern bank of the Nile, along which we were to travel when I escaped. During his absence I was to send Umm es Shole on weekly visits to her friends at Halfeyeh; as she was to escape with us, this arrangement was made for a twofold purpose. First, her visits would not excite suspicion at the critical moment, as the people both at Halfeyeh and Khartoum would have become accustomed to them; she was also to bring me the promised revolver concealed in her clothes, and then return to Halfeyeh for another visit. She and Abdallah would keep a watch on the banks of the Blue Nile for me and assist me in landing. My escape would have to be effected in my chains, and these, of course, would prevent my using my legs in swimming. I was to trust for support to the pieces of light wood on the banks, used by children and men when disporting themselves in the Nile, and to the current and whatever help I might get with my hands for landing on the opposite shore.

Abdallah went off, but never came back. I kept to our agreement for months, for the plan formed with Abdallah was similar to that arranged with Hawanein. Besides this, Abdallah, in the event of not being able to find revolvers at Berber, was to continue his journey to the first military post, obtain them there, and exchange his camels for fast-trotting ones, as those he had left at Berber were of a poor race. In order to prove to any officer he met that he was really employed to effect my escape, I gave him two letters couched in such words that, should they fall into the hands of the Khaleefa or any of the Emirs, their contents would be a sort of puzzle to them. Each day during those months I looked forward eagerly to a sign from any one of the people entrusted with my escape.

For various reasons I considered it advisable to interview Abdallah after my release, and did so; but to make certain of his explanations, I also arranged that others should question him on the subject of Rossignoli's flight and his reasons for not keeping his engagement with me, and this is what he says.

On leaving Cairo, he was given a sort of double mission; he was promised three hundred pounds if he brought me away safely, and a hundred pounds if he brought away any of the other captives. Seeing the difficulties to be encountered in effecting my escape, and appreciating the risks, unless we had revolvers and swift camels, he decided upon "working out the other plan," as he expresses it, viz. the escape of Rossignoli, as "he was at liberty and could go anywhere he pleased," whilst I was shackled and constantly under the eyes of my guards. Instead of returning for the camels, Abdallah arranged for Rossignoli to escape on a donkey as far as Berber. When some distance from Omdurman, Rossignoli got off his donkey, squatted on the ground, and refused to budge, saying he was tired. Abdallah tried to persuade him to continue the journey, but Rossignoli refused, said Abdallah was only leading him to his death, and demanded to be taken back to Omdurman. For a few moments Abdallah admits that he was startled and frightened. To go back to Omdurman was madness and suicide for him; to leave Rossignoli squatting in the desert made Cairo almost as dangerous for him as Omdurman, for who would believe his tale there? He felt sure he would be accused of having deserted the man, and there was also the chance of Rossignoli being discovered by pursuers, when a hue and cry would be set up for Abdallah.

One cannot help but admire Abdallah's solution of the difficulty. There was a tree growing close by; he selected from it a good thick branch, and with this flogged Rossignoli either into his right senses or into obedience to orders; then placing him on the camel behind him, he made his way to Berber. Here Rossignoli, instead of keeping in hiding, wandered into the town, was recognized by some people, and, when spoken to, told them that Abdallah was leading him to Egypt, but that he preferred to return to Omdurman. Fortunately native cupidity saved Abdallah; he baksheeshed the people into a few hours of silence, with great difficulty got his charge clear of the town, and with still greater difficulty hammered and "bullydamned" him into Egypt and safety. This is Abdallah's own tale. He assures me, and I believe him, that it was his intention, as soon as he had handed over Rossignoli safe, to have asked for the revolvers and started back to try and effect my escape, risky as he knew it to be; but as Rossignoli had betrayed his name in Berber, he knew well that the Khaleefa would have men waiting for him from Omdurman to the frontier, and he showed no better sense in flogging Rossignoli, than he showed in settling down with his well-earned hundred pounds rather than attempting to make it into four hundred by passing the frontier.

Rossignoli's absence was not noticed for a little time, and fortunately, for a donkey leaves better tracks to follow than a camel. The Khaleefa was not particularly angry about the affair, although he imprisoned for a day Mr. Cocorombo, the husband of Sister Grigolini, the former superioress of Father Ohrwalder's Mission, and Rossignoli's lay companion, Beppo; but the latter, after Slatin's escape, became my fellow-prisoner in the Saier.

One would be inclined to believe that either myself or some dramatist had purposely invented the series of accidents, which cropped up to frustrate every one of my plans for escape. On February 28, 1895, without a word of warning, I was so heavily loaded with chains that I was unable to move, and I was placed under a double guard in the house of Shereef Hamadan, the Mahdist Governor of Khartoum. At first I surmised that either Abdallah or Hawanein had been suspected and imprisoned, or had confessed, or that our plots had been divulged in some way, so that it was with no little surprise I heard the questions put to me concerning the escape of Slatin. I denied all knowledge of the escape, or any arrangement connected with it. I pointed out that I had not seen, spoken to, or heard of Slatin directly for eight years, as my gaolers and guards could prove. It was from no sense of justice to me, but to prove that he had not neglected his duty in keeping a strict watch upon me, that Hamadan took my part in the inquiry. I might have been again released, had Hawanein not put in his appearance a few days after the escape of Slatin was discovered.

Slatin's absence from his usual post had not been reported to the Khaleefa until three days after his escape; he was supposed to be ill. On the third day, Hajji Zobheir, the head of the Khaleefa's bodyguard, sent to his house to inquire about him. Not being satisfied with the reply he received, he informed the Khaleefa, who ordered an immediate search. A letter from Slatin to the Khaleefa was found sticking in the muzzle of a rifle, and was taken to Abdullahi. After the usual string of compliments and blessings, the letter continues—

"For ten years I have sat at your gate; your goodness and grace has been great to me, but all men have a love of family and country; I have gone to see them; but in going I still hold to the true religion. I shall never betray your bread and salt, even should I die; I was wrong to leave without your permission; every one, myself included, acknowledges your great power and influence; forgive me; your desires are mine; I shall never betray you, whether I reach my destination or die upon the road; forgive me; I am your kinsman and of your religion; extend to me your clemency.*

> * This letter was found on the fall of Omdurman, and came into the hands of people who, probably on the ground of its contents differing from those given by Slatin after his escape, published it in such a manner as to lead people to believe that the protestations of loyalty it contained were sincere. In my opinion the letter should be looked upon as a clever composition to humbug Abdullahi, so that, in the event of Slatin being retaken, the protestation of loyalty would at least save him

from the hands of the Khaleefa's mutilator or executioner.

SAID BEY GUMAA.

Abdullahi, on first realizing that Slatin had actually escaped, and had had about three days' start of any pursuers he might send after him, was furious; losing his temper, he anathematized him in the presence of the assembled Emirs, Kadis, and bodyguard. He reminded them that when Slatin first tendered his submission, he had been received with honours because he had openly professed the Mohammedan faith and had been circumcised while still the "Turk" Governor-General of Darfur; he reminded them also how Slatin had been allowed to bring into the camp his household, bodyguard, and servants, and had been attached to the Mahdi's personal suite, of which he, Abdullahi, was chief; how, with Zoghal, his former subordinate, he had been entrusted with the subjugation of Said Gumaa, who had refused to surrender El Fasher when ordered by him to do so; how he himself had treated him as his son and his confidant, never taking any step without his advice and guidance; but, suddenly pulling himself up, seeing the mistake he had made in showing how much he had been dependent on him, he broke off short to say what he would do to Slatin if he ever laid hands on him, and promised a similar punishment to any one else who returned him ingratitude for his favours. Reading out aloud Slatin's letter to him, he calmed down on reaching the protestations of loyalty, and ordered the letter to be read in the mosque and the different quarters of Omdurman. Abdullahi has been considered as an ignorant brutal savage, devoid of all mental acumen, and but little removed from the brute creation. As I may be able to show later, such an expression of opinion either carries a denial with it, or it is paying a very poor compliment to those who, once governors of towns and provinces, or high officials, should have bowed down, kissed hands, and so far prostrated themselves as to kiss the feet of the representatives of this "ignorant brute," by whom for years they had been dominated. Since Abdullahi respected me, as a man, by keeping me constantly in chains, I respect him for the intellectual powers he displayed, and which apparently paralyzed those of others who submitted to him.

Slatin, having given a good account of himself in his many fights, was, after his submission, looked up to as the military genius of the Mahdist army; he could not, as I did, play any pranks with the work he was entrusted with; the map he had drawn of Egypt, showing the principal towns and routes, and upon which the former telegraph-clerk, Mohammad Sirri, had been instructed to write the Arabic names, had given some the idea that no expedition might be planned without the aid of Slatin and this map. Abdullahi's object in having the letter publicly read will be divined; first, it would assure the dervishes themselves that there was no fear of Slatin, after his protestations of loyalty, returning at the head of the Government troops to overthrow the rule of the Mahdi, and without help from the exterior the wavering Mahdists could not hope to throw off the yoke of Abdullahi. Moreover, the reading of the letter to the Christian captives would confirm the opinion formed by many, that Slatin was at heart with the present Soudan dynasty, and that they could not expect any help as a result of his escape.

There is another incident, which must be here mentioned, to show how acute Abdullahi really was. Slatin had publicly proclaimed his conversion to Mahommedanism before his submission to the Mahdi, so that, when he did submit, he was accepted as one of the faithful, and treated as one of themselves. The remainder of the captives—those taken before and after the fall of Khartoum—had not, up to the time of the escape of Rossignoli, been actually accepted as Muslims. At the suggestion of Youssef Mansour, on January 25, 1895, the Khaleefa was gracious enough to take all into his fold as real converts to the faith, and, on the anniversary of Gordon's death, all the Muslimanieh (Christians) were ordered to be circumcised, the only two people not being operated upon being, I believe, Beppo, who was overlooked while in prison, and an old Italian mason, who pleaded old age as an excuse for not undergoing the operation. The Christian quarter was, therefore, at the time of Slatin's escape, considered as a Muslim community, and the practical immunity they had   enjoyed from a rigorous application of the Mahdieh laws was thereby put an end to.

Consequently, when Slatin escaped, leaving behind him such protestations of loyalty, the safest card the Khaleefa could play was to read to them his letter. The reading of it caused some little consternation and comment, no doubt, but I have already expressed my opinion as to the light in which this letter should be considered. It was a clever move of Abdullahi; the public reading of the letter blasted all hopes on the part of the discontented Soudanese of any assistance from Slatin in crumbling to dust the kingdom of the Khaleefa, and put an end to all hopes on the part of the former Muslimanieh captives of release, for the small proportion of old Government employés who had, up to then, firmly believed that Slatin was acting, as they express it, "politeeka" in all his dealings, now joined the ranks of those who believed differently. But in this they were, of course, mistaken.

After the public reading of the letter, the Khaleefa sent for the officials of the Beit-el-Mal and ordered them to take possession of Slatin's house, wives, servants, slaves, land, and cattle, at the same time giving them strict instructions, in the presence of all, that the household were to be treated gently, as being the property of a true Muslim. His Darfurian wife, Hassanieh, whom he had married when Governor-General of Darfur, was claimed from the Beit-el-Mal by Dood (Sultan) Benga as of a royal family, and was by him married to another of the Darfurian royal family. Desta, his Abyssinian wife, was within a few days of her confinement, and either, as a result of fright at the ransacking of the house and her reduction to the position of a common slave, or as a result of what would be to her, in her then delicate condition, rough handling, gave birth to a baby boy, who survived but a few weeks.

It was while the Khaleefa was awaiting the return of the scouts sent out to recapture Slatin that Hawanein put in his appearance at Omdurman. He was at once seized, accused of assisting in the escape of Slatin, and also of having returned to effect mine. Pleading ignorance of myself and Slatin, he was not believed; he was first sent into the Saier, and then, as he refused to confess, he was taken out and publicly flogged. Even this did not extort a confession; the Khaleefa, not being satisfied, ordered another flogging, but the Bisharas interceded for Hawanein, and succeeded in obtaining his release. As my would-be deliverer passed through the portals of the Saier, I passed in (March 26, 1895). Hawanein lost no time in returning to Assouan, where the relation of his experiences, with his torn back and unhealed wounds to bear him out, put an end finally to all attempts in that quarter to assist me in any way whatever.

It might be as well that I should not attempt to describe my mental condition on finding myself again in the Saier. I have a faint idea of what my state must have been; despair cannot describe it; insanity at blasted hopes might. Yes, I must have been insane; but I was mentally sound, if such a contradiction of terms is permissible. I remember that for days I shuffled about, refusing to look at or speak to any one. Perhaps what brought me round was that, in my perambulations, I came near the Saier anvil and heard a man crying. It was Ibrahim Pasha Fauzi, Gordon's old favourite, who was being shackled. My expostulations on his acting as a child and bullying him into a sense of manhood, again prevented that slender thread between reason and insanity snapping. It must, in some way, have calmed and comforted me to be brought to the knowledge that others were suffering as much as I was; and just as a child, which requires care and attention itself, gives all its affection and sympathy to a limbless doll, so must I have given my sympathy to Fauzi, and in so doing taken a step back from the abyss of insanity, which I was certainly approaching.

CHAPTER XVII
A NEW OCCUPATION

When Said Abdel Wohatt was transferred from the Khartoum to the Alti saltpetre works, his father-in-law, Ali Khaater, the storekeeper of the Omdurman arsenal, considered that he was no longer under the obligation of risking his neck by mixing the Khartoum product with the Fellati's, or substituting it with good saltpetre in stock. A consignment of mine was consequently sent direct to the powder factory, and was used in making what Abd es Semmieh and Hosny, the directors, believed would be a good explosive. The result, while being eminently satisfactory to myself, was just the reverse for the people responsible for making the powder. Not being certain where the fault actually lay, they mixed this powder with a quantity of really good powder made from the Fellati's product, only to succeed in spoiling the whole bulk. When my next consignment was sent in they carried out some experiments, and, discovering where the fault lay, sent me an intimation that if our works did not turn out saltpetre equal in quality to that formerly supplied by us, I should be reported to the Khaleefa. Nahoum Abbajee, hearing of the affair, came to me in a state of excitement, and pointed out the danger I was running into, and as he was then trying to think out an invention for coining money, he suggested that he should apply to the Khaleefa for my services in assisting him. This request Abdullahi was only too glad at the time to accede to; saltpetre was coming in in large quantities, and he was in great trouble about his monetary system.

As Khaleefa, he was entitled to one-fifth of all loot, property, taxes, and goods coming to the Beit-el-Mal; and as all property of whatever description was considered to belong primarily to this administration, it followed that Abdullahi was entitled to one-fifth of the property in the Soudan; but as he had not much use for hides, skins, gum, ivory, and such-like, he took his proportion in coin—after putting his own valuation upon his share. As the money he took from the Beit-el-Mal was hoarded and never came into circulation again, a sort of specie famine set in. Attempts had been made in the early days of Abdullahi's rule to produce a dollar with a fair modicum of silver; but Nur-el-Garfawi, Adlan's successor at the Beit-el-Mal, came to the conclusion, evidently, that a coin was but a token, and that it was immaterial what it was made of, provided it carried some impression upon it. The quantity of silver in his dollars grew less and less, and then was only represented by a light plating which wore off in a few weeks' time. When people grumbled, he unblushingly issued copper dollars pure and simple. All the dollars were issued from the Beit-el-Mal as being of equivalent value to the silver dollar, and when these coins were refused, the Khaleefa decreed that all future offenders should be punished by the confiscation of their property and the loss of a hand and foot. The merchants, though, were equal to the occasion; when an intending purchaser inquired about the price of an article, the vendor asked him in what coinage he intended to pay; the merchant then knew what price to ask.

As the silver dollars gradually disappeared, the few remaining went up enormously in value, until in the end they were valued at fifty to sixty of the Beit-el-Mal coins, so that an article which could be bought for a silver dollar could not be purchased under fifty to sixty copper dollars. Although a rate of exchange was forbidden, the Beit-el-Mal took advantage of the state of affairs by buying in the copper dollars, melting them up, recasting, and striking from a different die. These coins would be again issued at the value of a silver dollar, and the remaining copper dollars in the town were put out of circulation by the Beit-el-Mal's refusal to receive them. To make matters worse, the die cutters cut dies for themselves and their friends, and it was worth the while of the false (?) coiners to make a dollar of better metal than the Beit-el-Mal did, and these we re-accepted at a premium. The false coinage business flourished until Elias el Kurdi, one of the best of the die cutters, was permanently incapacitated by losing his right hand and left foot; and this punishment, for a time at least, acted as a deterrent upon others, leaving the Beit-el-Mal the entire monopoly of coinage.

Sovereigns might at any time be bought for a dollar, for their possessors were glad to get rid of them. Being in possession of a gold coin denoted wealth, and many people who attempted to change a gold coin returned only to find their hut in the hands of the Beit-el-Mal officials, searching for the remainder of the presumed gold hoard. Failing to find it, they confiscated the goods and chattels. The trade with the Egyptian frontier, Suakin and Abyssinia, was carried on through the medium of barter and the Austrian (Maria Theresa) trade dollar.

It was while the currency question was at its height that Abbajee came forward with his scheme for a coining press; and, in order that I might assist him, I was transferred to the Khartoum arsenal.

I was obliged to give up my quarters in the Mission buildings, and live with the bodyguard of thirty Baggaras in the house of Hamadan, the Mahdist governor of Khartoum. The arsenal was presided over by Khaleel Hassanein, at one time a clerk under Roversi, in the department for the repression of the slave trade. Although ten years had elapsed since the fall of Khartoum, the arsenal must have been in as perfect working order as when Gordon made it into a model Woolwich workshop. Power was obtained from a traction-engine, which drove lathes, a rolling-mill, drills, etc., while punches, iron scissors, and smaller machinery were worked by hand. In the shops proper were three engines and boilers complete, ready to be fitted into Nile steamers, and duplicates and triplicates of all parts of the machinery then in use were ready in case of accidents. Smelting, casting, moulding, and modelling were all carried on in the place. The storeroom was filled with every imaginable tool and article required for the smithy, carpenters' shops, and the boats. All the metal of the Soudan had been collected here. There were parts of cotton presses; sugar-mills; bars of steel and iron; ingots of brass and copper; iron, copper, and brass plates; the heavier class of tools and implements; and I was assured by Osta Abdallah, a rivetter in the shops in Gordon's time, that there was material in the place to build three more boats and keep the whole fleet going for many years. He did not exaggerate either. All other administrations were supplied by the Khartoum arsenal with whatever they required in the way of tools, furniture, iron and other metal work, cartridge presses and steel blocks for coinage; and very efficiently indeed was the work turned out.

The little time I spent in the arsenal was of course fully occupied with the coinage question. Two men were kept constantly engaged casting square steel blocks for the Omdurman mint; these blocks were polished and cut in Omdurman, and twenty-five sets were generally in use at the same time. Possibly two hundred men were employed in the melting of the copper and casting it into moulds the size and thickness of the dollars. The discs were next passed on to the people who gave them the impression; this was obtained by placing the disc on the lower block, and then hammering the upper block upon it. The impressions produced were in the main very poor; the coins spread and split, and the dies were constantly splitting and breaking. After we had studied the process, and Abbajee had explained his ideas of a press, I suggested that we should commence operations with the punching-machine. We experimented until we had succeeded in smashing dies, spoiling sheets of copper, and in the end smashing the machine itself; then Abbajee, as the chief of the operations, was roundly abused. Being of an excitable temperament, he wanted me to take part of the blame, but I only laughed at him. Then it was I learned that he had just reason to be angry; he had gone surety for me with the Khaleefa, and, as I was expecting Hawanein and Abdallah every day, I kept the quarrel going until Abbajee left the work in disgust, for I wished him to be out of the way when I escaped. His return to Omdurman, leaving me in complete charge of the invention, put an end to his surety for me. I might have saved myself this trouble, and the temporary misunderstanding with my old friend, for, before I had time to settle upon an idea for a coining press, Slatin escaped, and I was taken back to the Saier.

I have been frequently asked what estimate should be put upon the Khaleefa's buried treasure. It is next to impossible to say; one thing only is certain: all good gold and silver jewellery and coins have disappeared during the last fifteen years. Thousands of individuals may have their hoards here and there. Some idea of what the Khaleefa's treasure may amount to might be gleaned from an examination of the Beit-el-Mal books, for these were well kept. The real question is, Where is it? But this is a matter people need not trouble themselves about. It was generally believed in Omdurman that those who actually buried the money were soon afterwards buried themselves. "Dead men tell no tales." I doubt myself if the Khaleefa's hoards will ever be found—officially. The fortunate discoverers are hardly likely to exhibit any particular anxiety to ask their friends or the Government to share in their good fortune. Perhaps a small amount might be found, but it will be a very small one. The few millions he has buried in various places will, no doubt, be discovered some day, and we shall hear about it—a long time after the fact.

CHAPTER XVIII
MY SECOND IMPRISONMENT

It was some days after my return to the Saier before I learned that I had been incarcerated against the wish of the Khaleefa and Yacoub; but Hamadan and Khaleel-Hassanein, fearing that I might escape, declined to be responsible for me any longer, arguing that Slatin's escape had been effected through Government agents, and that mine would certainly follow. In deference to the wishes of Hassanein more than those of Hamadan, the Khaleefa ordered my return to the Saier, but it is very probable that he sent Idris es Saier instructions how to treat me; so that, taking it all in all, my life was not rendered so unendurable as it had been on my first entry into the prison. Added to Abdullahi's kindly interest (?) in me, Idris himself had become a sort of reformed character; he had tasted the sweets of imprisonment and the lash which he had been so generous with, and had also experienced himself what it was to be robbed on the Nebbi Khiddr account. The tables had been completely turned on him, and he had learned a lesson.

When Adlan was executed and his house searched for incriminating papers without result, Idris es Saier was accused by the Khaleefa of having assisted Adlan in disposing of the documents which he was in search of. Idris was imprisoned in his own house and flogged into the bargain; he was in disfavour for some time, and this gave released Baggara prisoners an opportunity of getting even with him. They explained the Nebbi Khiddr affair to Abdullahi, who ordered Idris to repay all the moneys he had collected on this account; he was deprived of all he had, but right up to the end, any former Baggara prisoner in want of a dollar knew where to find one. He presented himself to Idris, and asked for a further contribution towards a settlement of his claim.

These importunities drove Idris into begging from the prisoners, since the Nebbi Khiddr tale would only work with prisoners coming in from outlying districts, and they were few. As Idris never knew when the next call would be made upon him, he found it politic to be as kind and considerate to the prisoners as possible, and to relax discipline to the utmost. This state of affairs, added to the presumed instructions of the Khaleefa regarding myself, must have accounted for Idris' assembling the gaolers, and telling them in my presence that I was only brought into the Saier to prevent any Government people from carrying me off to Egypt; that if any one of them begged money from me or ill-treated me in any way, he would be imprisoned, flogged, and deprived of his post; Umm es Shole and her child were to be allowed to come into the prison at any hour they chose—but, and this spoiled all, I was never to be allowed to sleep out in the open, and must pass my nights in the Umm Hagar.

FAUZI PASHA IN DERVISH DRESS.

I have already described a night in this "Black Hole of Calcutta," but it might not be out of place to try and give a slight description of the first night Ibrahim Pasha Fauzi—one of Gordon's favourite officers—spent in that inferno, especially as he wishes me to do so. When taken to the anvil, as I have already remarked, Fauzi broke down completely, was carried off in a swoon to the Umm Hagar, placed sitting with his back in the angle of the wall furthest from the door, and there left—as I was, to "come round." When the first batch of prisoners was driven in at sunset, there was room for all to lie down on the foul and saturated ground. When the second batch was driven in about an hour and a half later, those lying down had to sit up with the new-comers, and Fauzi's outstretched legs gave a dry and comfortable seat to four big Soudanese. I was driven in with the third batch after the night prayers, and then all in the Umm Hagar had to stand up or be trampled on. Fauzi, still suffering from the effects of the shell wound he received in one of the sorties from Khartoum, with four people sitting or standing on him, and being heavily chained as well, was unable to rise to his feet. I could hear him from my place near the door feebly expostulating with the people who were standing upon him; I thought that maybe he was being trampled to death, and in my then frenzied state commenced to fight my way towards him, striking friend and foe indiscriminately, and striking harder as I received blows in return. A general fight was soon in progress over the few yards I had to travel, as none were certain in the darkness who struck the blow they had received, and struck out at random in retaliation. My friends told me afterwards that I was a "shaitan" (devil), a mad fool, and showered other dubious compliments upon me; but I reached Fauzi. The warders, hearing the uproar, had opened the doors, and, as usual, commenced to belabour the heads of all they could reach with their sticks and whips. While the uproar was at its height, and the prisoners swaying from side to side, I recognized the voices of one or two near Fauzi who were under obligations to me for occasional little kindnesses in the way of food; and, enlisting their services on most extravagant promises, we tackled the people standing on Fauzi's legs, pushed them away, and made a sort of barricade round him with our bodies. In clearing the space, we must have struck each other as often as we struck those whom we wished to get out of the way, and Fauzi could not tell whether an attempt was being made to murder or to rescue him. When we did at last get him clear, we had to use a bit of old rag as a sort of punka in order to bring him round; then he babbled.

At midnight, the doors of the cell were thrown open again, and about twenty men, each wearing a shayba, were thrust into the place; practically there was no room for them, but they had to be driven in by some means. To make space for them, the gaolers resorted to their favourite device of throwing into the cell handfuls of blazing straw and grass, and at the same time laying about the bare heads and shoulders of the prisoners with their whips. The scene must be imagined. Fauzi, seeing the fire falling on the heads of the prisoners, believed that he had really been sent to hell—but communed with himself in a dazed sort of way as to whether he was in hell or not. He appeared to call to memory all that he had ever read of the place of torment, and tried to compare the picture his brain had formed of it from the descriptions, with what he was experiencing, coming to the conclusion that he could not be in hell, as hell could not be so bad. At this stage I was able to get him to take notice of me, and we discussed hell and its torments until sunrise; but nothing could even now shake Fauzi's opinion that hell could not be as bad as such a night in the Umm Hagar, and the worst he can wish any one is to pass such a night. To Youssef Mansour he wishes an eternity of them.*

> * This Mansour was formerly an officer in the Egyptian Army, who had surrendered with the garrison at El Obeid. After this surrender, the governor of the town—Mohammad Said Pasha—arranged with his old officers and black regiments to seize their arms, on a given signal, and to turn against the Mahdists. Mansour, who, as one of Said's former subordinates, was in the plot, is thought to have betrayed it to the Mahdi. Said and his principal adherents were sent out of camp by Mohammad Ahmed, and quietly done away with; but Mansour became the favourite of the Mahdi, and commanded his artillery at the battle of Omdurman. It is also said that the Christian captives were circumcised on his representations, and that he suggested the imprisonment of Fauzi, lest, when the Government troops advanced, Fauzi should seize an opportunity of joining them. Yet Mansour is reputed to be coming to Cairo to claim his back pay and pension from the Egyptian Government.

Among others who spent that memorable night in the Saier, were Ahmed and Bakheit Egail, Sadik Osman, Abou-el-Besher and others from Berber, arrested for assisting in the escape of Slatin; they were later transported to the convict station at Gebel Ragaf on the evidence of the guide Zecki, who conducted Slatin from Omdurman to Berber. Zecki had been arrested with them on suspicion of complicity in the escape, and confessed that he had been engaged by Egail and others to bring away from Omdurman a man with "cat's eyes," but that he did not know who the man was.

Close to the common cell was an offshoot of it—a smaller one named "Bint Umm Hagar" (the daughter of Umm Hagar), which took the place of the condemned cell in Europe. On my return to prison, I learned that my old enemy, Kadi Ahmed, had been confined there for a year. The ostensible reason for his imprisonment was that he had been in league with the false coiners, and had made large amounts of money; but the real reason was that the Khaleefa was angry with him on account of the death of Zecki Tummal, who had conducted the Abyssinian campaign when King John was killed. Kadi Ahmed had been induced by Yacoub to sentence Zecki to imprisonment and starvation; so when Ahmed's turn came, the Khaleefa said, "Let him receive the same punishment as Zecki." He was placed in the Bint Umm Hagar, and after about ten months the doorway was built up; there Ahmed was left, with his ablution bottle of water only, for forty-three days according to one tale, and fifty days according to another. When, for days, no sounds had been heard from his living tomb, he was presumed to be dead; but on the doorway being opened up, to the astonishment, not to say superstitious fear, of all, he was still alive, but unconscious, though the once big fat Kadi had wasted to a skeleton. Abdullahi must have received a fright too, for he ordered Ahmed to be tenderly nursed and given small doses of nourishing food every twenty-four hours, until the stomach was able to retain food given oftener; but in spite of all care and attention, the Kadi died on or about May 3, 1895. He was regretted by no one but the Khaleefa, in whose hands he had been a willing tool, dispensing justice(?) as his master dictated it, only to die the lingering death in the end to which he had condemned so many at his master's nod.

Kadi Ahmed's place in the "Bint" was soon taken by his successor—Kadi Hussein Wad Zarah. His offence was that of refusing to sentence people unjustly, when ordered by the Khaleefa and Yacoub to do so. When first walled up in his tomb, he was given, through a small aperture left for the purpose, a little food and water every four or five days, but towards the end of July, 1895, the doorway was built up entirely, and Zarah, not being a big stout man like Ahmed, starved, or rather parched, to death in about twenty-two or twenty-three days. It is hot in the Soudan in July.

NEUFELD'S HUT IN THE SAIER, SHOWING THE
FAMOUS ANVIL.

During the first weeks of my imprisonment, Umm es Shole had little difficulty in begging a small quantity of grain, and borrowing an occasional dollar to keep us in food. But soon people became afraid of assisting us any further, and we were bordering upon semi-starvation, when, in the month of September, an Abyssinian woman came into the prison to see me under pretence of requiring medical treatment. She handed me a small packet, which she said contained letters from my friends, and which had been given to her by a man outside, who had said he also had money for me, and wished to know who he should pay it to. Three days elapsed before I found an opportunity of opening the packet unobserved, for with all letters received and written then, I had to wait until I found myself alone in the pestilential atmosphere of an annexe to the place of ablution. The packet contained a letter from my sister posted in 1891, another from Father Ohrwalder, and a note from Major Wingate. They were all to the same import—to keep up hope, as attempts were to be made to assist me.

Nearly two months must have slipped away before I succeeded in getting my replies written. I sent these to the guide, Onoor Issa, who promised that he would return for me in a few months' time. Father Ohrwalder has handed me the letter I sent to him. The following is in brief its contents:—

"I have received your letter enclosing that of my sister written four years ago, and the note from Wingate. Before everything else, let me thank you for the endeavours you are to make to assist me. Your letter was delayed in reaching me owing to the imprisonment of the guide, followed by the watch kept upon us after Slatin's escape, and my transfer to the Saier, from which I hope to be released soon. There is great need of coins here; up to the present, no one has been able to produce a silver-resembling dollar. If I could produce such a coin, it would lead to my release from prison, and lend probability to my chances of escape. Could you send me instructions for the simple mixing of any soft metals to produce a silvery appearance, and send me some ingredients? I should like also an instrument to imitate the milling of coins; the dies can be cut here. I should be glad of any tools or instruments which you think cannot be had here. If I am not released by the time these arrive, I feel sure that I shall be released through their agency. Please send the enclosed notes to their respective destinations, and when the answers arrive, send them on with the things I ask for. Can you give me any news as to how my business is progressing at Assouan, and the transactions of my manager? Our common friends here are in a sad way. Slatin will have told you all about the forced circumcisions; and now all the Christians have been ordered to marry three or four wives, and are engaged with marriage ceremonies. Beppo and I are in prison together in chains; other prisoners are Ibrahim Fauzi, Ibrahim Hamza, of Berber, who was arrested after Slatin's escape; Ahmed and Bekheit Egail; Sadik and Besher have been transported to Equatoria, with two of their relations. Your messenger brought with him seventy dollars, which have been given to Beppo, and I enclose his receipt for them. Kindly translate the letter I enclose for Wingate; I have written it in German, as no one here but me understands the language. Please keep these letters secret. For God's sake, do not let the newspaper people get hold of them, as you know, if they did, it would cost me my head. Perhaps, if you could get them to give as news something like this, it would help me: 'We hear that, after the escape of Slatin, Neufeld was secured against escape; he has rendered great services to Mahdieh with the saltpetre; he would be able to replace Osta Abdallah, who is now old and feeble; Neufeld is in the greatest distress, and in prison with his certain death close at hand; the people in the Soudan believe he is a relation of Slatin.'"

Onoor Issa went off with my replies, undertaking to return in a few months, after having made arrangements between Berber and Cairo for my escape; and during his absence I was to scheme for any excuse to get out of prison; escape from there was impossible. Onoor—or the translators of his accounts—are mistaken in saying that he actually met me in prison; all negotiations were carried on through the Abyssinian woman whom he employed to come into the prison for "medical attendance," or Umm es Shole, and days and days elapsed between the visits sometimes, in all amounting to maybe two months. There were times of mental tension in the Saier of Omdurman. To me ill luck and good luck appeared to be ever striving for the ascendency during my long captivity. Good luck gained in the end—the same good luck which had accompanied the Sirdar throughout his daring campaign to conquer, not only Abdullah, but the Soudan, and which, God grant, may ever accompany him in future campaigns; but the cup-and-ball-catch-and-miss strain was to me terrible. My one prayer was that an end might come. Liberty, of course, I hoped for to the end; but I often discovered myself speculating as to whether it was true or not that those suddenly decapitated by a single blow experienced some seconds of really intellectual consciousness, and wondering to myself whether, when my head was rolled into the dust by the Khaleefa's executioner, there would be time to give one last look of defiance.

Yet when I come to think of it, there was nothing very strange in such contemplations. What soldier or sailor has not often in his quiet moments tried to picture his own death, defiant to the last as he goes down before a more powerful enemy? And, after all, thousands and thousands of men and women in civilized countries are enduring a worse captivity and imprisonment than many did in the Soudan; but they are unfortunate in this—that no one has thrown a halo of romance over their sufferings. My lot was a hard, very hard one, I must admit; but the lot of some other captives was such that thousands in Europe would have been pleased to exchange theirs for it, and would have gained in the exchange.

CHAPTER XIX
RUMOURS OF RELIEF

Soon after the departure of Onoor Issa I was saved any further trouble in the way of scheming for excuses to get out of the Saier. Awwad-el-Mardi, the successor of Nur-el-Gerafawi as the Amin Beit-el-Mal on the appointment of the latter as director of the Khaleefa's ordnance stores, had been approached by Nahoum Abbajee and others on the subject of the extraction of gold and silver from certain stones which had been discovered in the neighbourhood. Awwad sent Nahoum to see me about the erection of a crushing-mill or furnaces. My interview with Nahoum was a stormy one. It commenced by his upbraiding me for the pranks I had played in smashing the arsenal punching-machine when we were associated in the establishment of a mint. The more I laughed the angrier Nahoum became; he is deaf, and like most deaf people, invariably speaks in an undertone, which is as distressing to the hearer as is the necessity he is under of bawling back his replies. It is next to impossible to hold a conversation with a deaf person without the natural result of raising the voice exhibiting itself in the features; the annoyance is there plain enough, but when the face flushes with the unwonted exertion, your deaf friend thinks you are getting angry, and follows suit. This is precisely what Abbajee did. He showed me his specimens, and I bawled into his ear, "Mica— not gold, not silver—mica;" and he yelled back, "Gold, silver, gold." The noisy discussion, accompanied as it was with gesticulations, attracted other prisoners around us, and Nahoum went off in high dudgeon.

ONOOR ISSA.

When he had gone, a few of my friends asked why I did not offer to assist him, and even if the thing was a failure, they thought I was clever enough to find something else to do; but, as they said, "promise anything provided it gets you out of the Saier." There were excellent reasons, but which I might not confide to them, why any work I undertook to do should occupy months, and, if necessary, years in completion. To offer to assist Nahoum in extracting gold and silver from such stones meant that two or three weeks at the outside would evidence our failure to do so, and then it was Saier again for me. Whether any work I undertook to do for the Khaleefa was to end in success or failure was immaterial to me; but it was very material that the result, whatever it was to be, should not be attained for months, as by the time my guides returned, the conditions surrounding my escape might have so changed as to necessitate an entire change in plans and programme. They might even entail the guides' return to Cairo or the frontier, and this occupied months. But the advice to accept Nahoum's proposals and trust to luck for discovering some other excuse for remaining out of the Saier when failure could no longer be concealed, appealed to me, and, in reply to my offer of assistance, a messenger came from the Khaleefa ordering the Saier to hand me over to the director of the Beit-el-Mal. His other instructions were that the bars and heavy chains were to be taken off my feet and legs, and that I was to be secured by a single pair of anklets connected with a light chain. While this change was being made I received the congratulations of the gaolers and prisoners, and (February, 1896) was escorted out of the prison by two guards to enter upon a new industry which had in it as much of the elements of success as would accompany an attempt to squeeze blood out of a cobbler's lap-stone. I had not forgotten Shwybo's fate.

When I reached Khartoum, Awwad-el-Mardi had not yet arrived. It was the month of Ramadan, and as all transactions were in abeyance until after sunset, I was not allowed to land until Awwad arrived to hand me over officially. I was left alone on one of Gordon's old steamers, moored at the spot where Gordon fell, and where the victorious Sirdar and his troops landed to conduct the burial service. During the hours I had to wait gazing at the ruined town and the dismantled palace which saw the martyrdom of as good a man and soldier as ever trod this earth, I ruminated over his blasted hopes and my own. I shall not pretend to call to mind all the thoughts which surged through my brain as I paced alone over the shell-and bullet-splintered deck; but you can imagine what they were when I reflected that I was the only European in the Soudan who had fired a shot for Gordon, and that I was now a captive in the hands of the successor of the Mahdi, gazing at the ruined town from which, just eleven years ago, we had hoped to rescue its noble defender. I should be ashamed to say that when Awwad did at last come I was not in tears.

I felt more acutely than I did when first taken to Khartoum to be "impressed," and still more acutely than when I was hurriedly bundled into the old Mission to start the saltpetre works. For the first time since my captivity I had been left absolutely alone. I was sitting on one of that fleet of "penny steamers" which, had Gordon not sent down the Nile to bring up his rescuers, might have saved him and the Soudan in spite of the wicked delay resulting from the attempt to make a theatrically impressive show of an expedition intended to be one of flying succour to the beleaguered garrison and its brave commander, praying for months for the sight of one single red coat. Gordon, I had been told, towards the end, called the Europeans together in Khartoum, and telling them that, in his opinion, the Government intended to sacrifice him, recommended them to make their escape. A deliberate attempt to sacrifice him could not have succeeded better. What wonder, when such thoughts as these and many others had been affecting me for hours, that when Awwad came, as darkness was setting in, the darkness of night had settled too upon my mind. He, believing that my chains were the real cause of my depression, ordered that they should be exchanged immediately for lighter and smoother ones, for the anklets and chains given me by Idris were rough in the extreme.

After being officially handed over to the Governor of Khartoum, the question arose as to my quarters. I was offered quarters in his house, but I had already experienced life amongst his Baggara bodyguard, and begged hard to be allowed to live in the same place with Nahoum Abbajee and Sirri—the former telegraph-clerk at Berber, with whom I was to work. We were given the house of Ghattas, an old slave-dealer, to live in. It was one of the best houses left standing in Khartoum, and boasted an upper floor, which was taken possession of by Nahoum Abbajee as head of what I might call the gold syndicate, while Sirri and I shared the ground floor. In the East the West is reversed; you climb to the garret with your rising fortunes, and descend with them, as they fall, to the lower floors. Instead of having Saier or Baggara guards to watch me, Awwad gave me some slaves from the Beit-el-Mal as guardians, and they had, in addition to watching me, to perform the household duties; in fact, they were my servants.

After the evening prayers, Awwad called together the employés of the arsenal and my guards, and explained to them that I was no longer a Saier prisoner; that my chains were left on only to prevent the Government people taking me; that I was "beloved" of the

Khaleefa, and was to be treated as his friend, and that if any one treated me differently, he would be sent to take my place in the Saier. Awwad then taking me aside under the pretence of giving me instructions from the Khaleefa, said, "I am your friend; do not be afraid; if you cannot find gold and silver, tell me of anything else you can do, and I will see that the work is given to you, so that you may not be sent back to the Saier." As Awwad was then a perfect stranger to me, I at first had suspicions in my mind as to the genuineness of his friendship; but he was a Jaalin, and I trusted him.

We were told to get to work at once with the extraction of the precious metals. As the engineer, I had to design and superintend the construction of the furnaces to be made by Hassan Fahraani (the potter), who also supplied the crucibles. Our first furnace crumbled to pieces after being started, and a stronger one had to be made. Then the crucibles gave out. We did all we could to coax gold and silver out of those stones, and obtained some extraordinary results. We added earth, common salt, saltpetre, oxide of lead—anything and everything to the split stones in the crucibles. Sometimes we found the crucible and its contents fused together. The only thing we actually found which gave an idea that we were working for metals was a small shiny black ball, very much resembling a black pearl, and this Hamadan at once took possession of and carried off to Abdullahi, telling him that it only required time for us to succeed. Hamadan, being our chief, was much interested in the work, and he was doubtless looking forward to the day when part of the contents of the crucibles would find its way to him.

But our experiments were destined never to be finished. About April, 1896, rumours first, and then precise news, reached Omdurman that the Government troops were again advancing. Then came the startling news that Dongola had been taken, only to be followed by the news of the capture of Abou Hamad. The fulminate factory presided over by Hassan Zecki had run short of ingredients, and as the stock of chlorate of potash ordered from Egypt had not arrived, it was believed that now the troops held all the country between Dongola and Abou Hamad, it would have no chance of getting through. Abdalla Rouchdi, the chemist of the Beit-el-Mal, had, with Hassan Zecki, failed to produce chlorine, as had also others, therefore we were ordered to experiment at once. Nahoum was sent over to the Beit-el-Mal to collect all appliances, chemicals, and anything else he chose to lay his hands upon. Our establishment was growing, and Hamadan was delighted at having under his charge people who were to do so much for Mahdieh. But the chlorine required for the production of the chlorate of potash refused to appear. Our laboratory was a dangerous place to visit, for we had jar upon jar containing mixed acids, and explosions were the order of the day. Nahoum had a lively time, deaf as he was. Once, and once only, Hamadan made pretence of understanding our experiments; he took a good inhalation from a vessel which had in it a mixture of various acids with permanganate of potash. He was almost suffocated, but he was much impressed, and told the Khaleefa what devoted adherents he had when we would work in such a poison-laden atmosphere.

There was good reason why I should do all in my power to keep Hamadan interested and hopeful of grand results. Onoor Issa had sent me word by a messenger from Berber that he was at that town with letters and money for me, but that he had been detained by the Emir; he hoped, however, to be able to get away very soon and arrange my escape. Then the consignment of chlorate of potash put in its appearance—about twelve hundredweight, I was told—and Sirri getting hold of a small sample of it, we showed it to Hamadan to prove that we were just succeeding with our experiments. He was satisfied, as was also Abdullahi, and we were told to continue our work.

However, the tales which were coming in every few days were causing no little anxiety to the Khaleefa. None of us believed that the troops were coming across the desert in "iron devils," and it was some time before we understood that a railway was being built. Indeed we could hardly believe it. Whatever the "iron devil" was, it behoved the Khaleefa to look well to his arms and ammunition. Sheikh ed Din was sent on a round of inspection of stores and arsenals,* and discovered that a large quantity of the powder had caked with the absorption of moisture, that other large quantities were of very poor quality, and that the powder-stores in general were not as he thought they were. The Khaleefa threatened to cut a hand and foot off both Abd es Semmieh and Hassan Hosny, the directors of the factory, if they did not work the powder up again into a good explosive. Awwad, as the head of the Beit-el-Mal, came and asked if it was not possible to make some sort of machine for pulverizing the ingredients for the powder; the work was then being done by hand. I tried to interest Nahoum Abbajee in the work, as it was about time we got clear of our alchemists' establishment on some excuse or another, otherwise I foresaw trouble if Sheikh ed Din should inquire too closely into our work. But Abbajee thought that he had had quite enough of me in connection with experiments and machinery, and decided to be out of the affair altogether; he thought his life had been in enough jeopardy already. Sirri elected to remain.

* A few errors have crept into the report submitted to the Earl of Kimberley in April, 1895, after the escape of Slatin.

On page 4 it is stated that the church of the Austrian Mission in Khartoum was utilized as the repairing shops of the arsenal. The church was never put to such a purpose. The account I have given of the purpose to which it was put is the correct one.

On page 7 it is stated "Neufeld started the first saltpetre refinery in Khartoum." This may or may not be correct, but it is very misleading. The refining of saltpetre for the Khaleefa was a big industry in Darfour and the environs of Omdurman and Khartoum long before I had anything to do with it. The account I have given as to how I came to be connected with this industry may be relied upon as being correct, while there are many living witnesses, irrespective of the stock of my saltpetre still existing, to prove that I deliberately prevented "the refining of saltpetre" so far as it lay in my power to do so.

In the following paragraph to that quoted, it is stated that the powder-factory was at Halfeyeh. It never was. It was first in Omdurman, and, after the explosion, was gradually removed to Tuti Island. The transfer was not complete when I left Khartoum for the Saier in November, 1897.

On page 10, when speaking of the coins in circulation, it is said, "This decrease in the intrinsic value of money is an interesting indication of the decline of dervish power and government." The inference to be drawn from my account of its depreciation is just the reverse, but is the correct inference to be drawn.

I invented a powder machine on the principle of the old German "dolly" toy. We spent a few weeks, assisted by Hamaida, the head of the carpenters, in making a model, which worked beautifully; and when it was shown to the Khaleefa, he was so delighted that he ordered my chains to be removed. The mortars were put in hand at once, also the beam which was to lift and let fall the pulverizers, and then it was discovered that the machine could not be made to my dimensions. I knew this when I designed it, but I had hoped that some one would have been sent south to try and find trees large enough to provide the beams, and so delay would be assured. Osta Abdallah and Khaleel Hassanein, jealous maybe of me, and fearing that their positions were in danger of being taken by myself, went to the Khaleefa, and told him that, in their opinion, I was only "fooling" with him. They also suggested that Awwad-el-Mardi was a friend of the Government, and was helping me on this account; but Yacoub, who was present, supported me. In the course of the interview, the Khaleefa said he had heard that in my country women and children made cartridges with machines, and as I must know all about it, I was to make him such a machine while the powder-mill was being constructed.

For ten years I had been so chained and weighted with iron that it was only with effort I was able to raise my feet from the ground in order to shuffle from place to place; the bars of iron connected with the anklets had limited the stride or shuffle to about ten or twelve inches. When freed from all this, I ran and jumped about the whole day long like one possessed; but the sudden call upon muscles so long unused resulted in a swelling of the legs from hips to ankles, and this was accompanied with most excruciating pains. I had just got the drawings ready for the cartridge-machine when I was compelled to lie up. This gave Osta Abdallah and Hassanein another chance to approach the Khaleefa, and again they suggested that I was "fooling."

Awwad was sent for, and in reply to the Khaleefa, said that he believed I was doing my best, and would certainly succeed; that had he not believed in me himself, he would never have recommended him to employ me on such important works. Yacoub again took my part, and said that whoever did not assist me, or whoever hindered me, would be considered an enemy of Mahdieh. Although, as he admitted, he did not understand the machines, yet in his opinion "there must be something in the head of the man who invented them, and he was better employed in the arsenal than idling his time in the Saier." Awwad also said that if Osta Abdallah and Hassanein had not and could not find the materials for the construction of the machines, he believed that I could make another one with such materials as they had. This decided the matter—both machines were to be proceeded with; but the Khaleefa agreed to my being put into chains to prevent my escaping, and on the thirteenth day of my freedom the chains were replaced. Being unable to move from my house, the joiners, with a lathe, their tools and material, were sent to me, as the Khaleefa wished the machine to be completed as rapidly as possible. Abdallah Sulieman, the chief of the cartridge-factory, was then employing upwards of fifteen hundred men, and the Khaleefa wished to release them for fighting purposes.

POWDER-MACHINES.

My efforts to obtain either the original models or photographs of them not having so far been successful, I have had models of the machines made here. Those interested in mechanics will discover for themselves the mechanical defects and unnecessary complications introduced into them. I was working under the supervision of fairly good mechanical engineers, so that defects might not be made too glaring. Some were detected and rectified, but the main defects were not seen, being beyond the powers of calculation of Abdallah; and Hamaida, who could and did see them, was enjoying the pranks which were played. The various ideas I had picked up while associated with Gordon's old corps were now standing me in good stead. When the model of the cartridge-machine was taken over to Abdullahi, instead of being pleased with it he was furious: Berber had been taken! He said, "I want cartridges, not models;" and gave orders that I should be taken from my house, kept at work all day in the arsenal, and locked up at night in the arsenal prison with the convicts employed there as labourers.

To gain more time, I insisted upon a full-sized wooden model of the cartridge-machine being first made for the metal workers to work from. Yacoub had given orders that all the material and labour of the arsenal was to be put at my disposition. While the wooden model was being made, I occupied myself in selecting the metal required, and in doing this I laid hands upon everything Osta Abdallah required for the ordinary works in hand. I appropriated the paddle axle of one of the steamers, as I said I required this to be cut with eccentric discs, and did my best to smash the best lathe with it, to give me still more time; but the lathe stood the strain, and four or five discs were actually cut in the axle.

It would have taken them another year to cut the remainder at the rate the work was progressing, and probably four years to make the machine; then when it was finished there would have been an accident, and some people would have been killed or maimed, for that paddle axle would have come tearing through the machine with the first revolution. I was taking a fiendish delight in destroying every good piece of metal I could lay my hands on under pretence of its being required for the machine; the copper and brass which I appropriated interfered considerably with the production of the cartridges, and the skilled workmen whom I kept employed delayed for months the finishing touches to the new powder-factory on Tuti Island. But there could be no going back now. Abdallah was my sworn enemy; but I knew that the more I destroyed under his own eyes, the less risk there was of his going to the Khaleefa again to induce him to believe that the whole of my work was, as he called it, "shoogal khabbass"—all lies, for Abdallah himself would get into trouble for not having discovered it before all the damage had been done.

While still engaged on collecting material for the machine (for no sooner was one lot cut up when it was discovered that some mistake had been made in either length or thickness, so that another raid had to be made on the stores), the steamer *Safia* was brought up and beached opposite Mokran fort for repairs. Instead of being allowed to settle on a cradle running the whole length of her keel, she was supported only amidships, and her bow and stern tore away. All the boats were at this time in the charge of the Beit-el-Mal, and when Osta Abdallah condemned the *Safia*, and said it was impossible to repair her, Awwad-el-Mardi, fearing the Khaleefa's displeasure at such a time, asked me if it was not possible to repair her. Taking with us a number of men discontented with Osta Abdallah, we examined the boat, and declared that she could be repaired. Awwad was pleased, and I was appointed superintendent of this work too. My superintendence consisted in hiding below and smoking surreptitiously.

Sometime in August, 1897, Onoor returned to Omdurman, and sent messages to me through Umm es Shole. The import of them will be seen from the following letter, which I was able to write and smuggle over to him; the letter was to be delivered to the first officer he came across:—

"In accordance with my arrangement with the bearer Onoor, I succeeded in getting liberated from the Saier, and moved over to Khartoum, where I have spent two years in the arsenal under surveillance. Onoor has been unable to meet me personally to consult over plans for escape, which offers little difficulty provided I had funds. In May, 1896, Onoor sent me, through his agent, your letter, and gave me to understand that the money mentioned in this letter was in his possession, and that he was awaiting an opportunity to bring it to Khartoum. Now (July-August, 1897) he has come to Omdurman only to find me in a difficult position, owing to the progress of the war. He tells me he was ordered to Suakin, where he was put in prison, and the money he had for me taken from him, as he had no reply from me to the letter sent, or any evidence to show that the letter had been sent. He has borrowed some money here, for which I have gone bail for fifty pounds, and Onoor promises to be back in three months' time with news from you and the money required for my support and escape. The course of the war will soon deliver us alive or dead from the hands of this savage rabble.

"The greater part of the arsenal has been moved over to the Beit-el-Mal at Omdurman owing to the war, and the remaining material will follow very shortly, and I will go over with it, when I may have an opportunity of meeting Onoor if nothing occurs to disturb the extremely good relations existing between myself and my present masters. Please give Onoor (here follows a list of medicines); practising medicine facilitates my communication with the outer world. I hope Onoor will find with you a letter from my family; I am in good health, as is also my daughter Bakhita, and her mother Umm es Shole. We send you greetings."

News was coming each day of the most alarming description for the Khaleefa; tales of big gunboats coming to reconnoitre Khartoum, and the "iron devil" (the railway) creeping forward, decided him on collecting everything under his eyes. All stores were hurried over to Omdurman; a hundred and fifty to two hundred men were sent over to destroy the mission house, mosque, and other buildings in Khartoum, as the Khaleefa was determined to leave no place of shelter for any troops who succeeded in landing there. I was looked upon with the greatest suspicion, as there was no concealing, try as I might, my anxiety to glean every bit of news possible about the expedition, and I was also in a fever of excitement expecting the return of Onoor. Each day was bristling with opportunities for escape, provided there was a man with a camel ready for me on the opposite shore. With the dozens of boats and hundreds of men employed in transferring the arsenal to the other side of the river, a successful escape was assured; but Onoor never came. Towards the end of November, 1897, I was taken over with the last of the arsenal material to Omdurman, and put into the Saier prison, only until, as I was told, a house could be got ready for me in the Beit-el-Mal, where we were to complete the powder-and cartridge-machines.

CHAPTER XX
PREPARING TO RECEIVE THE GUNBOATS

When I returned to the Saier in November, 1897, it was as a visitor—a distinguished one at that. I was told that I was only to remain there until my quarters in the Beit-el-Mal were ready for occupation, when I was to leave the prison and continue the construction of the powder-and cartridge-machines, to the completion of which the Khaleefa and Yacoub were looking forward with no little interest and anxiety. But once inside the gates of the Saier, Osta Abdallah and Khaleel Hassanein determined to keep me there, and succeeded in doing so. When Awwad-el-Mardi again interested himself on my behalf, these worthies succeeded in persuading Yacoub that Awwad's interest in me was sure evidence of his sympathies with the Government, and their schemes ended by Awwad also being sent into the prison with threats of what would happen to him if he attempted to hold any intercourse with me.

A GROUP—FROM PHOTOGRAPH TAKEN AT THE FEAST OF BEIRAM, 1899.

1. Mohammed Sirri, formerly telegraph clerk at Berber. He, with Hassan Bey Hassanein, cut the Khaleefa's communications.

2. Morgan Torjin. Imprisoned for two years for telling the Khaleefa that he insisted on being allowed to smoke tobacco and drink Marissa.

3. Khaleel Agha Orphali.

4. Said Bey Gumaa.

5. Osman Bey Daali, commandant of Irregular troops in Sennaar.

6. Hassan Bey Hassanein.

7. Sheikh Ali Toulba, formerly of the Khartoum Medrassa (college).

8. Ahmed Riad, formerly head clerk of Slatin at Dara. He it was who wrote the letters calling upon Said Gumaa to submit to the Mahdi, and who accompanied Slatin to Zoghal when Dara was surrendered.

9. Mohammad Farag, former officer of Dara troops.

10. Rhubrian Baalbal, clerk to Lupton.

11. Sheikh Taher Farrag, Kassala Medrassa (college).

12. Ahmed Yusef Kandeel, clerk to Wad Nejoumi.

13. Hassan Bey Abdel Minain, president of the Court of Appeal at Khartoum.

It was possibly a week after entering the prison that Umm es Shole came in to say that she had seen and spoken to Onoor Issa, who had not left Omdurman—the same Onoor whose return I had looked for so anxiously during the time of the transfer of the arsenal from Khartoum, when each day bristled with opportunities for successful flight! Fearing that he might play me false, and hand the notes I had given him to the Khaleefa as an earnest of his loyalty to him, I sent off Umm es Shole, and told her to say that I had a few notes to add to the letters which I had given him. Onoor at once suspected my reasons for sending for them, and replied that he was not pleased with my want of confidence in him, that he had a permit to proceed to Suakin for trade, but, having fallen under suspicion, he had so far been prevented from leaving, though he hoped to be able to leave any day. Upon this I again trusted him, and added the following to my notes, sending them out to him as soon as it was written:—

"News from here (the Saier); Slatin knows Omdurman prison. From the Beit-el-Mal to Morrada along the river are six semicircular forts with flanks; each fort has three guns, but the flanks are loopholed for musketry only. The parapets are of Nile mud, and appear to be three metres thick. Most of the forts are situated close under the high wall. There is a similar fort at the north end of Tuti Island, two more at Halfeyeh, and the same number at Hugra, north of Omdurman. Two batteries near Mukran sweep the White Nile and the arm which skirts Tuti Island, and I have just heard that some one has offered to lay torpedoes in the Nile to blow up the steamers. Slatin knows more about the army than I do; Wad Bessir has come in from Ghizera with about two thousand men. Osman Digna, with a force I have not learned the strength of, is at Halfeyeh. Onoor will tell you all about these troops. Ahmed Fedeel is at Sabalooka (Shabluka), and his strength is better known to you than me. The whole population left here is in the greatest dread of this savage rabble and their rulers, and pray God to deliver them out of their hands, and that you may save them from the fate of the Jaalin. I pray you to keep this letter an absolute secret. There are traitors among your spies" (this remark was confirmed a few weeks later); "if the least inkling of my communications with you reach the Khaleefa's ears, it will be all over with me. Answer me in German, as no one else here understands the language. It is a mistake to trust any Arab—civilized or uncivilized. Onoor is the only one who has brought me any news. He is the best man to go between us. In expectation of an early reply from you, I subscribe myself yours devotedly, and pray God he may enable me to join you soon. I have been moved from Khartoum to the Omdurman prison only until my house is ready in the Beit-el-Mal.

The Khaleefa has received news that steamers are coming to reconnoitre Khartoum."

It was not until the end of December that Onoor succeeded in obtaining permission to leave Omdurman; and then hurrying to Suakin, he handed in my notes to the commandant there, returning six months later with his thanks for the information given and money to keep me going. It is passing strange that my trouble in collecting information about the forts, writing to the advancing army, and giving what details I could, should have given those on the way to Omdurman the impression that it was "Neufeld's forts" which were being knocked to pieces. Even my good friend—that King of War Correspondents—Mr. Bennet Burleigh, was good enough to tell me that he believed I had designed and constructed them. They were all the work, from beginning to end, of Youssef Mansour.

At the time I am speaking of, the prison was filled with suspected sympathizers with the Government; the presence of Ibrahim Pasha Fauzi and Awwad-el-Mardi has already been alluded to. Hogal, who should have accompanied me on the expedition to Kordofan, was also a prisoner; but it was three months before I was able to steal an interview with him—about the time of the anniversary of my capture—and then I learned, at almost the hour of my release, the real history of my capture. Our circle of "Government people" was added to daily; one of the most interesting additions being a party of sixteen or seventeen spies, amongst whom was Worrak from Dongola, Abdalla Mahassi from Derawi, Ajjail from Kassala, and others from Suakin. They had been betrayed by other spies; I have forgotten the names of the traitors, but it is of little moment now, as doubtless the betrayed settled up their accounts on the taking of Omdurman. The betrayer or betrayers were Dongolawi— perhaps the only coterie of thieves on earth who have no honour among themselves.

Whatever may have been the excitement and anxiety in other parts of the world concerning the Sirdar's advance, we had our share of both in Omdurman. Strange tales had reached us of offers of assistance sent to the Khaleefa to resist the advance of the troops. Shortly before I left Khartoum, a field-gun had arrived from the south as a present for the Khaleefa; it was accompanied by a limited supply of ammunition—brass cartridges carrying a shell in the same way as the rifle carries its bullet. One of the cartridges was sent to the Khartoum arsenal, to see if others could be made like it. Various tales were told concerning its origin; but as the gun must have been taken at the capture of Omdurman, its real history has no doubt been traced.

It was only when I met in prison Ibrahim Wad Hamza of Berber, and Hamed Wad-el-Malek, that I learned from them what had transpired when the King of Abyssinia sent an envoy to the Khaleefa asking his assistance against the Italians. The envoy had been brought to the Khartoum arsenal to inspect it, but I was not allowed to speak to him. An arrangement had been come to by which the Abyssinians were to open up trade routes from Gallabat, and send in so much coffee and other articles of food monthly, in return for the promised assistance of the Khaleefa in attacking the Italians; but the contributions or tribute was paid for a few months only, as another envoy came with offers of assistance against the advancing armies. He was the bearer of a flag which he asked the Khaleefa to fly, as the troops might not fire at it; the conferences, like all conferences between the Khaleefa and strangers, were held privately, but at the end of the last conference, the Khaleefa gave his reply in the presence of the Emirs and others. Handing back the flag, he said, "My mission is a holy and religious one; I trust to God for help and success; I do not want the help of Christians. If ever I required the help of man, the Mohammedan boy Abbas is nearer and better to me," and with this he waved the envoy and his companions off. The only construction we could place on the concluding sentence, was that the Khaleefa wished every one to understand that, sooner than accept the help of a Christian power, he would surrender to the Khedive, and this meant never, for he was looking forward to the day when he would erect his scaffolds in the Cairo citadel, and haul up the Khedive and "Burrin" (Lord Cromer) as his first victims. To the Soudanese, Lord Cromer, or "Burrin," as they mispronounced Baring, held the same relation to the Khedive as Yacoub did to the Khaleefa.

From the day Mahmoud started until the arrival of the victorious army in Omdurman, I was pestered with questions day and night; the Mahdists wished to know whether the advancing troops belonged to the sheikh who sent the troops for Gordon in 1884; those against Mahdieh wished to know if they belonged to the other sheikh. From the Arabic papers which found their way to Omdurman, the Soudanese had learned that there were two tribes in England, each led by powerful sheikhs; one, the sheikh of 1884, and the other the sheikh who had said that when he started there would be no coming back until he had "broken up" (smashed) Mahdieh. To the Mahdists, it was the troops who "ran away" who were coming again; to the "Government" people it was immaterial which sheikh was in power; British troops were advancing, and that was enough. At night our circle would sift and discuss all the tales we had heard during the day, and although we were filled with hope, anxiety and fear got the better of us on most occasions.

When Mahmoud was sent off, his instructions were to wait at Metemmeh, and do all in his power to harass the troops as they crossed the river; if strong enough to attack them, he was to do so, but if they were stronger, he was to retire gradually to Kerreri, where an old prophecy had foretold that the great battle was to take place. Mahmoud disobeyed these instructions, and crossed to the east bank, upon which the Khaleefa sent him orders not to remain in a zareeba or trenches, but to attack the infidels in the open. Hardly had the excitement caused by Mahmoud's defiance of the Khaleefa's orders died down, when the news came that he had attacked and annihilated the English army. But other news than this followed on its heels; we learned the truth from a band of about thirty-eight blacks wearing the Egyptian uniform. They were dervishes taken at Dongola and Abou Hamad, and drafted into the army. At the Atbara they deserted to the dervishes, but suspected of being spies, they were sent to the Saier. The whole truth came out when Osman Digna came back to Omdurman to report to the Khaleefa.

"What news have you brought me, and how fare the faithful?" inquired Abdullahi. "Master," replied Osman, "I led them to Paradise." Now, Osman had been doing this at every battle for years, and the Khaleefa's patience was exhausted; he wanted victories, and not pilgrimages of his best troops to the next world. "Then why did you not go with them?" retorted Abdullahi. "God," replied Osman, "had not ordained it so; He must have more work for me to do; when that work is finished, He will call me." It was well known to the Khaleefa, and every one else in the Soudan, that Osman had an excellent eye for a field of battle, and knew an hour before any one else did, when to make a bolt for it on a losing day. Osman's appearance was quite sufficient to let people understand that all the tales of victory on the side of the dervishes were false, and it was useless for the Khaleefa to try any longer to conceal the truth, but some explanation had to be given for the terrible rout of his army. It was all the doing of an outraged Deity. Mahmoud had disobeyed the orders transmitted through Abdullahi by the Prophet, and this was the result! As other stragglers came in, extraordinary tales were told of enormous steamers with enormous guns which fired "devils" and "lightning"; this description probably referred to the rockets, which, I gathered, had ricochetted all over Mahmoud's camp, playing terrible havoc.

On the fall of Dongola, a Mograbin (from Tunis, or Algiers), named Nowraani, had offered his services to Yacoub, as a maker of torpedoes, and with these he said he could blow up every boat on the Nile. His offer at the time was refused, as the Khaleefa said that it was his intention to capture all these boats for himself; he did not wish them to be destroyed. But the tales which came in about them after the Atbara fight, showed that something must be done to secure them. Abdallah and Hassanein undertook to make a "boom" of chains across the Sabalooka (Shabluka) pass, and for this purpose almost every scrap of chain in Omdurman was collected. Their plan, as described to me, was as follows: the chains were to be laid across the stream, their ends made fast to posts on the opposite banks of the Nile. To prevent them from sinking to the bed of the stream, a series of large wooden buoys had been made, and these were to be fixed at intervals along the boom. It had been calculated that the buoys would, with the weight of the chains, be sunk just below the surface of the water, and also keep the chains in a series of loops; these loops were intended to entangle the paddles and propellers of the gunboats, and, while so entangled, Mansour's picked men were to shoot every one on board, and then, releasing the boats, bring them on to Omdurman. That was the arrangement.

Employed in the arsenal at the time was a man named Mohammad Burrai—a Government sympathizer, and a bitter enemy of Mansour and the others; he was entrusted with the attaching of the buoys at the fixed points in the boom. A few days after the boom was sent down the river, and, while I was "practising" the healing art at the gates of the prison, I received an interesting patient; it was Burrai, his head so wrapped up in cloths as to make him unrecognizable. He told me first of the arrangements made for the boom, and how he had succeeded in destroying it. The chains had been laid over the sterns of boats anchored in the Nile from bank to bank, and Burrai had fixed the buoys to them, but instead of making the buoys *fast* at these points, he merely slipped the rings round the boom so that the buoys could run from one end to the other. The word was given to slip the boom off the boats. The buoys with the force of the current were carried to the centre of the boom, and, with the resistance offered by them to the stream, the cables snapped and were lost. Burrai's object in coming to me will be divined; having been employed on the construction of the boom, he might, when the English arrived, be shot as a Mahdist, and he wished to tell me, as a "Government man," what he had done, so that I could speak up for him. This I promised to do.

There were no more chains left with which to make another boom, but those terrible boats must be stopped from coming to Omdurman, and Nowraani was sent for to explain his project again. He proposed to take two large tubular boilers, then lying at Khartoum, cut them in two, fill them with powder, seal up the open ends, and fire them by electricity as the boats passed over them. Sirri, the former telegraph-clerk at Berber, was asked to design the electrical apparatus, but he pleaded ignorance of such things. I was next sent to, to give my opinion as to the feasibility of Nowraani's plan. It was explained to me that each half of the boilers would contain thirty cantars (a ton and a half) of gunpowder; then it was mines, and not torpedoes, the man wished to make; however, the name "torpedo" was always used. I replied that I had heard, as Nowraani said, of torpedoes being used in the sea for the destruction of great ships, but had never heard of them being used in rivers, and I doubted his ability to make them. The Khaleefa was not satisfied with my answer, and sent word that he believed I could assist in the making of them, but would not. To this, again, I said I should be only too pleased to help Nowraani in his work, but what he proposed to do was very dangerous and risky. I said I felt sure that the only result would be an explosion while the torpedoes were being made, and that, while I did not mind being killed myself, I would not like to meet Allah responsible for the lives of others. Perhaps I made a mistake in putting forward religious scruples, for the Khaleefa never believed in my conversion; he took it for granted that I refused to help, and told the Saier to load me with an extra chain and bar.

Nowraani insisted that his plans were feasible, and a small experimental "torpedo" was ordered to be made; Mansour, Hassanein, and Abdallah superintended the work, which was carried out in almost absolute secrecy. When finished, the mine was taken over to the Blue Nile, made fast under a boat, and exploded. The result was most satisfactory—the boat being blown to matchwood, and a large column of mud and water thrown into the air, which was more impressive, evidently, than the destruction of the boat.

NEUFELD DOUBLY FETTERED.

The "torpedoes" were ordered immediately, and men were kept working night and day for their completion; the boilers were cut in two, plates fitted to the open ends, wires and "strings," as it was described to me, fitted to mechanism in the interior, and in maybe a fortnight's time I learned that four big and one small torpedo were fastened to gyassas ready to be lowered into the stream, while others were being made. Again I received a visit from Burrai; he had to assist in the laying of the mines, and wanted to know from me how they might be rendered useless. From his description of the wires and lines running in pairs, I came to the conclusion that electricity was to be the medium for their explosion, especially as Burrai's instructions were to take charge of these lines, pay them out as the torpedoes sank, and make the free ends of the line fast to posts, which had been fixed on the land just south of Khor Shamba. I told him that if either wire or string of the pairs of lines was broken, the torpedoes could not be fired, and suggested his giving a hard tug to one of the lines as soon as the "barrel" as he called the mines, was lowered to the bed of the stream.

What happened we know; how it happened we never shall. Burrai was seen on the *Ismailia*, which towed down the stone-laden gyassas with the torpedoes; the gyassas were to have a hole knocked in them, and the boat and torpedoes allowed to sink gradually. One torpedo had been lowered, and an explosion immediately followed. The boats with Nowraani and between thirty and forty men were blown to atoms; the *Ismailia* was blown in two—the stern floating a few yards down stream and sinking. Burrai was picked out of the water with the whole of the flesh of the calf of his left leg blown clear away, and also the flesh from his ribs on the left side. He lingered for seven days, asking repeatedly for me; but all that I was allowed to do was to send him carbolic acid for his wounds—I was not allowed to go and see him. To all inquiries as to how the accident happened he could, or would, only say that all he did was to pull in the slack of the lines, to prevent their becoming entangled.

Sorry as I am for poor Burrai's death, I cannot consider that I am in any way to blame for it; I can only think that some system of fuse, or detonator, had been fixed to the "torpedoes," and that the very action which I had suggested to render them useless had exploded them. About the time that the mines exploded, Onoor returned, or, at least, I received the news of his return, by receiving the letter and money he had brought from Suakin. Every one with leanings towards the Government was now coming to me in prison under one pretext or another, to give me information as to all that was going on; it was to their interest to do so, as to the end I was looked upon as an official. Owing to this, I was able to send out to Onoor slips of paper giving as nearly correct details as possible of the number of various arms possessed by the dervishes, the stock of ammunition, and the Khaleefa's plans as far as they were known. In one of my notes I informed the army of the explosion of the "torpedoes," and the existence of two other mines ready to be sent off, with details concerning the forts. I asked Onoor to get away with these as quickly as possible, and he promised to do so. I do not know who he handed these notes to, or whether he handed them over himself; he replies to my inquiries by writing me from Omdurman saying that he was arrested on the Nile by Osman Digna, but whether coming or going from the army it is impossible to say. My own opinion is that Onoor, not knowing how the day would go, remained in Omdurman the whole time. If the English won, his life was safe as a well-known spy; if the dervishes won, he was among his own people, and could take credit for having contributed towards the victory. He was not the only one in the Soudan who debated chances and probabilities as did Hassib Gabou, and Hogal when Gabou talked him over on April 1, 1887.

No sooner had my "latest intelligence" been sent off by Onoor, than an arsenal carpenter, Mohammad Ragheb, came to me on the subject of the remaining torpedoes. He had been ordered to assist in the laying of them, and was particularly anxious to learn from me how he might render them useless, and no less anxious that I should make a mental note of the fact so that I could say a "good word" for him if ever he was accused of trying to impede the advance of the "Government." Associated with him was a no particular friend of mine—Ali Baati, and others; but there was no mistaking their earnest desire and real anxiety to circumvent all the schemes of Mansour, Hassanein, and Abdallah in favour of the Government troops.

Ragheb could give me no more information as to the firing medium of the mines than could Burrai; all he could tell me was that the "barrels" had the wires wrapped two or three times round them to prevent their being pulled or dragged in removal. I suggested first that he should chip away any cement which he thought filled any hole or crevice; this would allow of the water penetrating. Next I suggested that he should, as the boats carrying the mines went down the river, try and "snip" any or all of the wires running round the "barrel," but cutting the wires in different places, so that the trick would not be discovered. Ragheb must have succeeded, for neither of the mines exploded, although Mansour had appointed people to fire them as the gunboats passed.

It is impossible for me, away from the spot where association would bring to memory the incidents of those stirring times, to remember the names of all who came to me asking what they might do to evidence, before the arrival of the troops, their loyalty to the Government, and it must not be forgotten that they were running risks in fighting Mahdieh. It is but right that I should record the one or two striking examples which occur to me, especially in the face of my oft-expressed opinion that there are one or two released captives, who should not even be allowed the formality of a drum-head court-martial.

CHAPTER XXI
NEARING THE END

Events were now following each other in rapid succession. In the universal excitement prevailing, sleep was almost unknown, drums were beaten and ombeyehs blown continuously day and night, days and dates were lost count of; even Friday, that one day in the week in Mahdieh, was lost sight of by most, and the prayers were left unsaid.

Councils of war were the order of the day—and night; and what tales we heard! The Emir Abd-el-Baagi had been entrusted by the Khaleefa and Yacoub with keeping in touch with the advancing armies, and sending to Omdurman information of every movement. Never was a general better served with "intelligence" than was Abdullahi by Abd-el-Baagi; his messengers were arriving every few hours in the early days, and hourly towards the end. It was with no little astonishment that we heard Sabalooka was to be abandoned. The boom of chains which was to entangle the paddles of the gunboats had snapped, therefore it was the will of Allah that the boats were to come on. Then the mines exploded. Again it was Allah, who in this showed that he would not have His designs interfered with. The real truth of the matter was, that the troops at Sabalooka, hearing that the gunboats had guns which could send one of the "devils" (shells) half a day's journey, and over hills too, took upon themselves to retire out of range.

There was an old prophecy to the effect that the great fight would take place on the plains of Kerreri. Here the infidels were to be exterminated, and all the waverers on the side of the faithful were to be killed, the remnant collecting afterwards and then starting off, a purified army, on the conquest of the whole world. Again, it was decided that the faithful were to collect in Omdurman, and allow the infidels to come on. While attacks were being made against them on the western flank and rear, a great sortie was to be made from the town, when the infidels, pressed back to Kerreri plains, would be caught between three fires, and exterminated. The gunboats, with their "devils," would be afraid to shoot, as they would kill their own people. But no sooner had this been decided upon when objections were raised. Those gunboats could anchor half a day's journey off, knock Omdurman to pieces, and bury the faithful under the ruins.

Again the prophecy was alluded to, and a move out to meet the armies finally decided upon. Every man was to be taken out of Omdurman, so that, if the infidels should succeed in reaching the town, they would find only women and children, and instead of their being the besiegers, they would become the besieged.

Omdurman was overrun by Abdullahi's spies, who, professing to be friendly towards the "Government," tried to wheedle out of known friends of the Government expressions of opinion as to the chances of success to the Mahdists' arms, and at the same time to ascertain the general feeling of the populace. Their favourite hunting-ground was of course the Saier, where the more influential people were incarcerated. From the persistence with which these spies pressed their inquiries as to the chances of success which might attend large bodies deserting to the Ingleezee under cover of darkness—their anxiety to learn how they might approach the camp without being fired upon before they had been given an opportunity of evidencing their peaceable intentions—we came to the conclusion that Abdullahi had been advised to make a night attack. Few knew better than we did what might be the result of such a tactic. At close quarters the dervish horde was more than a match for the best-drilled army in Europe. Swift and silent in their movements, covering the ground at four or five times the speed of trained troops, every man, when the moment of attack came, accustomed to fight independently of orders, lithe and supple, nimble as cats and as bloodthirsty as starving man-eating tigers, utterly regardless of their own lives, and capable of continuing stabbing and jabbing with spear and sword while carrying half a dozen wounds, any one of which would have put a European *hors de combat*—such were the 75,000 to 80,000 warriors which the Khaleefa had ready to attack the Sirdar's little army. Artillery, rifles, and bayonets would have been but of little avail against a horde like this rushing a camp by night.

We had heard from the prisoner deserters how, at the Atbara, the armies had advanced by night and delivered their attack at dawn, first shelling the zareeba with their "devils," which "came from such a great distance." With Fauzi, Hamza the Jaalin, and others, I came to the conclusion that the same tactics would be employed for the attack at Kerreri; therefore, to the spies we swore that the English never did things twice in the same way; that they would on this occasion march during the day and attack at night, since the Sirdar would be afraid to let his soldiers see the Khaleefa's great army, as they would all run away if they did. Our advice was that the faithful should remain in their camp, and await the attack. It would have been very awkward for me had the Sirdar planned a night attack, for he would have found the dervishes on the *qui vive* awaiting him, and then I might have been blamed for the advice I had given. However, I believed that a night attack would be the very last thing he would resort to, and any tale from our side was good enough, provided doubts were raised in the minds of the Khaleefa and his advisers as to the chances of success which would attend his attacking by night.

The population at this period may be said to have divided itself into three camps; the one praying—and sincerely, for the victory to Mahdieh; the second praying openly to the same end, but breathing prayers to Heaven for just the reverse; the third camp—and this the bigger of the three, consisting of those waiting to see which side would probably win in order to throw in its lot with it. Dozens of people, who really were friends of the Government, came to me in prison asking advice as to what they might do before the troops actually arrived to evidence their loyalty, and it must not be forgotten that they were risking death at the hour of deliverance. To most I was still the "brother of Stephenson el Ingleezee," and there were "brothers" of mine coming up with the Government troops.

I was able, through these people, to collect the information I was sending off daily by spies. Abdallah-el-Mahassi, who had received some message from Major Fitton, asking about me, and also asking for all information procurable concerning the arms and ammunition possessed by the dervishes, sent to me the spy Worrak, who had been released from prison, for any information I could give. Worrak, doubtless looking forward to a reward, decided upon delivering my messages himself. He was to be accompanied by two others; so, besides giving him notes with the numbers of rifles, etc., issued to the troops, and a last warning about the mines near Halfeyeh, I gave the information verbally to the three, so that, in the event of it being found necessary to destroy the papers, the verbal messages would get through. Worrak and his companions left, but were intercepted by Abd-el-Baagi's scouts. Inflating their water-skins, they took to the river under a shower of bullets. Worrak must have been killed or drowned, as he was not seen again; but the two others reached the British lines, delivered the messages, and said that they would be confirmed by Worrak, who they then thought must have been carried by the current to the east bank of the Nile. These were the last messengers I actually sent off.

One of the Saier gaolers had worked himself into a state of frenzied excitement in describing, for the edification of the prisoners—and mine in particular, the coming destruction of the infidels. He gloated over the time when the principal officers— their eyes gouged out to prevent their looking upon the benign face of his master, would be brought into the Saier, and there baited for the amusement of the populace. How little the Sirdar thought, on that September evening, that one of the gaolers grovelling at his feet had, but a few days previously, looked forward to the time when he, blinded and shackled, would be lashed round the place, and, with the rest of my "brothers," spend the nights in the "Umm Hagar." This gaoler, in his mad enthusiasm, rushed at me, and nearly succeeded in gouging out my left eye. There was a struggle, and getting up almost breathless, and certainly driven to desperation, I turned stupidly round, and prophesied, for his edification this time, that the destruction he had predicted for my "brothers" was the destruction which was to fall upon Mahdieh.

SHEREEF, THE "FALSE FOURTH KHALEEFA."

It was fortunate for me that, for a few days previous, Idris es Saier had been sending for me, under one pretext and another, and asking what action he should take in case the English won the battle. I promised that if he treated me well, I would say "good words" for him; but perhaps Fauzi's tale made the greatest impression upon him. Fauzi related that when the English took Egypt there was one gaoler at Alexandria and another at Cairo. The gaoler at Cairo treated his prisoners well, and so the English promoted him; the gaoler at Alexandria killed his prisoners, and ran away to another country across the seas, but the English brought him back, and hanged him in his old prison. Knowing that the troops were close, Idris took me under his especial care, for he knew I had sent messages to my "brothers" telling them I was alive, and he feared that if they came and found me dead, they would hang him on the same scaffold with my corpse. Although he warned the gaolers and spies to say that I was mad, and did not know what I had been saying, my little speech by some means got to Yacoub's ears. I was carefully watched, and no one from outside was allowed to speak to me. I should have been taken out of prison to see the great fight, but I believe that I was the only Christian not called out to the field of battle. I had asked Idris not to remove my chains if I was sent for. I had no wish to be found alive or dead on the field as a practically free man, and, dressed as a dervish, any attempt on my part to escape to the British lines during the fight could only end in my being shot down.

The Khaleefa had been sitting for eight days in the mosque in communion with the Prophet and the Mahdi, and it was either on the Tuesday night or Wednesday morning immediately preceding the battle that the decision to move out of town was arrived at. On the Wednesday afternoon a grand parade of all the troops was held on the new parade ground, and, while it was being held, alarming news was brought by Abd-el-Baagi's messengers. Instead of returning to the town as intended, the Khaleefa set off with the whole army in a north-westerly direction. It was this hurried movement which accounted for the greater part of the arms and ammunition he required being left in the Beit-el-Amana, for Abdullahi had intended distributing the remainder of the rifles only at the last moment, when his troops would have to use them against the infidels in self-defence; he could trust none but his Baggara and Taaishi. Sheikh ed Din, with Yunis, Osman Digna, Khaleefa Shereef, and Ali Wad Helu, moved off first in command of the attacking army of 35,000 rifles and horsemen. Yacoub followed in command of a similar number of spear and swordsmen; in all, the army assembled must have numbered between 75,000 and 80,000 men. As every male had been taken from Omdurman, the Khaleefa issued a hundred rifles to the gaolers with which to shoot down the prisoners in case of trouble.

That night the rain came down in torrents, and the following day the army arose uncomfortable, and maybe a little dispirited, but Abdullahi restored their good spirits by the relation of a vision. During the night the Prophet and the Mahdi had come to him, and let him see beforehand the result of the battle; the souls of the faithful killed were all rising to Paradise, while the legions of hell were seen tearing into shreds the spirits of the infidels. While this tale was going its rounds, the gunboats were creeping up, and a further move to the north was ordered, for it had been reported that the English were landing the big guns on Tuti Island, to shell the camp.

We, too, in prison heard that the gunboats were approaching, and then we heard the distant boom, boom of the guns gradually nearing and growing louder. Before we had time to speculate as to whether the great fight had commenced or not, a boy whom I had stationed on the roof of a gaoler's house, came running down to say that the "devils" were passing Halfeyeh. At the same moment we were smothered in dust and stones; a shell had struck the top of the prison wall, ricochetted to the opposite wall, and fallen without exploding in the prison of the women. All we prisoners hurried off and squatted at the base of the north wall, believing this to be the safest place. The air was now filled with what to us chained wretches appeared to be the yells and screeches of legions of the damned let loose. We shuddered and looked helplessly from one to the other. Then I noticed that the shells were all flying high over us. Getting to my feet, I rushed—as far as my shackles allowed—stumbling to the middle of the open space, tried to dance and jump, called on all to come and join me. I shouted that my "brothers" had got my messages; that only one place in Omdurman would be left—the Saier; my brothers would spare all their lives for me. Yes, I had gone mad; reason had left me, and I was raving, laughing, crying, singing, kissing my hands in welcome to those terrible messengers of death screeching and yelling overhead; throwing open my arms, and leaping up to embrace the shell which a second later was to gather in death seventy-two then praying in the mosque.*

> * The flight of the shells overhead had a most extraordinary effect; they appeared to compress the atmosphere and press it down to the earth; we could actually feel the pressure on our bodies, and with some it brought on nausea.

I was only saved from death at the hands of the infuriated Baggara prisoners by Idris es Saier locking them all up in the Umm Hagar, and leaving myself, Fauzi, the Jaalin, and other Government sympathizers in the open. Then the tales of the fight came to us; two of the gunboats had been sunk, and the remainder had run away again! Fauzi and I sat there distracted, heartbroken. The attack on Khartoum, in 1885, had been enacted over again. I sat in a daze; the reaction from the madness of joy to that of despair was more than the strongest man could stand, after nearly twelve years' captivity, but fortunately I broke down and sobbed like a child.

During the night we could hear the pat, pat, pat of at first a few dozen feet, until eventually we could tell that thousands were running into the town. It is no use relating the tales then told us, I will relate what actually occurred. After the bombardment of the forts, the Khaleefa sent messengers to bring in all news from Omdurman. When told that all the forts had been destroyed, he ordered a salute to be fired in token of his having gained a victory, and called out, "Ed deen mansour"—the Faith is Triumphant! But other messengers were hurrying in, and as they came with grave faces and asked to see Yacoub before delivering their news to the Khaleefa, it was soon noised abroad that the volley from the rifles was only to try and hide something serious which had occurred. First, it was learned that, instead of the gunboats having been destroyed, it was the forts which had been battered to pieces. Then the more superstitious lost heart when it was related that one of the "devils" had entered the sacred tomb of the Mahdi, and numbers deserted desertwards, afterwards striking back to town. Later on, it became known that not only had one of the shells destroyed the Mimbar (pulpit), but had also destroyed the Mihrab—that sacred niche in the wall of the mosque giving the direction of Mecca. What rallying-place was there now for Mahdieh? And so more deserted.

Between ten and eleven at night a riderless horse from the British or Egyptian cavalry came slowly moving, head down, towards the dervish lines. The Khaleefa had related how, in one of his visions, he had seen the Prophet mounted on his mare riding at the head of the avenging angels destroying the infidels. This apparition of the riderless horse was too much; at least one-third of the Khaleefa's huge army deserted terrified. When Yacoub told him of the desertions, Abdullahi merely raised his head to say, "The prophecy will be fulfilled, if only five people stay near me," His Baggara and Taaishi stood by him, but they too were losing heart, for the Khaleefa, on his knees, with head bowed to the ground, was groaning, instead of, as customary, repeating the name of the Deity. However, he pulled round a little as the night progressed, and invented visions enough to put spirits into the remaining but slightly despondent troops.

CHAPTER XXII
AT LAST

It will, I believe, surprise but few when I admit that it is next to impossible for me to remember and relate the incidents which occurred during my last night and day in the Saier. Added to the general excitement shared by every one, I had also to contend against the mental excitement which, earlier in the day, had almost deprived me of reason. From where I lay chained to a gang of about forty prisoners, I could hear the infuriated Baggara in the Umm Hagar heaping their curses on the head of that "son of a dog—Abdallah Nufell," and promising what would happen when they laid hands upon me. These were no idle promises that they made. Apart from the threats which may not be spoken of, those of "drinking my blood" at the moment my brothers reached Omdurman almost froze that blood in my veins.

The whole night through we could hear the soft pat, pat, pat of naked feet, and sometimes the hard breathing of men running a race. Not having heard any firing, we made all sorts of conjectures. At one moment it was thought that the troops had rushed one of the zareebas under cover of darkness, and that these were the fugitives coming into town; at another moment it was believed that the Khaleefa had altered his plans, and had decided to stand a siege in Omdurman. Next it was thought that the dervishes had rushed the camp of the troops; but this idea was soon discarded, for the people running back to town would have still had breath to yell out the news of victory. I have already given the reasons for these people returning, but I only learned them later; to us prisoners, the night passed in anxiety, and amidst alternate hopes and fears.

Daylight was only creeping through the skies when we heard a low boom, followed by an ever-increasing volume of yells and screechings as of Pandemonium let loose, and then a terrific explosion which positively shook Omdurman. The town could not stand this sort of thing for ten minutes; we gave ourselves up for lost, but the bombardment ceased as suddenly as it began. I asked one of the gaoler's boys to climb to the roof of the Umm Hagar to see what the gunboats were doing, as it was believed that the shells had been fired by them. He called back that they were "standing still" near Halfeyeh, and not firing at all. As we could hear the distant booming still going on, we knew then that the English were holding their own if nothing more, and hope returned.

It did not need the boy to call out when the gunboats moved down stream that they, too, were opening fire on the dervish camps; we could almost follow the tide of battle in that furious artillery duel from the alternate roars and silence as of waves breaking on a rock-bound coast. There was no doubt in our minds now that the tactics of the Atbara had been repeated, and that the zareebas were being shelled preparatory to being stormed; the conjecture was wrong, as we learned later. Then the rattle of musketry was borne down on the wind; it was not the rattle of dervish rifles either; we knew the sound of these when fired. Then followed a long silence, only to be succeeded by another terrific fusillade; to us prisoners, it was the reserve zareeba which was now being carried. But the tale of the battle is old, and who has not heard of that second fight on the day of Omdurman, when MacDonald's brigade withstood the combined attack of the armies of Sheikh ed Din and Yacoub?

One must go amongst the survivors of that attack to learn the details of the fight. Those having glasses in the British lines must have noticed Yacoub prancing about on horseback in front of his lines; this was in imitation of the man he could see on horseback in front of the brigade which was mowing down his men by hundreds at each volley. They have learned since who the man was, and "MacDonald" with "Es-Sirdar" is now a name to conjure with in the Soudan. It was not the first time MacDonald had so terribly punished the dervishes, while commanding troops which they had expected would throw down their arms and bolt, as in olden days.

While all this was occurring on the field of battle, I in prison, to hide my excitement—and really to calm my overstrung nerves,—took the Ratib of Ibrahim Wad-el-Fahel, and occupied myself with "illuminating" its pages with red-and black-ink designs; this was an occupation I had often earned a few dollars at, but Fahel still owes me for my last exploit in "illumination." I left the work unfinished about noon to attend to two young men attached to the prison, who had come in from the fight, one with a bullet over the left temple, and the other with a bullet in the muscle of the left arm. Provided only with a penknife, I made a cross cut over the spot where I could in one case see, and the other feel the bullet imbedded, and pressed them out; both bullets had kept their shape, and must have been encountered at extreme range, or rather beyond it.

Maybe, with a European, chloroform might have been necessary for the extraction of the bullet in the arm, but with a Soudanese— have I not already said that a dervish can continue leaping and stabbing with half a dozen severe wounds in his body? A dervish can and will kill at the moment when the ventricles of his heart make their last contraction. Bodily pain, as we understand it, is unknown to them. Many a time have I applied, and seen applied, red-hot charcoal to sores, with the patients calmly looking on. With my present patients, after dabbing a little carbolic acid over the wounds, I asked what news they had brought. Yacoub, they said, was killed; almost all the faithful were killed or wounded; the Khaleefa himself was running back to town, but they had outstripped him. While still questioning them, Idris es Saier told me that the Muslimanieh who had been taken out to fight had made their way back to town, and were rummaging for European clothes in which to array themselves to receive the troops when they arrived.

THE FLAG OF KHALEEFA SHEREEF.

Line 1. "In the Name of God, the most Compassionate and Merciful."

Line 2. "Thou Living, Thou Existing and most Glorious Source of generosity."

Line 3. "There is no God but God. Mohammad is the messenger of God."

Line 4. "Mohammad El Mahdi is the Khaleefa of the messenger of God."

I should here take up the tales of those who were fighting in the dervish lines in order to present a complete narrative. At sunrise on September 2, Sheikh ed Din determined on attacking with his army of riflemen and cavalry, leaving Yacoub, with whom was his father, the Khaleefa, as a reserve. The shells which fell amongst his men did not knock them over or mow them down in lanes, they "blew a hundred men and horses high into the air"; then, when the rifle fire struck them, it "rolled them about like little stones." The carnage was so frightful that Sheikh ed Din himself led the way to the shelter in a khor to the west of Surgham hill.

And now, to understand clearly what followed next, and in a measure to explain the post of honour being given to Sheikh ed Din, I must refer to an incident occurring at the last moment before the army left Omdurman. Khaleefa Shereef, since his insurrection against Abdullahi, had not been allowed to exhibit the white flag made specially for the family of the Mahdi. It was believed that Abdullahi intended to nominate his son to succeed him, but this was against the expressed order of the Mahdi that Wad Helu and then Shereef should do so. While Sheikh ed Din was given the principal command, Shereef was not allowed any command at all, nor was the white flag of Mahdieh brought out of the Beit-el-Amana. Discontent was openly expressed at this, and some of the more religious or fanatic of the Mahdists demanded to know whether it was Abdullahi or Mahdieh they were to fight for. Abdullahi was advised to bring out the white flag, and it was carried at the extreme left of his army, but Sheikh ed Din Abdullahi had hoped would return as the victor of Kerreri, and thus his succession could be assured with the aid of a vision.

Seeing the repulse of Sheikh ed Din, the Khaleefa ordered the advance of Yacoub's army, and, as they were advancing, Sheikh ed Din collected his men and joined it. Then it was that the determined attack was made on MacDonald's brigade. The Khaleefa had dismounted, and, sitting on his prayer-skin, surrounded by his Mulazameen six deep, he held communion again with the Prophet and the Mahdi, while his army was being thinned by the thousands. Yacoub, with his Emirs and bodyguard of horsemen, rode in front of the troops and did his best to incite them to a final rush on the brigade. The white flag of Mahdieh was pushed close to where the 2nd Egyptian battalion, under Colonel Pink, was posted, and five standard-bearers in succession were shot down; others ran to raise it only to be shot down in turn, until the flag was buried under the slain.

Almost at this moment a well-aimed shell blew Yacoub and his bodyguard "high in the air," and before the Khaleefa's eyes; the black flag was planted, but the dervishes had had a lesson. Yunis, breaking through Abdullahi's bodyguard, ran to him, saying, "Why do you sit here? Escape; every one is being killed;" but Abdullahi sat still, dazed and stupefied with what he had seen. With the help of others, Yunis raised him to his feet, and actually pushed and bundled him along. Then Abdullahi started running on foot. He refused to mount a horse or camel; after stumbling and falling three times, Yunis persuaded him to mount a donkey. His army was now in full retreat, and "Where, oh, Abdullahi—where is the victory you promised?" assailed his ears. Calling his camel syce, Abou Gekka, he told him to hurry on a fast camel to Omdurman, collect his wives, children, and treasures, and conduct them to the Zareeba-el-Arrda (parade-ground) to the west of Omdurman, where he would meet them, and then all were to fly together. On reaching the zareeba, his household were not visible, and hearing that were still thousands of his troops in Omdurman, he was persuaded to enter the town, and make a last stand at the praying-ground. When nearing the mosque, Abdullahi saw Yacoub's eunuch waiting there. Telling him to collect Yacoub's wives, children, etc., and take them to the zareeba, the eunuch asked, "Where is my master?" Abdullahi then probably for the last time exercised his power of life and death. Turning to one of those near him, he said, "Who is this slave, to question my orders?" and the eunuch fell dead at Abdullahi's feet with a bullet through his head.

Reaching the large praying enclosure, Abdullahi ordered the drums and ombeyehs to be sounded, but few or none obeyed the summons; some came, looked at him sitting there mute, and slunk off; some, I have heard, jibed at him by asking if he was "sitting on his farwah." The farwah, or prayer-skin, is what the leaders formerly stood upon when the day was lost, and awaited their death. Finding himself deserted by all, he called for his secretary, Abou-el-Gassim, and asked what could be done. Gassim, whether in a sarcastic vein or not, recommended that he should continue praying where he was, and, maybe, his prayers would still bring victory; but there being none to join in the prayers, he asked Gassim to collect his household, and bring them to him. Gassim went off, and did not return.

At this time the Taaishi, Baggara, Berti Habbanieh, Rhizaghat, Digheem and other tribes, whom he formerly depended upon for support, were streaming off to the number of probably fifteen thousand, from the south of the town. Calling two men, he asked them to go outside the town, and see how far the Government troops were distant. The messengers, on reaching the Tombs of the Martyrs, about twelve hundred yards from where Abdullahi was sitting, suddenly came across the Sirdar and his staff standing at the angle of the great wall; they watched the staff move off towards the Beit-el-Mal, and returned and reported this to Abdullahi. Slipping through the door communicating with his house, he changed his clothes, collected the remainder of his household, and quietly slipped off while the Sirdar was making the complete circuit of Omdurman with the exception of those twelve hundred yards. It is a thousand pities, as things actually were, that the staff did not continue in the direction they were then taking, for a few minutes' trot along the deserted street leading to the prayer-ground would have allowed the Sirdar to lay his hands upon Abdullahi, as he sat there absolutely alone, on the spot where he had hoped that his faithful would make their last stand.

The sun was falling, and still we in prison did not know exactly how the day had gone. We had heard the drums and ombeyehs, which told us that Abdullahi was calling upon the faithful to assemble at the prayer-ground; a cloud of dust on the desert and the gunboats slowly steaming up, meant that the troops were advancing on the town. Idris es Saier came and asked me what he was to do—to go to his master or wait for the English. I advised him to close the gates of the prison, use his rifles upon any of the Baggara trying to force an entrance, and wait and see who would ask for the keys—the expected Sirdar or the Khaleefa. In all cases, I told him, it was his duty to protect the prisoners in his charge, and reminded him of Fauzi's tale of the two gaolers. When we heard the shrill cries of the women, we knew that some one was being welcomed, and guessed correctly that it was the English at last. Idris, in his anxiety to secure his prisoners, had us all chained in gangs earlier than usual, and this linking of my gang to the common chain had only just been completed when Idris came, frightened out of his life, as one could tell by his voice, to tell me that the "place was filled with my English brothers," that a big, tall man, who, he was told, was the dreaded Sirdar, had asked for me, and that I was to come at once.

It seemed an age while the chain was being slipped from my shackles, and then, led by Idris, I made my way to the gate of the Saier. I was crying dry eyed; I could see a blurred group, and then I was startled out of my senses by hearing English spoken—the only words of a European language I had heard for seven long years. From that blurred group, and through the gloom, came a voice, "Are you Neufeld? are you well?" And then a tall figure stepped towards me, and gave my hand a hearty shake. It was the Sirdar. I believe I babbled something as I received a handshake from one, and a slap on the shoulder from another, but I do not know what I said. Looking down at my shackles, the Sirdar asked, "Can these be taken off now?—I am going on." I believe a second's discussion went on with Idris, and then I heard the last order I was to receive and obey in the Saier, "Neufeld, *out you go!*" It was the Sirdar's order, and, half carried by the friendly and strong arms supporting me, I obeyed. The next thing I remembered was a British officer slipping off his horse, lifting me into the saddle, and trudging along at my side after the terribly trying and arduous day he must have had.

I was taken to the "head-quarters' mess" at the camp; the Sirdar had, I believe, allowed himself the luxury of a broken angareeb on which to rest; the staff were lying in all positions on the sand, fagged out, but hard at work with despatches and orders by the light of guttering candles. It was a hungry, thirsty, and deadbeat head-quarters' mess I had been invited to on the night of the memorable 2nd of September. While the comfort of the troops had been looked to, the Sirdar and his staff had evidently neglected themselves. Their canteen and mess were miles away on slow-travelling camels; one of the most brilliant victories of the nineteenth century was being celebrated by a supper of a few biscuits, poor water, some of my prison bread, which I shared with others around me, and Cairo cigarettes, with the sand of the desert for seats, and the canopy of heaven as the roof over our heads.

Soon after reaching the "mess," I heard a voice calling, "Where's Neufeld?" and the inquirer introduced himself to me; it was Mr. Bennet Burleigh, of the *Daily Telegraph.* I had heard, and yet had not heard, much English spoken to me, but the flood of language he poured out when he found me still in chains came as a revelation to me; it was as picturesque as his description of the battle which I have since read. Rushing off, he was back in a few moments with some farriers with their shoeing implements to try and remove my chains; off again, he came with some engineers, and amidst a running torrent of abuse, anent cold chisels and other implements which he required and which were not forthcoming, he questioned me. Every one had a try at those chains; some one I heard use language concerning the Khaleefa when he found his thumb between the hammer and the links, but with a great deal of strong language, and equally as strong blows, the links connecting with the anklets were cut through, but the anklets themselves were only removed, owing to want of appliances, on board Colonel Gordon's steamer a few minutes before he led the way to the troops who were to take part in the funeral-service at the spot where his hero uncle fell.

While Slatin's countryman, Joseppi, was imprisoned with me, I was able to exercise my mother tongue, and correct his broken German, which gave me, at all events, some little amusement; but after his murder, and the escape of Father Ohrwalder, I never had another opportunity of speaking a European language except in my dreams, and when I discovered myself talking to myself. For seven long years, with the exception of the word "torpedo," by which name the Algerian called his mines, I had not heard a syllable of a European tongue. The last Europeans I had spoken to before leaving Egypt were English; the first language I was to hear on my release was English, and then a strange thing happened. As far as language was concerned, my brain became a blank from the moment I left Wadi Halfa, to the moment when the Sirdar called out, "Are you Neufeld?" so that when the German Military Attaché spoke to me in German, while hearing, and in the main understanding what he said, I could not, much to his very evident annoyance, find words in my mother tongue to reply. It was weeks after my return to Egypt before I was able to express myself properly in the German language. While to myself this was not to be greatly wondered at, yet the fact might be of interest to some scientist, who has made cerebral affections his particular study.

CHAPTER XXIII
THE SIRDAR AND SAVAGE WARFARE

On the morning following the battle of Omdurman, a number of the townspeople came out to the camp, complaining of the rough usage which they had been subjected to at the hands of the Soudanese troops left in charge of the town, and of the looting of their houses. The majority, not knowing that the Sirdar and his staff were fluent Arabic scholars, brought their complaints to me, and asked me to interpret for them. In my then excited and half-dazed state, I rushed off to report the matters. Colonel Maxwell at once called up a hundred men, and with an officer and sergeant, instructed me to proceed to the town and see the men posted to the houses of the complainants. The real truth of the matter, of course, only came out later, and as I do not know of any one else who is in as good a position as I am to relate it, I submit the following.

Long before the troops reached the town, the inhabitants were busily engaged in looting the Mahdieh institutions and the deserted houses of the fleeing Baggara and others. Their local knowledge obviated the necessity of *searching* for loot; they knew where there was anything at all worth taking and took it, anticipating the troops by half a day. Into every occupied house loot was being carried, if not by the head of the household, then by the servants and others attached to the establishment, while the head mounted guard. True, the soldiers did loot towards midnight; but what? angareebs (the native seats and bedsteads combined), on which to rest themselves instead of lying down on the filth-sodden ground of Omdurman. Heaven knows they richly deserved the temporary loan of these angareebs. Wherever residents were looted, it was their own fault. The victorious and therefore happy and grinning Blacks kept an eye on their hereditary enemies—the lighter coloured population, as they passed backwards and forwards, always entering their huts loaded and emerging empty-handed. In their eagerness to collect all they could, they threw down their loot, and hurried off for more, and during their absence the Black "Tommy" annexed whatever he thought might be useful to him.

TROPHIES TAKEN AT OMDURMAN.

The Sirdar himself could not have made a better arrangement than that which came of itself. The troops were enabled to keep at their posts with an eye open for any lurking Baggara; the looting was being done for them by the residents, who knew exactly where to lay their hands upon anything worth taking, instead of time being wasted by searching empty houses, while the soldiers were kept in good spirits by having the fun of the looting without running the risk of being suddenly confronted with half a dozen Baggara concealed in some hut or room. When some one came staggering along under a particularly heavy load, a Black would assist him with his burden; some of his comrades would join in, and when the looter protested that he did not require any help, a little Soudan horseplay was indulged in, and later on these little pleasantries came up as grave charges of assault.

The only people in Omdurman who had anything worth looting were the real Mahdists themselves—and they deserved to be looted of their ill-gotten gains. In dealing with any claims for compensation for having been looted, three things should be kept in mind—the complainant should prove that he was not a real Mahdist; that what he was looted of on the evening of the 2nd of September was not the proceeds of his own looting during the day; and, having got so far, should reconcile the fact of his having been looted of property and valuables with his tales of abject misery, poverty, and semi-starvation.

It did not take me long to grasp the situation, for after seeing the soldiers posted to the houses of the "Government" people, I started on a voyage of discovery after the houses of the principal

Baggara and others, and having had them pointed out to me, I recommended the soldiers to take their cleaning rods and bayonets, and probe the walls of the hareem rooms for hidden valuables. I am pleased to say that the suggested operations were not entirely without some gratifying results; but a very small find indeed gratifies the native troops. Whoever possessed property in Omdurman was either a thief or murderer. Most had bolted with the Khaleefa, and it was through no fault of theirs that they left a few dollars behind for people who could make good use of them. I regret now that I did not organize a looting party, and place myself at the head of it.

I have heard of, but I have not read, the article or articles written by one of the correspondents who accompanied the Khartoum Expedition, consisting of a series of wholesale charges brought against the Sirdar and the troops in connection with "Khartoum Day." I gauge what the articles must have been from some of the letters written in reply. As every one appears to have criticized and shown how much better than the Sirdar they could have carried out the reconquest of the Soudan, as the "oldest resident" I think I am entitled to express an opinion, and to criticize also.

The Sirdar, in my opinion, made one grave error—he gave quarter; and I have no doubt that, in doing so, he knew that he was doing a positive injustice to his Black troops in order to pander to an ignorant public opinion which he knew existed elsewhere. I know that some people, profoundly ignorant of the Soudan and its tribes, and their history, religion, laws, customs, and legal rights, will hold up their hands in holy horror, and jump to the conclusion that my long captivity has engendered a spirit of vindictiveness against my captors which has deadened in me every sense of humanity—and in this they will be wrong. Lord Kitchener of Khartoum made a grave error in extending to a horde of murderers the advantages of civilized warfare, *and the clemency he felt called upon to extend to them will cost England the loss of many a gallant life yet.*

There was not a man in the Black Battalions who had not, by the old Law of Moses, the laws of his country in which he was then fighting, the law of the Prophet, and the religious law, irrespective of the law handed down from the remotest ages, more right to take a life on that day than any judge in a civilized country has to sentence to death a man who has personally done him no wrong. Every man there was entitled to a life in retaliation for the murder of a father, the rape of a mother, wife, daughter, or sister, the mutilation of a brother or son, and his own bondage. To prevent, as the Sirdar did prevent, these soldiers from exercising their rights, was doing them an injustice, and running a risk as well, when it is remembered how they had slaved for this "Day of Retaliation." There may have been, doubtless were, many cases of the killing outright of wounded dervishes; this was no more murder than a judicial hanging; and looking at the matter from a humanitarian point of view, would it not have been better to send those Blacks over the field to put the wounded out of their misery, and thus kill two birds with one stone? For let it be remembered, that when a dervish sits and lies wounded, he is wounded to death, and only by force of will keeps himself alive until he dies happy at the moment when he sends his spear through the heart of his would-be saviour. I repeat, the Sirdar committed a grave error in extending to the dervishes the advantages of civilized warfare. I who have lived amongst the people, who have discussed with their greatest exponents of the religious law, and made comparisons between the administration of their and our laws, consider that I am well qualified to express an opinion, and better qualified than those who, with a command of language, can so present their views to the public that the cant, ignorance, and humbug—not to say hankering for notoriety which underlies it all—is hidden.

You who have held up your hands in holy horror at the foregoing, prepare to hold them up again.

The day after the battle of Kirbekan an outpost was being sent forward. Moving to its position, it espied a wounded dervish making signs for water. One of the soldiers slipped off his camel to give him some, and his comrades moved on. As time went on, and their chum did not catch them up, they came back to see what had happened. There he was, still attending to the wounded dervish, his hand resting on his shoulder, but there was no movement from either. Approaching—this was the tale plainly written. The lines on the ground showed that "Tommy" had taken the wounded man in his arms, and half supporting and half dragging him, had placed him in a sitting posture in the shade, with his back against a rock; then, taking his water-bottle, he began to pour the life-giving drops down the throat of the dervish, for he still grasped the empty water-bottle. With returning life came, of course, returning strength—sufficient strength for the dervish to slip off his knife, poise his hand for a second of time behind "Tommy's" back, while he was occupied with his mission of mercy, and then, plunging it in with sufficient force to divide the spinal column, the dervish died happy as "Tommy" fell dead across his shoulder. That dervish was glorified in the Soudan, and thousands of others were awaiting the opportunity of dying as gloriously. Do you like the picture now? These are the sort of people you howl for the protection of. If you wish the wounded dervishes to be attended to against their will, then institute some special decoration for those who return alive from their mission of mercy, and when you have discovered that for each decoration given, a few hundred valuable lives have been sacrificed, perhaps you will agree to the issue of orders which I, knowing what I do know, should issue now.

If I had my say in the matter, when next the Government troops come face to face with the tribes, whom Lord Kitchener in his clemency spared to gather again around the Khaleefa, I should make it a drum-head court-martialling business for any doctor who risked the lives of his wounded in hospital by attempting to throw away his own in attending to a wounded dervish who does not want to live. He is wounded to death or would not be lying or sitting there, and he wants to die—but to die killing; he wants your life's blood, not your aid and succour. As he wants to die—as he *must* die—then shoot him at once and put him out of his misery. In doing this, you are but acting humanely to a dying but still ferocious animal in the guise of a man. You are not taking a life needlessly, but in all probability saving a better one; and as the troops pick their way over the field of battle, another bullet should be put into the "dead" and "wounded" from a distance a yard beyond the point to which a dervish can throw a spear, to prevent any more accidents. The number of soldiers killed by "dead" and "wounded" dervishes is great enough already, and it would be criminal to add to it. Have you no thought for some English mother mourning the loss of her brave lad, who threw away his life in attending to a wounded dervish, when she had been looking forward to his return as the hero of the village? How many cottages in England have been made desolate by the hands of "dead" and "wounded" dervishes?

If none of the foregoing suggestions are acceptable, then let each correspondent accompanying an expedition into the heart of Africa declare whether he votes for first aid to the wounded dervishes or not. If he does not, then let him hold his peace if he sees things which he would not expect to come across, were he witnessing the sequel to a fight between civilized peoples. If he declares for first aid, then give him a packet of bandages and a water-bottle, and let him put his principles into practice, while his more enlightened brother knights of the pen tag on to their despatches his obituary notice.

CHAPTER XXIV
BACK TO CIVILIZATION

I must leave it to my readers to try and imagine what my sensations were as I sailed away from Omdurman on the first stage of my journey to civilization and liberty. Remembering the reason which I gave my wife, manager, and friends, when I was begged to abandon my projected journey into Kordofan, knowing that others knew how I had comported myself before my captors and Abdullahi, I was conscious that I had nothing to be ashamed of in the production of a worse than useless saltpetre, which I could easily have refined—but the real refinement of which I prevented. Nor was I ashamed of having designed impossible machines for the manufacture of powder and cartridges, in order to keep out of that terrible Saier; nor of the wilful destruction of so much good material for their construction, especially as there were living witnesses to bear me out. Thinking, therefore, that the small, very small, risk I ran in the collecting of information to send to the advancing armies might have been appreciated, I built up on my journey what proved to be a house of cards to be blown down by a breath as soon as I reached Cairo. I was much disappointed in the reception awaiting me; so also was every other released captive, and not a few Mahdists. Perhaps I am to blame for delaying at Berber for the purpose I have "admitted" in my chapter "Divorced and Married," when my arrival had been announced by a certain train; but I have been punished for this, though even now I am too uncivilized to feel ashamed of the action, or to appreciate the justice of the strictures passed upon me in consequence.

When at last I did reach Cairo, it was but to learn that although I had taken as "jokes" the compliments which I received on my way down, on the "manufacture of gunpowder with which to kill English soldiers"—on the "'damned clever' design and construction of the forts to oppose the advance of the gunboats," on my "smartness in galloping away from the field when I saw it was all over for Mahdieh, and reaching the prison just in time to get on my chains again before the Sirdar put in his appearance"—yet these, and a great many other tales, were implicitly believed in. Moreover, they had lost nothing in being translated into the many languages spoken in Cairo, which include every language of Europe, with a few of the East.

It was heartrending to me, after what I had gone through, to return to my own flesh and blood to be spurned and shunned as the incarnation of everything despicable in a man. I, who had defied my captors and had looked for death, wished for it more now that I was amongst my own people; but fortunately the persecution I was subjected to, added to my change of life, caused me to break down completely, and when I recovered from my delirium it was to find myself in the hands of a few friends. Do not think that I had worried myself over what was mere idle gossip; all the charges were made in sincerity, and this owing to the influential quarters whence they were emanating.

A few days after receiving the generous offer of my publishers, I was told that I was a prisoner of war, and as such was debarred from entering into any engagements; moreover, my experiences were said to be the property of the War Office. Later on, I was told that, in consideration of the subscriptions raised by a newspaper group in England for the purpose of effecting my escape some years ago, I was to write my experiences for the benefit of the subscribers. Then, after keeping me waiting weeks for a reply, they offered me £100—a sum not sufficient to pay the guides already in Cairo—and asked me to repay them the moneys they had lent me while in prison. When in reply to this offer I pointed out the ruined condition I am in, and offered to repay the subscribers the monies spent from the money I am to receive for my book, I was first threatened with an injunction upon the book, and then with the publication of "interesting" disclosures (?) concerning me.

When H.R.H. Duke Johann Albrecht, the Regent of Mecklenburg, graciously writes to me himself, instructing me to call at the German Consul-General's, in Cairo, for some money sent there to "give me a new start in life," I am met, when I do present myself, with accusations of ingratitude and broken engagements towards people whose names I had never heard of. However, these people wrote disclaimers to the *Times*, saying that they knew nothing of the claims made against me in their names; yet, in spite of the disclaimers, the money was impounded for about five months in all, and then some claims paid from it, but on whose account I am still ignorant.

While all these charges are being levelled at me, I am warned that if I dare contradict anything published formerly concerning myself or Soudan affairs, certain correspondence will be communicated to the London Press; yet what am I to do but contradict them wherever I can find a scrap of evidence to support my contradiction? Surely I cannot be expected to confirm such reports in the face of the threats made verbally and in the columns of a newspaper, especially as I and mine must remain the social outcasts we have been since my release, until my narrative appears. I am writing more in grief than in anger; these are all subjects I should have preferred not to mention in my narrative, and I am touching on them as lightly as is possible, but as others have chosen to publish them, by keeping silence I should be doing myself an injustice. My hand or tongue has been forced, therefore those who have taken the initial action against me must be responsible for the inevitable result which will follow when, questioned as to the foregoing by those entitled to ask for the evidence, I hand over for publication the whole of the correspondence. For the public, having been led to form opinions about me on the strength of the reports and explanations printed, have the right to know the whole truth before pronouncing a second judgment; but my narrative ought not to be burdened with such a voluminous correspondence. Surely a kind Providence kept watch over the few documents which I have been fortunate enough to find after all these years, and which are of such value to me in substantiating my story.

Amongst the many articles published concerning me, one printed in the London and Provincial papers on the 5th and 6th of September last caused me considerable injury in England and Egypt, and, maybe, irreparable injury in my native country, to which I have appealed for the rights of citizenship which my capture and long captivity precluded my returning to claim during 1887. To this appeal I have as yet received no answer—and little wonder. On the appearance of this article, some of my countrymen attacked me in no measured terms, and I was shunned by them as they would shun a pestilence. The communication made was on the presumable authority of General Hunter, as his name is mentioned; but so sure am I that he was no more capable of communicating such a report for publication than he is of turning his back in the face of an enemy, that I have not so much as written to him asking his denial. I was advised to allow these reports to accumulate and circulate, and reply to them *en bloc* in my narrative, leaving a deceived public to take up the matter. The article I refer to reads as follows:—

"Twice had every preparation been made. The relays of camels to take the exile across the desert were ready. Nothing remained but for Neufeld to pluck up courage and quit Omdurman. Each time he backed out at the last moment. At length he confessed the truth, namely, that he did not care to come away. He had married a black wife. His friends in Germany were dead or had forgotten him. He would stay where he was."

Is it not possible to find some one to swear that *more* than two attempts were made during those long twelve years to extricate me? I have in my narrative said all that I know of the visits of any guides to Omdurman. Having been promised the publication of interesting documents concerning me, perhaps the proofs of the above will be forthcoming; let it be proved that on even *one* occasion relays of camels were posted to effect my escape, and at the same time let it be proved that the guide who posted those relays ever came to me.

It is quite possible that there are a sheaf of letters waiting to be published bearing my signature; and maybe when they are, I shall learn their contents for the first time. I had to sign many letters the contents of which I was ignorant of, as is evidenced by the letter to my manager, and the letter to General Stephenson, in reply to the one he entrusted me with when I went on my expedition. This letter was photographed, and a translation is given on p. 338. The reply was dictated by Abdullahi to his secretary, and handed me to sign. Let the note, letter, or report, on which my refusal to escape is founded, be produced, and then see if the date of it does not correspond with the date of the maturing of one of my many plans for escape. But do not press me too closely for my reason for writing or giving such a message. If I gave it I should be committing as great an injustice as did poor Lupton, when sending back part of the monies sent him by his friends at Suakin, who were trying to effect his escape, wrote. . . . Those friends are still living, and as they have not chosen to tell the world what they did for their countrymen, and how it was that their schemes fell through, I may not do so—at least, not yet.

If I lied, as I have been told to my face that I did, when I denied some of the charges made against me, why should more credence be given me for sincerity in notes refusing to escape than was given to Slatin's protestations of loyalty in his letter to the Khaleefa when he escaped? If during my capture and my long captivity my behaviour was unmanly, or such as I, a European, ought to be ashamed of, then let the proofs be at once forthcoming. Do not weary me out and keep the world against me with threats of coming disclosures; moreover, have I not good reason to complain of the communication of everything damaging to me while everything in my favour is suppressed?

The sources of information, reference, and assistance thrown open to Ohrwalder and Slatin when compiling their experiences have been closed to me. When Slatin arrived in Cairo, he was handed the statements of guides reporting his "persistent refusals to escape," and allowed to be the first to inform the world of their existence. When I arrive in Cairo, I find that similar reports concerning me have been given wide publicity and believed in. Why, I ask, should it have been believed that the guides' reports were false in Slatin's case and true in mine? and why should I not have been given the opportunity of first announcing their existence to the world? Perhaps, before I have completed my narrative, people will come to the conclusion that some of those privileged to look at all my papers have, for some reason or another, felt that it was necessary thoroughly to discredit me, so that, when my story appeared, I should not be believed in; but then, who could have foreseen that I should ever be so fortunate as to collect any evidence in support of it?

It has been suggested that maybe I have taken too much to heart the "tales being told about" me; that they were but gossip. It was no idle gossip for me. I was persuaded, much against my wish, to attend a hotel garden-party, my first and last appearance in public in Cairo, for this was the sequel: One of my few friends connected with the Press there handed me some cuttings containing the usual inaccuracies and slanders, and while sitting down in a corridor, my amanuensis at my side taking notes as I read them over, I heard, "Hello, how is that book of Neufeld's getting on?" The speaker, when asked if he knew Neufeld, blurted out, "Know him—no, nor do I want to know him, considering the number of English soldiers he has sent to eternity with his gunpowder. I would not even look at the fellow's face." And as my companion whispered, "This is Neufeld," I raised my head just in time to see the representative of a great news agency hurrying through the doorway. Maybe, on the appearance of this, Reuter's Cairo Agent may not be averse to telling me on what or whose authority he made this charge in my own hearing. The incident for the moment is closed, but if it is re-opened, it must be re-opened somewhere where highly placed officials may not be successfully appealed to to go around asking lawyers not to take up my case. Memo. for that News-Agency representative—"Walls have ears," and "Don't shout till you are out of the wood."

I trust that when I send up my card to the London correspondent of the newspaper from whose article I have quoted, he will, instead of imitating his brother knight of the pen in Cairo, at least receive me, and examine the originals of the documents inserted in my narrative, disproving the charges which he was the medium of circulating in England and on the Continent. Then, if satisfied with their genuineness in the first place, and in the second place convinced that during my long captivity I was striving more than any other captive to effect my escape, he will at least, when next writing to his readers, try to do what little he can towards repairing the great injury which he did me in England, though it was without malice, I admit, and then try to have his error corrected in the German papers. I ask nothing more than this. Is it too much to ask?

But from the sea of slander and uncharitableness in which I was struggling, there rose some kindly hands to help me. When pressed by the War Office to repay the £20 I had borrowed from it on the way down—with my old guides in Cairo asking me to redeem the receipts they had for monies lent me while in prison—with the monies kindly sent me from Berlin to give me a "new start in life" impounded—with the hand of every one against me, after calling at one bank and being refused, I went to Mr. Hewett Moxley, an old friend of the Bleichröders, of Berlin, and now the Director of the Imperial Ottoman Bank in Cairo. Handing him my file of letters and telegrams, I asked if he thought that they contained sufficient guarantees for my being able eventually to repay the money which I wished him to advance to me. He left me for a few moments, and then returned, and as he went over one letter after the other, my hopes fell, for he remarked that my "guarantees were not of the very highest order," and that my "credentials were not of a very satisfactory nature." But I knew a few moments later that these were pithy, maybe sarcastic, remarks upon the letters which he was glancing through, for while engaged upon these running comments, his clerk was counting out £150 in gold for my immediate needs, and opening a credit for a further £250. I thoroughly enjoyed his joke, so different from those I had so far encountered, for his action was the first kindly one which I received in civilization.

It was late on a Saturday night when, for the first time, I rose from my bed of sickness to meet the proprietor of one of those great English papers, which I had been promised were to hound me. In spite of the assurances given me, it was with no little nervousness that I approached him; but instead of the ogre whom I had expected to meet, I found myself being supported by a kindly spoken English gentleman, assisted to an easy-chair, and tucked up in rugs. A few waiters were in attendance, and the "ogre" was blaming himself for having asked me to call and see him, and begging my forgiveness, as he did not know that I was so ill. The "ogre" was Sir George Newnes. He listened patiently to all I had to say, went through my correspondence, ventured the opinion that certain actions directed against me were "monstrous," told me not to believe that the English Press would attack me without reason, and recommended me, as soon as I was well, to go ahead with my book and collect every scrap of evidence which I could in support of my own story. I have followed his advice, but the collecting of the little evidence which I have got has been no light task, groping as I was in the darkness of a twelve years' oblivion.

I must not forget either to acknowledge the handsome treatment which I have received at the hands of my publishers, who have kept me in funds, and with extraordinary patience awaited the completion of my narrative; but the absolute necessity of collecting proofs for what I state, in face of the threats dangling over my head, accounts for the long delay.

CHAPTER XXV
HOW GORDON DIED

When the news of the Sirdar's splendid victory reached England, the British nation may be said to have breathed again, and when the great rush was made for the cheap edition of "Ten Years' Captivity," which was extensively advertised with my portrait to catch attention, the few known details of Gordon's death became as fresh again in people's minds as they had been years before. I was constantly asked to relate all I had heard concerning Gordon. When I had done so I was invariably met with quotations and readings from "Mahdism," "Ten Years' Captivity," "Fire and Sword," and other works; for what I had been told of Gordon's death by eye-witnesses was an entirely different history to those published.

The first to relate the story of Gordon's death was a man whose tongue Gordon had threatened to cut out as the only cure for his inveterate lying, and when he escaped and reached Cairo, in telling his tale he sustained his reputation. All accounts of Gordon's death have apparently been based upon this first one received. Gordon, the world has been made to believe, died as a coward, for what other construction may be placed on the assertion that he turned his back upon his assailants, and in his back received his mortal wound? It is an infamous lie; but, then, what was to be expected from a man whom Gordon knew so well, and who, maybe, had good reason to invent the tale he did? I quote, side by side, what may be called the three official accounts of Gordon's death:—

MAHDISM.

"He (Gordon) made a gesture of scorn with his right hand, and turned his back, where he received another spear wound which caused him to fall forward and was most likely his mortal wound. . . . He made no resistance, and did not fire a shot from his revolver."

". . . One of them rushing up, stabbed him with his spear, and others then followed, and soon he was killed. . . . He (Nejoumi) ordered the body to be dragged downstairs into the garden, where his head was cut off."

OHRWALDER.

"The first Arab *plunged his huge spear into his body. He fell forward on his face,* was *dragged down* the stairs, many stabbed him with their spears, and *his head was cut off and sent to the Mahdi."*

SLATIN.

"The first man up the steps *plunged his huge spear into his body; he fell forward on his face* without uttering a word. His murderers *dragged* him *down* the steps to the palace entrance, and here *his head was cut off and* at once *sent* over *to the Mahdi."*

It will be noticed that Father Ohrwalder's account appears to be a condensation of the first given, while it is hard to believe that a coincidence only accounts for Slatin giving the history in almost the identical words used by Ohrwalder. It is still more extraordinary that the first account should ever have been believed and published, and still *more* extraordinary that it was not corrected by Ohrwalder and Slatin, for when I arrived in Omdurman, in 1887, the real details of the death of Gordon were the theme of conversation whenever his name was mentioned, and there are many eye-witnesses to his death—or were until the battle of Omdurman, who could tell a very different tale.

KHALEEL AGHA ORPHALI.

Those who knew Charles George Gordon, will believe me when I aver that he died, as they must all have believed that he died—in spite of the official and semi-official accounts to the contrary—as the soldier and lion-hearted man he was. Gordon did not rest his hand on the hilt of his sword and turn his back to his enemies to receive his mortal wound. Gordon drew his sword, and used it. When Gordon fell, his sword was dripping with the blood of his assailants, for no less than sixteen or seventeen did he cut down with it. When Gordon fell, his left hand was blackened with the unburned powder from his at least thrice-emptied revolver. When Gordon fell, his life's blood was pouring from a spear and pistol-shot wound in his right breast. When Gordon fell, his boots were slippery with the blood of the crowd of dervishes he shot and hacked his way through, in his heroic attempt to cut his way out and place himself at the head of his troops. Gordon died as only Gordon could die. Let the world be misinformed and deceived about Soudan affairs with the tales of so-called guides and spies, but let it be told the truth of Gordon's death.

A week before the fall of Khartoum, Gordon had given up hopes. Calling Ibrahim Pasha Fauzi, he ordered him to provision one of the steamers, get all the Europeans on board, and set off for the north. To their credit be it said, they refused to leave unless Gordon saved his own life with theirs. Finding him obdurate, a plot was made to seize him while asleep, carry him off, and save him in spite of himself; but he somehow heard of the plot, smiled, and said it was his duty to save their lives if he could, but it was also his duty to "stick to his post." As the troops must be near, then sail north, he told them, and tell them to hurry up.

Each day at dawn, when he retired to rest, he bolted his door from the inside, and placed his faithful body-servant—Khaleel Agha Orphali—on guard outside it. On the fatal night, Gordon had as usual kept his vigil on the roof of the palace, sending and receiving telegraphic messages from the lines every few minutes, and as dawn crept into the skies, thinking that the long-threatened attack was not yet to be delivered, he lay down wearied out. The little firing heard a few minutes later attracted no more attention than the usual firing which had been going on continuously night and day for months, but when the palace guards were heard firing it was known that something serious was happening. By the time Gordon had slipped into his old serge or dark tweed suit, and taken his sword and revolver, the advanced dervishes were already surrounding the palace. Overcoming the guards, a rush was made up the stairs, and Gordon was met leaving his room. A small spear was thrown which wounded him, but very slightly, on the left shoulder. Almost before the dervishes knew what was happening, three of them lay dead, and one wounded, at Gordon's feet—the remainder fled. Quickly reloading his revolver, Gordon made for the head of the stairs, and again drove the reassembling dervishes off. Darting back to reload, he received a stab in his left shoulder-blade from a dervish concealed behind the corridor door, and on reaching the steps the third time, he received a pistol-shot and spear-wound in his right breast, and then, great soldier as he was, he rose almost above himself. With his life's blood pouring from his breast—not his back, remember—he fought his way step by step, kicking from his path the wounded and dead dervishes—for Orphali too had not been idle—and as he was passing through the doorway leading into the courtyard, another concealed dervish almost severed his right leg with a single blow. Then Gordon fell. The steps he had *fought* his way—not been dragged—down, were encumbered with the bodies of dead and dying dervishes. No dervish spear pierced the live and quivering flesh of a prostrate but still conscious Gordon, for he breathed his last as he turned to face his last assailant, half raised his sword to strike, and fell dead with his face to heaven.

Even had I not been specially requested, as the last of the Soudan captives, to relate in my narrative all that I had heard and learned concerning Gordon, I should have done so to a certain extent at all events, for he was no more the hero of the British people than he was mine, and the belief that he was still alive had no little to do with my ill-starred journey in 1887. The truth about his death, which is now published for the first time, is ample justification for what follows concerning him while still alive. It is true, as I have been told, that all I can have to say will be from "hearsay;" but then all the reports published concerning Gordon's last days are from hearsay. I have the advantage over all others in this—that I was maybe the one man, captive or not, in Omdurman whom Mahdist and "Government" man alike could trust implicitly and confide in, for there was no questioning what my attitude was towards Abdullahi and Mahdieh. The consequence was that old "Government" people and the powerful men who from time to time became my fellow-prisoners, and, as a consequence, enemies of Abdullahi, gave me confidences which, if given in other quarters, might have resulted in the loss of a head.

Again, almost all the tales told about the Soudan may be classed in one of two categories; the first, tales like mine, related by people interested in putting their own version upon events and incidents with which they were personally connected, and the second, tales told by people with versions for which they believed their questioners were hankering, so that what was white to "A" became black to "B," if it was considered that this colour pleased "B" best. The system scarcely puts a premium on accuracy.

But before proceeding to my comments on the criticisms, a few introductory remarks are called for to prevent misconceptions and misunderstandings arising in the minds of my readers. As an evidence that the following is not intended—far from it—to lacerate the feelings of any of those who suffered with me, I might mention that I have read over the notes of this chapter to many of my fellow-captives, and have, at their suggestion, cut out a series of incidents well known to Gordon, which influenced him in the stand he took towards certain people, and other incidents which prove how clear and long-sighted he was, and how events justified his taking up the stand which he did. One incident ought to be written, to punish on this earth, if possible, the man whose escape has not been recorded, and whose deserted and broken-hearted wife lies by the side of their unshriven baby-boy in the sands of the Soudan. However, maybe Gordon, had he come back alive to meet all the calumnies directed against him, would have hesitated to help his "clearance" by stabbing the living with a dead hand, and out of respect to his memory this incident, with a number of others, has been expunged.

I have already told Father Ohrwalder that, in commenting upon what he says in "Ten Years' Captivity," when speaking of Gordon's actions, the remarks I may feel called upon to make are not intended for him personally, and although I foresee that I must in the main have to speak as to the second person, I think Father Ohrwalder quite understands that the second person in this instance is his book, not himself. I do not, as I have told him, consider that he is directly responsible for the opinions he is credited with in "Ten Years' Captivity," and this notwithstanding the remark, "The reader is reminded that all opinions expressed are those of Father Ohrwalder." Considering that Father Ohrwalder is a priest and missionary, and has ventured upon thin ice in attacking Gordon's memory, such a statement is hardly fair to him, as in the preface to the book it is stated, that "Father Ohrwalder's manuscript, which was in the first instance written in German, was roughly translated into English by Yusef Effendi Cudzi, a Syrian; this I entirely rewrote in narrative form; the work therefore does not profess to be a literal translation of the original manuscript. . . ."

I should have thought that when Gordon was being attacked the original manuscript might have been treated a little differently. Of course it is easily understandable that when a Syrian, with Arabic for his mother tongue, translates from one difficult language which he has picked up into another equally difficult, and translates roughly too, when moreover this rough translation is handled in the manner admitted, errors may have crept in or been passed unnoticed, whilst salient points were lost sight of. It is also quite possible that the peculiar idioms of the Arabic, German, and English languages got into a hopeless tangle, and were left so. Whatever the cause, there is no gainsaying the fact that Father Ohrwalder is credited with the expression of opinions which he, as a priest and missionary, ought to be one of the last on this earth to give utterance to. That he did not appreciate to the full the real import of the opinions he is credited with, I feel certain of after my long interview with him, when, with the Bible in one hand and a copy of "Ten Years' Captivity" in the other, we compared the opinions expressed in the latter with the teachings of Christ in the former.

Father Ohrwalder may or may not have been ill-advised in omitting or suppressing the relation of well-known incidents, which accounted for Gordon's attitude in certain cases. It was only by omitting to mention these incidents that the criticisms on Gordon were rendered possible, or I should say that, had those incidents been included, the criticisms would not have lived a day. It would have been far better to tell everything to the generous and sympathetic world which he and Slatin met when they escaped, and to leave it to condone, if any condoning was called for, and to sympathize with them in the parts force of circumstances compelled them to act, which must have been so repugnant to them; for to omit, when criticizing Gordon, the relation of the very acts which compelled him also by force of circumstances to act as he did, was, to say the least of it, very unwise.

In "Ten Years' Captivity" the reader is led into a maze of opinions, and left there. Once inside, you discover that you can neither gain the centre of the maze or return to the starting-point; you must either wander round for an eternity, or do as I shall do, cut your way through the hedges planted to bewilder you, and thank Heaven when on the outside that you are clear of the tortuous passages. Compare, for instance—

"He (Cudzi) added that Gordon should have no anxiety about Berber as long as Hussein Pasha Khaleefa was Mudir,"

with,

"Gordon himself committed a mistake by which he gave a deathblow to himself and his mission. On his way to Khartoum, he stopped at Berber, and interviewed the Mudir Hussein Pasha

Khaleefa; he *imprudently* told him that he had come up to remove the Egyptian garrisons, as Egypt had abandoned the Soudan."

Gordon cannot be blamed for confirming, as Governor-General of the Soudan, the news telegraphed to his subordinate, the Mudir of Berber, *through whose hands the retiring garrisons must pass*, nor can he be blamed if, when his suspicions were aroused, he deferred to the opinion of the man who was acting British Consul, Government representative, and his own agent, when he wrote and telegraphed as he did, "Trust in Hussein Pasha."

"The catastrophe which had overtaken Hicks filled the inhabitants of Khartoum with indescribable dismay. Several of them returned to Egypt, and the members of the Austrian Mission, with their blacks, quitted Khartoum on the 11th December, 1883."

I therefore take it for granted that Father Ohrwalder's fellow-workers saw that all was hopeless *two months before Gordon's name had been suggested to the Egyptian Government*, yet, in the face of this, we are first asked—

"What could Gordon do alone against the now universally worshipped Mahdi?"

and then told—

"General Gordon's arrival in Khartoum gave fresh life and hope to the inhabitants."

Then,

"As it appeared to us in Kordofan, and to the Mahdi himself, Gordon's undertaking was very strange; it was just as if a man were attempting to put out an enormous fire with a drop of water,"

and,

"I have not the slightest hesitation in saying that had the Egyptian Government not sent Gordon, then undoubtedly the evacuation originally ordered could have been carried out without difficulty."

One is simply staggered by such an assertion. When Gordon arrived in Khartoum, the whole of the western Soudan had fallen. The town was overrun with the mourning women and children— the widows and orphans, I should say—of the troops who, under Hicks Pasha, had been annihilated a few months before on their way to extricate the garrisons. Slatin had surrendered Dara to Zoghal. Said Bey Gumaa, the last man to fight for the Government in the western Soudan, was compelled to capitulate very shortly before Gordon's arrival, and this only after a second siege when his men were dying with thirst. Bahr-el-Ghazal fell before Gordon had had time to turn round, and, for all that he or the Mahdi knew, the Equatorial province had fallen also. The town was hemmed in by the Mahdists, and the commanders of the garrisons which Gordon was expected to extricate were holding various commands in the dervish army, while Slatin had taken part already as a Mahdist in the subjugation of his subordinate, Said Bey Gumaa of El Fasher, who had refused to surrender. Am I not justified in saying that only the suppression of such facts made possible such attacks upon Gordon?

We are next told—

"Those who escaped massacre in Khartoum have often told me that they were perfectly ready to leave, and it was only Gordon's arrival that kept them back, but Gordon's arrival without troops had rather disappointed them. Had he been accompanied by five hundred British bayonets, his reputation in the Soudan might have been maintained, and probably the Mahdi would never have left Kordofan."

Why did not those perfectly ready to leave leave with the members of the Austrian mission, or leave between the date of their departure, December 11, and the early days of February, when the news of Gordon's mission first reached Khartoum? Who prevented their leaving during that interval of at least two months from the moment when they were all thrown into "indescribable dismay" until they heard of Gordon's appointment? And if, when he did arrive, they were so bitterly disappointed at his not being accompanied with five hundred British bayonets—much good these would have been against the "universally worshipped Mahdi" in extricating those who had surrendered to him—why did they stay on? Did not Gordon beg them to leave? did he not try and compel them to do so? did he not put boats at their disposal to sail north or south as best suited them? And has not Gordon himself given the real reason for their staying on?—though to this should be added their unbounded faith and confidence in Gordon.

Gordon, I venture to believe, sustained his reputation in the Soudan up to the end—up to the moment when, with the hand of Death on him, he fell facing his last assailant. True, he lost his reputation for telling the truth, but there are few men in this world whose telling of an untruth would startle and astonish a community. The people of Khartoum, their eyes dry and wearied with looking for a sign of the returning steamers which Gordon had sent off three months before to bring up the troops expected to arrive at the beginning of November, turned to each other, and, in an amazed whisper, said, "Gordon has told a lie," and were startled and afraid at their own words.

Having dealt as tersely as possible with this curious collection of contradictions, I proceed to the quotation of and replies to the criticisms passed upon Gordon in the book I have already quoted from.

1. "Looking back on the events of the siege of Khartoum, I cannot refrain from saying I consider Gordon carried his humanitarian views too far, and this excessive forbearance on his part added to his difficulties."

2. "It was Gordon's first and paramount duty to rescue the Europeans, Christians, and Egyptians, from the fanatical fury of the Mahdi, which was especially directed against them. This was Gordon's clear duty, but unfortunately he allowed his kindness of heart to be made use of to his enemy's advantage."

3. "Thus, in his kindness of heart, did Gordon feed and support the families of his enemies. It was quite sufficient for a number of women to appeal to Gordon, with tears in their eyes, that they were starving for him to order that rations of corn should be at once issued to them, and thus it was that the supplies in the hands of the Government were enormously reduced."

4. "Gordon should have recognized that the laws of humanity differ in war from peace time, more especially when the war he was waging was especially directed against wild fanatical savages, who were enemies to all peace."

5. "He was entirely deceived if he believed that by the exercise of kindness and humanity he was likely to win over these people to his side; on the contrary, they ridiculed his generosity, and only thought it a sign of weakness. The Soudanese respect and regard only those whom they fear, and surely those cruel and hypocritical Mahdists should have received very different treatment to civilized Europeans."

6. "I also think that Gordon brought harm on himself and his cause by another action, which I am convinced led to a great extent to his final overthrow. Such men as Slatin, Lupton, Wad-el-Mek, and others, had offered, at the risk of their lives, to come and serve

him. . . . Gordon would not, however, vouchsafe an answer to the letters of appeal these men wrote to him."

In the first five extracts, Father Ohrwalder, from an initial mistake in forgetting or being unaware of the presence in Khartoum of the thousands of widows and orphans of the soldiers of Hicks' army, flounders on until, as I have said, he is credited with opinions which he should be the last to give utterance to. It is passing strange that any missionary should place limits to the humanitarian views and forbearance of a military commander in time of war, who may invariably be depended upon to err on the wrong side from the biblical point of view. Gordon, in keeping in mind the Sermon on the Mount, and acting up to its precepts as far as the exigencies of a state of war permitted, performed no act derogatory to him as a military commander. Gordon was no worse a Christian than he was a soldier—and the world never saw a better soldier. And whatever Gordon's paramount duty may have been, it certainly was *not* his paramount duty to weaken his little garrison by sending an expedition into Kordofan to rescue, say, a dozen people who, as far as Gordon and every one else in Khartoum knew, had disavowed the Christian religion and adopted that of the Mahdi.

There is another aspect to the case. Gordon's troops were Muslims. The "Christians" had adopted the "true faith" and become Muslims also. Why, then, should Muslim lives be sacrificed to "rescue" them from Islam and bring them back to Christianity? And it must not be forgotten that Slatin, so far from denying his conversion, excused himself on the ground that his religious education had been neglected at home. Gordon is not to be blamed for having believed that the "Christians" had sincerely adopted Islam, for apart from the mere adoption of the religion, people sworn to celibacy and chastity had entered the matrimonial state, which was considered a further evidence of their conversion. While the gardener of the Khartoum Mission was bewailing the money he had sent to the "apostates," Consul Hansal wrote, asking that the matter be kept secret, to the Austrian Consul-General in Cairo, informing him of what had occurred. Had there been any "Christians" to rescue from the Mahdi, doubtless Gordon's paramount duty would have exhibited itself in some action. Nor is there any evidence that the Mahdi's "fanatical fury" was in any single instance especially directed against the "Christians," but there is a great deal of evidence to the contrary. With the exception of putting Slatin in chains, when he believed that he was playing him false, I know of no case of wanton cruelty practised by the

Mahdi towards the "Christians," and I am not sure whether "clemency" would not be the proper word to use in Slatin's case, when it is remembered what happens to prisoners of war who break their parole, for Slatin and the others had sworn the oath of allegiance.

Extract No. 3, apart from the extraordinary censure on Gordon for feeding the families of his enemies, and being moved to pity at the sight of the tears of starving women, calls for a more detailed reply to the criticism. Gordon, according to "Ten Years' Captivity," ought to have turned these women out of the town to be at the tender mercies of the "wild fanatical savages" and been responsible for the rehearsal under his own eyes of the hunt for lust which followed on the fall of Khartoum. Father Ohrwalder can never have heard of England's proud roll of heroes who on land and sea have given their lives to save those of helpless women and children. In feeding these women—even had all been the wives of his enemies, which they were not—Gordon committed no graver military crime than did the commander of the troops on board the *Birkenhead*, when, instead of seeing first to the safety of the soldiers for whose lives he was responsible, he placed the women and children in the boats which could have saved the troops, and called upon his men to present arms as the boats left the side of the ship—and to stand to attention as the vessel sank under them. So much for British principle, apart from Christ's teachings, in peace and war; now for the facts in Gordon's case.

When Gordon arrived in Khartoum, he found wandering—hungry and helpless—the thousands of widows and orphans of the soldiers who a few months before constituted Hicks Pasha's army. Throughout his journals you will discover constant reference to the food question, with accounts of his successful search for the *stolen* biscuits, which had "enormously reduced" the supplies in the hands of the Government. Gordon had calculated that the relieving army would reach him at the beginning of November, so that we find him writing on the 2nd of that month that he has six weeks' food supplies. In making this estimate he was allowing for full rations to the troops (who were also in receipt of the money with which to buy those rations), and the wants of the poor. On the 11th of that month he discovers nearly a million pounds of stolen biscuits. On the 21st he writes, "I do not believe one person has died of hunger during the months we have been shut up." On December 14—that is a month after the latest date he had estimated for the arrival of the relief expedition, he says that unless the troops come in ten days the town may fall, and this because he had on November 12 written, "Omdurman fort has one and a half months' supply of food and water." With the fall of this fort, he knew that the end would soon come.

But up to this date the soldiers, who were not entitled to rations since they received money for their purchase, were given full rations, and there is every reason to believe that the pinch only came when Omdurman fort fell on January 14 or 15, and the town was completely hemmed in. Food was short, no doubt, but, eight days before the fall of the town, Gordon could spare from the stores fifteen hundred pounds of biscuits to provision a boat for the Europeans. One should only be filled with amazement that Gordon held out so long after the date when he had expected relief, and it is not only ridiculous but monstrous to attack him, because he did not calculate that the expedition would only arrive *seventy-eight* instead of seventy-six days late, when we know for certain that his troops were receiving full rations which they were not entitled to for at least a month after the date of the expected arrival of the expedition.

It is true that Gordon, seeing the food supplies giving out, recommended people to leave him and join the Mahdi, but this was only after more days had slipped away after the "ten days from December 14." He had then abandoned all hope, and saw that his prophecy was to come true—the expedition would arrive just "too late." In comparison with the number of widows whom Gordon had had to support for ten months, without the slightest assistance or aid from outside, the number of wives of his "enemies" in the Mahdi's camp was so insignificant as to be unworthy of notice. But even supposing that all the starving women who went to Gordon crying for the bread which Father Ohrwalder suggests should have been represented by a stone, were the wives of his enemies, his own writing justifies Gordon's feeding of them, for he says, "These crafty people thus assured themselves that, should the Mahdi be victorious, their loyalty to him would ensure the safety of their families and property in Khartoum, while, on the other hand, should Gordon be victorious, then their wives and families would be able to mediate for them with the conquerors."

It is quite evident, then, that these people who went over to the Mahdi's camp did so, not from conviction of his divine mission, but to save the lives of their wives and families, whom by preference they entrusted to Gordon even at the last hour, and nearly a year after the date when his arrival without five hundred

British bayonets is supposed to have ruined his reputation in the Soudan. I am inclined to think that the "craftiness" displayed by some in trying to secure their wives and daughters against violation and death, was no less justifiable than the "craftiness" displayed by others for an entirely different purpose. What a tribute these "crafty" people paid to Gordon! I mean the crafty people who left Khartoum in January, 1885, and trusted Gordon with the lives of their wives and children. In discussing this food question with Khartoum survivors, I laid particular stress upon the feeding of the women and children, and I can do no better than give the summing-up of it in the words of a native survivor, after I had translated to him the criticisms I am replying to—"What! Would Gordon Pasha send away the hungry women and children of soldiers who had been killed fighting for the Government?"

I pass over extract No. 5 for the moment to refer to No. 6. The use of my portrait in advertising the book I am quoting from led most to believe that I approved of the criticisms it contained, and I have taken this opportunity of showing how thoroughly I disagree with them. To say that Slatin and others had offered, at the risk of their lives, to join Gordon is hardly correct, and if Gordon did not vouchsafe a written answer to the letters he received, he probably had good reason for not doing so, especially as it appears likely that some of Said Bey Gumaa's letters addressed to the Governor-General before Gordon's appointment had succeeded in getting through to Khartoum, and from these and deserters from the Mahdi, Gordon must have learned all.

Under pretence of intending to submit, Gumaa gained time, and tried to hurry up reinforcements, but this having been suspected, Zoghal ordered Slatin, Tandal, the President of the Civil Court, Aly Bey Ibrahim-el-Khabir, Slatin's head-clerk Ahmad Riad, and a few others, to send in an ultimatum to Gumaa, and await his reply. The reply travelled quickly; as soon as he read the letter, Gumaa opened fire upon the spot where Slatin and his companions were awaiting him. During the first siege of El Fasher, Gumaa must have accounted for at least fifteen thousand dervishes, and utterly defeated the army which retired to Walad Birra, from whence a party was sent off to Dara to bring up the ammunition which, as appears from Gordon's Journal, was handed over to the Mahdists by Slatin when he surrendered the province. This occupied eleven days, and then the second siege was laid. The wells were filled up, thus depriving the garrison of water; but for seven or eight days they held out, dying of thirst, while the town was constantly bombarded with Government ammunition. Said Bey Gumaa has always protested that had it not been for the ammunition handed over by Slatin to the Mahdists he could have held out—and more.

The knowledge of these things must have influenced Gordon, especially when Slatin writes to him, through Consul Hansal, offering to place his services at his disposal, but only on condition that Gordon should guarantee never to surrender, for, if he did, Slatin would be maltreated by the Mahdists when they laid hands upon him. Gordon was the best judge as to the value of services offered under such conditions. For "moral and political reasons," Gordon considered it unadvisable to have anything whatever to do with what he called "apostate" Europeans in the Mahdi's camp, but appreciating the enormous responsibility thrown upon his shoulders, he appealed to the Ulema for their advice, as these apostates were now their co-religionists, and they decided to have nothing whatever to do with their "proposals of treachery," as no good could come of it. Matters were made still worse by Slatin writing to Gordon asking him to be a party to proceedings very foreign indeed to Gordon's nature at all events. Slatin's request to Gordon was to write to him personally one letter in French, and another letter in Arabic, "asking him to obtain permission from his Master to come to Omdurman and discuss with him the conditions of his (Gordon's) surrender," which letter he could use in order to obtain permission to come to Omdurman. If Gordon had written that Arabic letter. . . .

If all these facts were not known to Father Ohrwalder before 1892, six years is quite long enough time to have learned them, and now I have no hesitation in saying that to assert that Gordon brought about his downfall by refusing the services of people willing to risk their lives in reaching him is, to put it charitably, pure fiction.

Irrespective of the opinions expressed in the first four extracts given, extract No. 5 makes out a very good case for the Sirdar to write in large letters at the Soudan Frontier, "No Missionaries Admitted," for Father Ohrwalder proves conclusively that they can do no good. Honestly I believe that for many years to come the only religious teachers allowed to penetrate into the Soudan should be enlightened exponents of the Quoran. Consider that for sixteen years the Soudan has been in the throes—is still in the throes of one of the greatest religious upheavals known. While this revival of Islam has been in progress in the Soudan proper, the converts at Uganda and elsewhere have been snicking each other's throats to evidence their zeal for the rival Christian creeds. In the Soudan, missionaries have openly avowed to thousands their acceptance of the "true faith"—Islam, the very religion from which they had gone out to convert the Blacks. I have not the slightest hesitation in saying myself that for some time to come religious revivalism in the Soudan will, if permitted to take place, very soon spell REBELLION. Time must be given for the bad (?) effect produced on the native mind by the conversion of the Soudan missionaries to die out, and goodness knows the poor country requires a rest. If missionaries must be sent, then let them be honest traders, the best missionaries for savage countries. When the Soudan has again been opened up, and the natives have become a little more civilized through their contact with trade, and so Europeanized that their simple faith, "There is one God, and He is God," is not sufficient for them, but they must needs snarl and fight over creeds, then and only then remove the "No Admittance" signboard.

I trust that no religious body or society of earnest Christians will think from the foregoing that I am either sneering or scoffing at religion, or that their disinterested efforts to spread the gospel of peace to the remotest ends of the earth have not my sincerest sympathy. I have spoken plainly and to the point, for I consider that the occasion calls for it. The missionaries required in the Soudan now are clean-minded, honest traders, who will do more for you by a few years' preparing the ground for "talking" missionaries than the missionaries can do in a score of years of preaching. It is men like Gordon who, though not preaching religion, yet practise it in their every act, whom the Soudan requires. Ask any one in the Soudan what is his opinion about Gordon, and he will reply, "Gordon was not a Christian; he was a true Muslim; no Christian could be so good and just as he was," and I believe that this saying, or estimate of him, emanated from the Mahdi himself. I draw your particular attention to the word "just," which proves that, in the eyes of the Mahdists and Soudanese alike, his justice ranked with his goodness. If any Soudanese or Mahdist ridiculed to Father Ohrwalder Gordon's generosity, and considered it a sign of weakness, it must have been done for a purpose. During my twelve years amongst all shades of people of the Soudan, I never heard a single word against Gordon, nor did I hear one until I came amongst his own flesh and blood. I cannot do better than relate another example of the esteem he was held in, and this example is from a Christian source.

My friend Nahoum Abbajee, when he reached Cairo, prepared a petition which he had intended forwarding to her Majesty the Queen, asking that the British Government should restore part of the fortune accumulated by him during his twenty-three years' residence in the Soudan. His argument was that, trusting to Gordon, he had delayed in Khartoum until Stewart's departure was arranged for, when, acting on the advice of Gordon, he sold off his goods, realizing but half their value, accepted Gordon Bonds in payment, bought a boat, as no one then would hire one out, set off with Stewart, and was captured by the dervishes. This would not have happened, had not the commander of the gunboat disobeyed Gordon's orders by steaming off to Khartoum, instead of bombarding Berber for three days, and Gordon was consequently responsible for the delinquencies of his subordinate.

On being asked what his personal impressions of Gordon were, he said that his thoughtfulness for every one, his goodness, justice, and innumerable virtues would take years to relate; and then when he was told that his claim could only be sustained on his proving that Gordon was to blame for the loss of Stewart's party, ill as he was, he rose from his couch, tore up the petition, and, with his hand raised, prayed Heaven that if the bit of bread to save him from starvation should be purchased with money obtained through laying a fault upon Gordon, it might choke him. One had to witness the scene really to appreciate it. Ruined, broken down in health, too old to make a new start in life, his eyes lost their dulness and glistened as he breathed his prayer and fell back on his couch exhausted with the effort. Nahoum, I am afraid, will have joined Gordon by the time this appears in print.

HASSAN BEY HASSANEIN.

APPENDICES

APPENDIX I HASSAN BEY HASSANEIN

When Gordon heard of the murder of Colonel Stewart and his companions, he held a sort of court-martial on himself, and, after reviewing all the arrangements which he had made for their safety, he came to the conclusion that Stewart must have been invited on shore and murdered. Then, as if endowed with second sight, he almost exactly described what actually happened. The *Abbas*, drawing less than two feet of water, ought not to have stranded, as it was High Nile. Treachery on the part of the crew he had guarded against by sending a bodyguard of highly paid Greeks. The cutting adrift of their boats just after passing Berber contributed to the catastrophe, for had they been with the steamer at the time she struck, it is hardly likely that the inhabitants of the village would have planned the treachery they did. As interpreter to the party, Gordon gave them the man he could least spare, and one in whom he had every confidence—Hassan Bey Hassanein. Gordon himself writes, "thus the question of treachery was duly weighed by me and guarded against," yet, in "Ten Years' Captivity," we find the contrary stated. "It is said that the interpreter, Hassan, arranged the betrayal." Moreover, to clinch the matter, and to show that Gordon had selected a traitor in the very man whom the lives of the party might depend upon, it is added, "And I was afterwards told that, when he got into difficulties later, he sent a petition to Mohammad-el-Kheir, in which he said that he was entitled to reward for having secured Colonel Stewart's death. He is still living in Omdurman."

Hassan Bey Hassanein has lived to come back to Egypt and bear witness to the goodness and virtues of the heroic defender of Khartoum. The only bit of treachery Hassan Bey acknowledges is that—with his fellow-clerk, Sirri—he cut the Khaleefa's telegraph and telephone communications as the troops were advancing, to prevent communication between Omdurman and Khartoum and the outpost at Khor Shambat. It was Hassan Bey who ran out of the telegraph-hut as the gunboats advanced and attempted to get on board in order to warn them of the mines. He succeeded in attracting attention, and barely got off with his life, for his shouts in English were drowned by the report of the rifles as the men "potted" at his dervish dress.

Hassan Bey Hassanein, speaking English, French, and Arabic, was sent to Khartoum in July, 1883, for telegraphic work. When Gordon arrived, in 1884, he wrote an official letter detailing him for his special service. Orders were given that he was to have access to him at all hours of the day and night. It was Hassan Bey who used to mark the words Gordon required to use at a forthcoming interview, in his Arabic dictionary. Before giving his version of the murder of Stewart's party, a few words concerning him and his relations with Gordon will prove that, in selecting him as interpreter to the party, Gordon "well-guarded against treachery."

One of Hassan Bey's first missions after the arrival of Gordon was to seek out the widow of Bussati Bey; for, on arrival at Berber, he had telegraphed to Bussati Bey, not knowing that he had been killed with Hicks. Having found the widow and her children in dire straits, he returned with one of the children to Gordon, and then took the child back carrying a handkerchief containing a hundred pounds. "Bis dat qui cito dat" was certainly Gordon's motto in Khartoum, from the hundreds of tales which I have heard. On handing the money to the widow, she brought out her husband's uniform and sword, and, handing them to Hassan Bey, said, "As you take the place of my husband at Gordon's side, then take his sword and uniform." Hassan Bey took it to Gordon, who asked what it was worth, and being told "perhaps ten pounds," sent twenty pounds to the widow to make sure, and told Hassan Bey to keep the uniform, as it might yet come in useful.

Later on, when Hassan Bey, who was then but "effendi," had had a particularly hard spell of night and day work, Gordon asked him which he would prefer—an increase of pay or a rank. Hassan Bey left the matter to Gordon, and he gave him both, writing the "firman" himself. On the Friday following, Hassan Bey presented himself to Gordon in Bussati's uniform—for uniform was worn on Fridays and feast days. Gordon was evidently much amused at his interpreter and telegraph-clerk appearing in the uniform of a lieut.-colonel, although the rank he had bestowed upon him was nothing more nor less. Telling Hassan Bey that such a uniform did not look well without a decoration, he pinned on to his right breast one of the decorations he had had struck to commemorate the siege of Khartoum, and Hassanein walked off a proud man to delight the eyes of his wife, then nearing her confinement. Fifteen days before the departure of the *Abbas*, he presented himself to Gordon, and told him that he was the father of a boy. "No, I am the father," replied Gordon, and, knowing Hassan Bey's house, he hurried off at a quick walk, which Hassan Bey had to run to keep up with. Pushing his way through the women assembled in the outer room, he tapped gently on the door where mother and child were lying, and asked, "Mary, tyeeb-tyeeb?" ("Is all well?") and then, as the child's "father," he insisted upon entering, took the child in his arms, crooned to it, kissed it, and then hurried off and wrote a note to the Finance Office to pay a hundred pounds *from his salary* "to his boy." Mother and child were to meet with a tragic death.

Two days before the departure of the *Abbas*, Gordon told Hassan Bey that he had selected him to accompany Colonel Stewart as interpreter. He was to accompany the party as far as Dongola, at all events, but there was the possibility of Stewart requiring him as far as Cairo, therefore his wife collected a number of presents for her relatives in Cairo, which Hassan Bey was to present in uniform and decorations, so that all should understand how highly she had married. I must now, having given an idea of the relations existing between Gordon and the man who "betrayed" Colonel Stewart, and who had left with Gordon his wife and fifteen-day-old boy, give his account of what actually occurred. I purposely leave out all the incidents of the voyage until the boats reach the island opposite the village of El Salamanieh.

A discussion arose between the two Reises (pilots) as the island was neared, as to what course to take; the river was running strong, and between the island and mainland resembled a mill race. One reis contended for the left bank and the other for the right. Stewart, who spoke Turkish and Arabic, asked what was the matter, and decided that judgment was to rest with the oldest of the reises, and he selected the right bank. Instead of coming through the race stern first, it was decided to put on full steam and "shoot" what might be called the rapids. While the decision was being given, the steamer had come end on with the island, and when full steam ahead was signalled, she steamed ahead at an angle of about seventy-five degrees to the southern spit, and before reaching the race proper, struck—swung round, and struck again. Colonel Stewart took down his revolver, and threatened to shoot both reises, upon which they dived overboard and swam to the right bank of the Nile, but thirty or forty yards distant. Colonel Stewart did not fire at them as they swam off. This occurred about an hour before mid-day.

About an hour later, the two reises—Mohammad el Dongolawi and Ali el Bishtili—returned to the vessel, said they had spoken to the people of the village, who had declared they acknowledged the authority of Mustapha Pasha Yawer, the Mudir of Dongola; they at the same time begged that Stewart would not molest them in any way, and they would provide camels to take the whole party to Dongola. Colonel Stewart spiked the cannon, and threw it overboard along with the ammunition. He then ordered Hassan Bey, with one of Gordon's cavasses, and the clerk Mahmoud Ghorab, to go on shore and interview the people. At first they demurred, as, being Egyptians, they felt sure they would be murdered, and asked that the small boat should be sent as far as a village near Derawi, where it was certain "friends" would be met with. Colonel Stewart, after first threatening to throw them into the river, took his revolver again and threatened to shoot all three if they did not obey instantly. They obeyed, and went on shore to meet the men awaiting them—a blind man named Osman, and two men of the Wadi Kamr tribe. On reaching the reception-room of the Sheikh-el-Belad (headman of the village), a copy of the Quoran was produced, and upon this Osman and his companions swore loyalty to the Government. Osman remained behind while the other two accompanied Hassan Bey and the others to the island where Stewart's party had then landed. Here again the oath of allegiance to the Government was taken, and the men left, promising to send for camels to be ready on the following morning.

At about ten o'clock the next day they returned, and suggested that all should come to the right bank and pack up their effects, to be ready for the camels when they arrived. About two hours after mid-day, while all were either seated on the bank or fastening up their effects, a man came, said that the Sheikh-el-Belad had arrived, and invited the "Pasha" and the Consuls to his house. Colonel Stewart ordered Hassan Bey to accompany him as interpreter. On reaching the reception-room, they found about forty or fifty people assembled to receive them. The Sheikh-el-Belad was seated in the centre of the room on the left. Two angareebs were placed at each side of the doorway: Stewart and Power seated themselves on the angareeb on the right, and Hassan Bey and Herbin on the angareeb to the left. Some minutes were taken up in the usual salutations, and before they had time to speak about the journey, the natives rose, and, saying the camels were approaching, left the room, only to rush back a few minutes later shouting, "Salaamoo tisslaamoo ya kaffarah" ("Become Muslims, you infidels, and you will be spared"); but at the same moment Herbin had his head smashed in with an axe, and Hassan Bey was stabbed in the right arm with a crease knife, and, as he was falling, received a large spear wound in the left leg. He fell unconscious, and did not see how Stewart and Power were killed. While the bodies were being dragged out of the room, some time after sunset, Hassan Bey was found to be still alive; it was proposed to kill him, but the brother of the Sheikh-el-Belad, he heard afterwards, pleaded for him, as his "stomach felt sick."

After the murder of Stewart and the others, the party made their way to the river, and a long fight ensued between them and the crew of the vessel, the latter being killed to a man. Hassan Bey was given some engine-oil from the steamer with which to dress his wounds, and, when he recovered, was sent to attend the flocks of the tribe. About fifty to sixty days later, he was sent to Berber on the orders of Mohammad-el-Kheir, and there imprisoned for four months, and, on the death of the Mahdi, was, with other prisoners, sent to Omdurman, to take the oath of allegiance to Khaleefa Abdullahi.

In 1889–90 he was sent to Kassala, and, on the breaking out of the famine, he, with his wife and child, and many others, made up a party to return to Omdurman. Hassan Bey's group consisted of his family, a man named Ismail, with his wife and daughter, and a man with two women. They ran short of water, and, leaving the others, who were worn out, to rest under some shrubs, Hassan Bey and Ismail set off in search of water. In about four hours' time they reached some pools near the Atbara, and filling their water-skins, set off to rejoin their families. On reaching the spot, they found that they had been devoured by lions; the heads of Hassan's wife and boy—then between six and seven years of age—and the heads of Ismail's wife and daughter were all that remained. No trace was left of the heads of the man and the other two women, and it is surmised that they must have escaped, for the lion never eats the head of its victim. Half mad, the two wandered on, living on roots and leaves, until, on reaching the village of El-Mughetta, on the banks of the Atbara, they were taken prisoners and made slaves. Ismail had to work at the ferry, but Hassan Bey, being weak and ill, was allowed to wander about until, meeting with a caravan bound for Geddaref, he joined it, and then made his way to Omdurman, being employed, first, as clerk under Abdallah Sulieman, the head of the cartridge-factory, and then transferred to the telegraph service.

APPENDIX II ORPHALI

The account which I have given of how Gordon died differs so very little in essentials from the account which I have since received from Khaleel Agha Orphali, and which has been read to Khartoum survivors with the idea of comparing the statements made with what was related at the time, that I think it advisable to allow my account to stand, and to append that of Orphali, giving a few details concerning Orphali himself. I might mention that Gordon was credited with having killed a much greater number of dervishes than I have given, but the error arose from his being credited with the killing of the dervishes on the "Gouvernorat" (E) staircase; but these were killed by the guards. The fact of his having killed so many as he did, is to be accounted for in two ways; first, the people who first assailed him on the private staircase were unaccustomed to the use of the small spears they carried—indeed, it is safe to say that they had only been dervishes outwardly for half an hour or so; and, secondly, as they were packed on a narrow staircase, every shot told on the mass. To assist the reader in following Orphali's narrative, I have drawn from memory a rough plan of the palace as I remembered it while it stood intact, and, with the assistance of Fauzi Pasha and others, have been able to name each of the rooms.

Khaleel Agha Orphali joined the army for service in the Soudan in the Coptic year 1591 (1873–74). After taking part in a number of engagements, he was promoted to the rank of Bulok Bashi (commander of twenty-five men), and when Gordon reached Kulkul, in 1878–79, Orphali and his men had been without pay for months. They presented themselves to Gordon and clamoured for their pay; he recommended them to go to Khartoum for it, upon which they became abusive, and Gordon drew his revolver. Orphali followed suit, but neither fired. Gordon quietly ordered the cavasses to remove their chief in custody, which they did. Shortly afterwards, Gordon sent for Orphali, told him he was a "man," gave him a present of money, and offered him the post of cavass to himself, which Orphali at once accepted, accompanying Gordon to Khartoum, and remaining with him until he left.

On Gordon's return, in 1884, he found Orphali then in Khartoum, and made him his chief cavass. Orphali is one of those men who know but one master, and believe that master to be the ruler of the universe. He, therefore, was no great favourite with some in the administration, as, during the siege, he was never away from Gordon's side, and his cavasses were allowed to do nothing but keep their arms clean, and be ready to surround Gordon in case of trouble. They were strictly forbidden to leave their posts to carry coffee, bread, run messages, or perform all the other little services which they had been accustomed to perform for the katibs (clerks). Orphali's ideas as to the duty of his cavasses were the cause of constant bickerings, which came to a climax about twenty days before the fall of Khartoum, when he espied one of them carrying an ink-bottle behind Geriagis Bey—the head-clerk, who succeeded Rouchdi Bey. This was too much for Orphali. Grasping the brass inkstand, he drove it with all his force against Geriagis' chest, and this assault Gordon could not pass over. Orphali was in disgrace for eight days, and "confined to barracks," that is to say, the palace precincts, but he slept at Gordon's door as usual. Twelve days before the fall, he was re-instated in favour, and never again left Gordon's side for a moment.

Orphali—as Gordon is not alive to speak for him, and as so many knew from Gordon himself of his threat to shoot him many years before—has been afraid, since his return, to talk about his relations with Gordon, and was not a little surprised when I assured him that, if he appeared in "Londra," he need have nothing to be afraid of from the English people. Having introduced the man, I now give his description of the night of the 25th January, keeping as much as possible to his own words, and only, to give a complete account, mentioning the incidents occurring in other parts of the palace while Gordon and he fought the upper floor:—

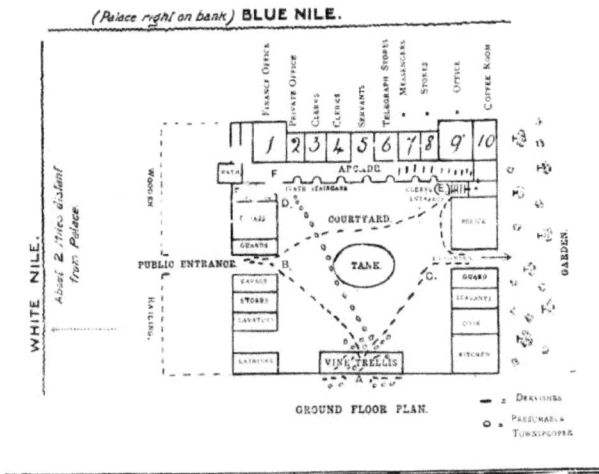

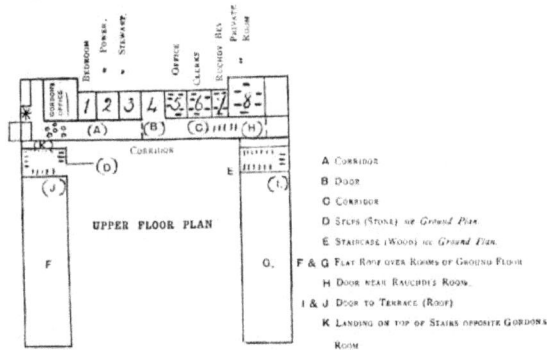

PLANS OF PALACE AT KHARTOUM ILLUSTRATING
THE DEATH OF GORDON.

see better image

His excellency was not an early sleeper, and on the night the dervishes entered Khartoum he was in his room. At eight o'clock, Consul Hansall, Consul Leontides and the Doctor, Abou Naddara (he of the spectacles), came to see him, and remained until midnight. After their departure, he did not go to sleep, but sat reading and writing letters, and sometimes pacing the room. At one o'clock in the morning, he sent me to the telegraph-office to inquire about the enemy's movements, as he had received confirmed news of the intended attack, and his excellency had issued general orders to the soldiers and employés to be on guard to attack and withstand the dervishes. Ali Effendi Riza, Mohammad Effendi Fauzi, and Youssef Effendi Esmatt were on duty, also the messenger Mohammad Omar. They reported all was quiet, and this news I gave his excellency. Half an hour later, perhaps, firing was heard from the land side (*i.e.* to the south); I was sent to seek information. Bakhit Bey, from Buri, telegraphed that a few dervishes had attacked, but had been driven off, and when I told his excellency, he prepared to sleep, and gave me the customary order to bolt his door, and this I did. Then I closed the door of the terrace (I, plan), then the door of the Gouvernorat (H), near Rouchdi Bey's room, and returning along the corridor leading to the private apartments, closed the door in the middle (B), and then went down the private staircase (D), gave the usual orders to the guards, and returned to my sleeping place opposite the pasha's room (K), after I had told the telegraph-clerks to bring information as soon as any news came from the lines. About three o'clock, Mohammad Omar, the messenger, with Cavass Ali Agha Gadri, roused me and said that an attack was being made at Kabakat (boats) on the White Nile. I informed the Pasha, who told me to run to the telegraph-office for more news, and there I met Hassan Bey Bahnassawi, who was on duty, and we heard that an attack had been made, but had been repulsed.* On informing the Pasha, he told me to close the door of his room again, which I did, and sat down to make coffee. Then we heard more firing from the White Nile, and the cavasses, having run to the terrace, called to me that the dervishes were coming into the town. I ran down to Buluk Bashi Ibrahim El Nahass, who had twenty-four men; fifteen we placed at the windows (rooms on right ground-plan), and nine on the terrace overlooking the garden (G). There were also twenty-four cavasses and ferrashes; thirteen were placed at the windows (left of ground-plan) under my second, Niman Agha, eight on the terrace (F), and three at the door of the palace (B). Each man had ten dozen cartridges, besides which, each party had a spare case of ammunition. All these arrangements did not take five minutes, as each knew his place. I then ran up to the Governor-General's room, and informed him of the arrangements. The day had now come (dawned). The dervishes who ran to the front of the palace were killed by the fire from the steamer. About seventy were killed in the garden by the soldiers firing on them from the terrace, and then we saw the dervishes coming over the rukooba (vine-trellis A), and they were met with the fire from the windows and terraces. They came in great numbers very quickly. Some ran to the entrance (B), killed the guards and opened the door; then they all ran to the Gouvernorat door and killed the telegraph-clerks, all except Esmatt, who hid among the sacks in the storeroom; they then went to the terrace (G) and killed the soldiers, and Nahass, seeing the massacre, jumped from the window. Four men were on guard at the private stairs, but when the dervishes came back from the Gouvernorat door (E) they were soon killed, and some of the dervishes ran to the terrace (F), and killed the soldiers there; others came up the steps to the private apartment, and broke the door; Gordon Pasha met them with his sword in his right hand and his pistol (revolver) in his left, and killed of them two who fell at the door, and one who fell down the stairs,† and the others ran away. Then we heard the dervishes breaking the private door (B), while the Pasha was loading his revolver. I went forward and received a little wound in the face, and when the Pasha came, he received a wound in the left shoulder; the man who wounded him was a half-blood slave. We followed them to Rouchdi Bey's room, killing three and wounding many, and the others ran away and fell down the stairs. We went back to the Pasha's room and reloaded, but the dervishes came back, and I received a slight wound in my right leg from a sword, but I warded the blow, and the cut was nothing. We attacked the dervishes on the private stairs (D), and while we were passing the door a native of Khartoum, dressed as a dervish, stabbed the Pasha with a spear on the left shoulder; seeing this man's hand coming from behind the door, I cut at it, and he ran and fell on a spear held by one of his companions on the steps, and was killed. At this time more dervishes were coming along the corridor (from H), and we returned to meet them; I received a thrust in the left hand, but the Pasha cut the man down with his sword, and kicked him on the head and he died; then the dervishes ran into the clerks' offices (5, 6, 7, upper-floor plan), and while we were standing in the corridor, a tall negro fired a shot from the door (H) near Rouchdi Bey's room, and the bullet struck the Pasha in the right breast, and the Pasha ran up and shot the man dead. The dervishes then came out of the offices, and we turned, and they ran to the private stairs, and we fired into them, but the Pasha was getting weak from loss of blood. We fought these dervishes down the stairs till we reached the last one, and a native of Katimeh speared the Pasha in the right hip, but I shot him, and the Pasha fell down on the cavasses' mat at the door, and he was dead, and as I turned to seek refuge in the finance-office (F plan), I was struck down and lost my senses, and I was lying down with the dead. In the afternoon, a man of El Katimeh—Abd-el-Rahman, whom I knew, helped me to go to the river for water, and I saw the body of the Pasha at the door (D), but the head was not there. I was helped to my house, and found my wife and children and property all missing. ... I was taken by a friend and Abd-el-

Rahman to El Dem-el-Darawish, and left on the plain all night, and in the morning I was taken before Wad en Nejoumi . . . and I was stripped to see if I had any money and papers, but I had not; and when I said that I was ignorant of any treasure, I was heavily beaten, though much wounded, and was very ill for seventeen days, and my wife found me.

> * This is a literal translation. What Orphali intends to convey is, that on telegraphing to the lines, Bahnassawi Bey, who was on duty, was at his post, and replied to the inquiries sent by telegraph. The distance between the palace and Bahnassawi's post was about two and a half miles.

> † That is to say, fell dead or wounded.

All who were taken to see the steps where Gordon fell remarked upon the number and extent of the blood stains, for they could not believe that all had come from one body. These stains were shown to me in 1887. It has been stated on good authority that "Stains of blood marked the spot where this atrocity took place, and the steps from top to bottom for weeks bore the same sad traces." Here is what I choose to consider not only a confirmation of Gordon having died fighting, but a confirmation of Orphali's narrative, for there were only two people on the upper floor—Gordon and Orphali, and all the fighting must have been done by them. It is quite impossible that the steps "from top to bottom"—four flights-could have been stained as they were stained with large patches of blood left by a body which had been dragged downstairs some time after death. The steps *were* stained with the blood of the dervishes through whom I have said Gordon shot and hacked his way in his heroic attempt to reach his troops.

APPENDIX III Translation of the letter which the Khaleefa dictated in reply to the letter given me by General Stephenson, in Cairo, before leaving for Kordofan.

"In the name of God the Most Merciful, and thanks to God the Omnipotent and Generous, with prayers on Mohammad our Lord and his descendants; Greeting.

"From the servant of his Lord Abdallah-el-Muslimani-el-Brussi (the Prussian), formerly named Karl Neufeld, to Stephenson the Englishman, at Cairo.

"We have to inform you that, in conformity with your letter, dated March 1, 1887, addressed to us, and recommending us to Sheikh Saleh Fadlallah-el-Kabashi with regard to your projects,

"We started from Halfa, with his men bearing the arms and ammunition and other things sent him by the Government.

"We proceeded on our course, and were constantly on guard on ourselves and our property, until we arrived at a well called Selima, from where we took the water supply, and continued our way to our destination.

"It was our fate to be met in the desert by six fakirs, followers of the Mahdi, who attacked us, so that we and Saleh's men had to defend ourselves, our number being fifty-five men.

"The six fakirs were later reinforced by others, all of them being men of Abd-el-Rahman en Nejoumi. Thus there remained for us no way of escape, and in the space of half an hour we were defeated, many being killed, and the rest taken prisoners. The rifles, ammunition, and things destined for Saleh were seized, and I, my servant Elias, and my slave-girl, Hasseena, were among the prisoners, and we were thus conducted to Abd-el-Rahman en Nejoumi, to Ordeh or Dongola.

"From this place we were sent to the Khaleefa of the Mahdi, on whom be peace, at Omdurman, to whom we were presented. We were certain that we were to be killed, taking into consideration our great crime against him.

"The Khaleefa of the Mahdi, on whom be peace, however, pitied our condition, and proposed to us to avow the Mohammedan faith. We accepted, and became Muslims by pronouncing the two declarations in his presence, and by publicly professing that there is no God but God, and that Mohammad is the Prophet of God, and I then added that I believed in God and his Prophet Mohammad, and in the Khaleefa of the Mahdi. We then asked him for his clemency and pardon, which was granted. He thereupon embraced me, and named me Abdallah. I was then accepted of the Mohammedan religion.

"It was on these conditions that the Khaleefa of the Mahdi, on whom be peace, pardoned me and spared my life, which was already forfeited.

"This was done to the honour and glory of the Mohammedan religion.

"We further inform you that although Dufa'Allah Hogal deceived us, notwithstanding his perfidy, we cannot sufficiently thank and reward him, as his treachery turned to our great benefit, and he has allowed us to enjoy great prosperity.

"Finally, we inform you confidentially that Saleh Fadlallah Salem has lost all his power and influence, and has taken refuge in the desert. This is the truth. I write this for your advice.

"The 17th Shaaban, 1304."

APPENDIX IV IBRAHIM PASHA FAUZI-GORDON'S FAVOURITE OFFICER

When Gordon arrived in Khartoum, in 1874, Ibrahim Pasha Fauzi was then a second-lieutenant. Gordon had applied to the then Governor-General of the Soudan, Ismail Pasha Ayoub, for four companies of soldiers to accompany him to the Equatorial Provinces. Ayoub was not at all pleased at Gordon's mission, as he took it as a slight upon his administration, so that when Gordon's application for troops was received, Ayoub selected for the purpose his most worthless men, with the double object of getting rid of them, and making Gordon's mission a failure. Fauzi, anxious to see some service, had volunteered to accompany Gordon, and, for doing so, Ayoub placed him under arrest. Gordon, hearing of the matter, sent to Ayoub demanding that the officer who had volunteered his services should be sent to him immediately. Fauzi was sent to Gordon's head-quarters, when Gordon first asked him, "Are you the officer who volunteered your services?" following up the question, when Fauzi in reply said, "Yes, sir," the only two words he then knew of English, by asking why he had done so. On learning that Fauzi wished to see service, he promised that his wish should be gratified. "But," added Gordon, "I wish you to answer me as an officer—why did the Governor place you under arrest?" Fauzi gave the reason—Ayoub was afraid that Gordon would discover, before departure, that he had been sent the worst troops. Sending back the four companies, he requisitioned four companies indicated by Fauzi, and, Fauzi being too young for a command, he appointed him commandant of his body-guard, and a sort of adjutant-major to the little force.

FAUZI PASHA IN UNIFORM.

Fauzi accompanied Gordon to the Albert Nyanza, returned with him to Khartoum, was gazetted major in consideration of his services, and appointed Mudir (Governor) of Bohr, but given two months' leave of absence before taking up his post. Gordon left for England, and Fauzi came to Cairo for his leave, on the expiration of which he set out for the Soudan, but, on reaching Berber, he found a telegram awaiting him from Gordon telling him not to go further than Khartoum, as he (Gordon) was returning as Governor-General. When Gordon reached Khartoum, it was to hear that Darfur was in revolt, and that the Bahr-el-Ghazal province was joining the rebels. A council of war was held, when Gordon asked the officers present to select one of themselves to head an expedition to the Bahr-el-Ghazal province, while he took another into Darfur; he had expected all of them to volunteer for the command, but they believed that such an expedition had more the elements of defeat and death in it than of glory and distinction. Told that they must name an officer, they named Fauzi, who was not present, and Gordon at once accepted him, sending him off with 4000 troops and the clerks for the civil administration. Fauzi succeeded in setting the province to rights without fighting, and while travelling about setting the administration right in the districts, he often met, and assisted with food and money, a holy man then living as a sort of hermit at Abba and the neighbourhood. The man's name was Mohammed Ahmed—whom the world was to hear of six years later as the Mahdi.

Breaking down in health, Gordon ordered Fauzi to Khartoum, for rest, promoted him to the rank of full colonel, and named him Governor of Equatoria, in which province he spent about a year carrying out Gordon's instructions to the letter, and making a host of enemies amongst the officials whose peculations and interest in the slave-trade he put a stop to. He accompanied Gordon to Cairo in 1879, and when Gordon decided upon resigning, he asked Fauzi whether he would prefer to remain in Cairo or return to the Soudan. Fauzi saw that, without Gordon to back him up, his tenure of office would be but of short duration, unless he engaged himself in the maladministration of the provinces; he elected to remain in Cairo, where, at Gordon's request, he was gazetted Colonel commanding the 1st Regiment of the 3rd Brigade. Gordon made it a point to be present at Fauzi's first parade, congratulated him on the handling of his men, and bidding him farewell, gave him three hundred pounds as a souvenir of their days together in the Soudan. At the outbreak of the Arabist rebellion, Fauzi's regiment, with others under the command of Kourschid Pasha, was ordered to Rosetta, and after the defeat of Arabi, at Tel-el-Kebir, he was, with other colonels, ordered to surrender to Sir Evelyn Wood at Kafr Dawar. Sent to Alexandria, he was tried, degraded, and then dismissed in disgrace.

Some days before the arrival of Gordon, in 1884, H. E. Nubar Pasha and Sir Evelyn Wood sent for Fauzi, and told him to be in readiness to proceed to the Soudan, as Gordon had asked for his services. When Fauzi said that he had been dismissed, and was no longer on the army-list, Nubar Pasha replied, "General Gordon will see to the matter." It had not been Gordon's intention to call at Cairo, and Fauzi was to have gone to Suez or viâ the Nile, as Gordon might decide. However, Gordon was stopped at Port Said, and asked to come through Cairo; Fauzi went to the station to meet him, and Gordon, on alighting, went up to his old Soudan lieutenant, and asked how it was that he was not in uniform. Fauzi detailed his dismissal, upon which Gordon turned to Sir Evelyn Wood, and asked him how it was. It appears that when Gordon saw Fauzi's name amongst the names of the colonels to be tried, he wired, or wrote—or both—to Sir Evelyn Wood, asking him to look after Colonel Ibrahim Fauzi. General Wood did do so, but there was another Colonel Ibrahim Fauzi; and while Gordon's Fauzi was dismissed in disgrace, the other Fauzi retired in glory and with a pension.

Gordon had some difficulty in seeing Fauzi reinstated, for his enemies were powerful; but, not to be thwarted, he took Fauzi direct to His Highness the Khedive, and carried his point. Two days later, Fauzi took his seat in the carriage with Gordon and Stewart, and left Bulac Dacroor station on that journey from which he only was to return alive, and that fourteen years later.

On the way to Khartoum, Gordon named Stewart sub-Governor-General of the Soudan, and Fauzi Director of Military and Marine, and, in communicating these appointments to Cairo, he wrote of Fauzi, "I especially recognize in Fauzi Bey the desired activity which he has displayed with me while previously in the Soudan; he has already given proof of his abilities, and I am more than ever satisfied with him."

Soon after his arrival at Khartoum, Fauzi was entrusted with the clearing out of the rebels from Khor Shambat and Halfeyeh, and the restoring of the telegraphic communications which they had cut. Fauzi won his dual victory, and restored the line, but, in leading his men, he was hit in the right leg with a bullet fired from an elephant-gun, which split and shattered the bone. Owing to want of skill on the part of the Greek doctor, the broken bone was allowed to overlap, and a suppurating wound set in from the unextracted fragments, which kept Fauzi confined to his official residence for about six months, although he was able to transact the executive part of his duties. On the departure of Stewart, Gordon named Fauzi Governor of Khartoum and Commandant of Troops, calling a special parade for the occasion. Fauzi Pasha must be left to relate, at some future date, the incidents of the siege of Khartoum; I pass on to January 25, 1885.

About three o'clock in the afternoon, Gordon called Fauzi to the roof of the palace, to see the activity taking place in the dervish camp. He had a large tripod telescope fixed on the roof immediately over his room.*

> * It has been repeatedly stated that Gordon had a gun on the roof of the palace, with which he used to shell the dervish camp. In one account of the fall of Khartoum, it is averred that Gordon, in his sleeping suit, served this gun for an hour until it was rendered useless, as it could not be depressed sufficiently to bear upon the dervishes surrounding the palace. There never was a gun on the roof of the palace, for the roof would not have supported its dead weight, much less the shock of its recoil.

About 3.30, Fauzi, riding a donkey, accompanied Gordon on what proved to be his last visit to the lines. Most of the troops were lying down exhausted and hungry; as they saw Gordon approach, they wished to present arms, but he kept calling out to them, "Rest, rest; but keep your eyes open." At sunset they regained the palace, and walked up and down for some time discussing the situation. As the dinner-hour approached, Gordon told Fauzi that he was sorry he could not invite him to dinner, as he had nothing to eat. Fauzi said he had, for himself and guards, the hearts of four date trees, and would send one to the palace, upon which Gordon ran in and brought out his dinner—also the heart of a date tree. This was the last Fauzi was to see of Gordon.

At midnight, Fauzi Pasha, as usual, went his rounds of the posts in the town, reaching his guards at about 2 a.m. While giving orders in the courtyard of his official residence, a sound as of shouts in the distance was heard. This was towards dawn. Fauzi went to the roof, and, through his binoculars, could faintly make out hand-to-hand fighting going on in the lines. Hurrying down, he drew up his men, and set off for the palace, being joined by ten Greeks who had been on duty. On coming in sight of the palace, they were met by two bands of dervishes, but succeeded in cutting their way through one, only to be met by a troop of dervish horse. The little party was forced back, fighting every step, and when close to his house all rushed inside, closed the doors, and commenced to fight through the windows, but for every shot they fired, a score came back in reply. The little garrison assembled in the courtyard for a last stand as the dervishes were then beating down the doors. Fortunately, the sight of other dervishes rushing past with loot drew the besiegers off on a similar errand, and the party was able to hold its own against successive parties until the Mahdi sent word to stop the massacre. When Fauzi was taken before the Mahdi, he was asked, "Why is it that you, a good Muslim, have never written to me when every one else has done so, expressing their loyalty? Have you forgotten the days at Abba, and the instruction I gave you? If you have, I have not;" and, kissing him, the Mahdi told him to "go in peace." The Mahdi was very wroth at the death of Gordon, for he really admired and respected him, and he had given strict orders that he was not to be harmed in any way.

As, during his captivity, Fauzi used to receive moneys from Cairo, he had, to explain his being able to live, to engage in some occupation, and took to lime-burning, a business which cost him more than he ever got out of it. As an Egyptian, he was under the surveillance of Youssef Mansour, who, after the escape of Slatin, refused to be responsible for Fauzi any longer. Failing to get him executed for having assisted in Slatin's escape, he succeeded in getting him committed to the Saier, where he remained as a prisoner for four years, until released by the Sirdar.

APPENDIX V AHMED YOUSSEF KANDEEL

Ahmed Youssef Kandeel, though actually a civilian employé, held the rank in Khartoum, where he was born, of Lieutenant in the 3rd Soudan Artillery. He took part in many of the attacks on the dervishes during the siege, and fought with Bakhit Bey on the night the town was taken. He managed to fight his way to his house, and held out until the Mahdi's orders came to stop the massacre of the inhabitants, when he gave himself up. His father, uncle, and brother had already been killed fighting. For some time he supported himself at Omdurman by cutting firewood, living in a state of semi-starvation. Being a good clerk, he offered his services to Wad Nejoumi, who, it appears, would employ no one but old Egyptian employés as "katibs" (clerks). He was with Wad Nejoumi when I was taken prisoner to Dongola, and throws an interesting light upon Nejoumi's attitude towards Mahdieh, which more than confirms the impressions I had formed, and which I have given expression to in Chapter VI.: "Dongola to Omdurman."

AHMED YOUSSEF KANDEEL.

Kandeel tells me that, on the arrival of our party at Dongola, Nejoumi called a meeting of emirs, and asked what should be done with us. All voted for instant execution, but this Nejoumi would not sanction. Among the emirs was a Taaishi wakil (spy or agent of Abdullahi)—a similar wakil being appointed to each army not actually led by one of the Khaleefa's relatives. This wakil's name was Messaad Geydoom-el-Taaishi. When Nejoumi insisted upon saving my life, and, as an alternative, sending me to the Khaleefa, leaving him to decide what should be done with me, he instructed Kandeel to write a letter saying that, as I was a "hakeem" (doctor), I might be useful to him (Nejoumi) and also to the army. Geydoom, having his suspicions about Nejoumi's loyalty to

Mahdieh, used his sparing of my life as a proof of his sympathies with the Government, and Nejoumi was ordered to Omdurman, and kept a prisoner in his house for some months.

Geydoom's treatment of the army during Nejoumi's absence caused so much discontent that Abdullahi determined to send Nejoumi back to Dongola, but with strict instructions to at once commence the march for the conquest of Egypt. He was given a hundred and twenty rifles only, and very little ammunition.

When General Grenfell sent the letter to Nejoumi, calling upon him to surrender, Nejoumi called a council of emirs, said that the army could not possibly fight, as they were tired, hungry, and thirsty, and suggested surrender, for they must either be killed upon the field or die in the desert on the way back. The emirs, being of the Taaishi family, first accused Nejoumi of cowardice and then of treachery. They threatened to report him to the Khaleefa when the fight was *won*, and to ask that one of themselves should be given the command when the further advance into Egypt was ordered. There appears to be but little doubt that, had it not been for the Taaishi emirs, the army would have followed Nejoumi unarmed to the lines of the Government troops. The emirs dictated the reply which Nejoumi was to send to General Grenfell, and when Nejoumi dashed down into the plain as the dervish army was in retreat, it was doubtless with the object of reaching the Government lines, but under pretence of rallying the few remaining troops, so that they should not shoot him down if they thought he was deserting them—or follow him if they thought he was charging, for this would have drawn the fire of the brigades upon them. After the death of Nejoumi, spies reported to the Khaleefa that he had attempted to open up negotiations with the Government troops, and Kandeel, being suspected as Nejoumi's "katib," was loaded with chains and sent to Omdurman, where he was imprisoned for fourteen months, and then released to become the clerk of Yacoub, the brother of Abdullahi.

APPENDIX VI THE SOUDAN: ITS PAST, PRESENT, AND FUTURE

To the present generation the history of the Soudan may be said to commence with the date of its partial conquest by Mohammad Ali Pasha, the Viceroy of Egypt. To go further back than this is to compile from various sources, all more or less inaccurate, a mass of information which, where not misleading, would be next to useless to the would-be correct historian. Even the recent history of the benighted country has from force of circumstances been compiled from sources not the most reliable, and it is extremely difficult for the moment to sift the facts from the legends. The Soudan is still an unknown and unconquered land. Small tribes have been magnified into nations, and petty chiefs and sheikhs into kings and sultans who evidenced their exalted position in the possession of a few more sheep, goats, donkeys, and slaves, than their neighbours. No single tribe or sheikh ever held general supremacy over the others; Zubeir was within an ace of making himself the Sultan of the Soudan, when he accepted an invitation to visit Cairo; that was twenty-five years ago, and he is still here. The Soudan was nothing more nor less than a collection of little commonwealths; occasionally a number of these would acknowledge allegiance to one particular headman, and, in such instances, the "nation" might have boasted almost as great a population as some small and obscure provincial town. But that such instances were rare is proved by the facility with which Mohammad Ahmed and Abdullahi set the various sections of tribes fighting among themselves.

When Mohammad Ali established his government, and when later Ismail Pasha attempted to extend his empire, they each took advantage of the chronic anarchy reigning in the Soudan to further their schemes, but the tribes soon found that they had but stepped from the frying-pan into the fire, and waited patiently for the strong man who was to rid them of the thraldom of the now hated and detested Turks, from whom they had hoped so much. From the time when, what the Soudanese call the "Turk" rule, was established, until the rebellion of 1882, nothing whatever was done to develop the natural resources of the country—indeed, the reverse. The only trade the officials fostered was that of slaves, and these were invariably drawn from peaceful and agricultural districts; the adult male population of whole districts was swept away in those raids organized to supply the hareems of Arabia, Algeria, Egypt, and Turkey, with eunuchs and concubines. The mineral wealth of Sennar, Darfur and Kordofan was neglected, as when the soldiers reached the gold, silver and copper mines, they discovered that the precious metals did not exist in the pure blocks they had expected to find, and that to extract the metals meant work.

The population of the half-conquered provinces was robbed in every conceivable manner by tax-collectors, who were seldom or never paid their salaries of from twenty-five to thirty shillings a month, and they were assisted in the duties of tax collecting by companies of irregular soldiers whose salaries also were never paid. Where money was not forthcoming, the taxes were collected in kind, and it may be imagined what the result of tax collecting was. The people were driven farther and farther away from the cultivated lands and watercourses. The "Sudd," that rank growth of weeds which obstruct the navigation of the Nile and its tributaries, was left to accumulate year after year, the little clearances which the inhabitants themselves made formerly, being abandoned as they but aided the passage of boats conveying soldiers on tax collecting or conquest of territory expeditions.

Admitting, for the sake of argument, that some of the Soudan tribes may have risen to the dignity of independent kingdoms, their history may be written with one word—"anarchy," and when the "Turk" government was established, general rebellion was rife from the beginning until it culminated in the rising of Mohammad Ahmed.

The population of the Soudan was, and still is, divided into three great classes, (1) the pure Arab to whom manual labour has been unknown since the day his ancestor Ishmael mixed the mortar with which to cement the stones of the Kaaba or House of God, which Abraham built at Mecca; (2) the Negroid, who will perform a few light duties, but who has absorbed all the worst to the exclusion of the few better qualities of his progenitors,—and, (3) the Black— naturally indolent and too lazy to work,—without ambition, and whose presumed avarice only extends to the possession of a little more than he can eat. For centuries the Black has been the slave of the Arab, and performed all the manual labour, such as the collection of gum and senna leaves, indiarubber, ivory, the cultivation of cereals, and the navigation of the rivers; but taking it all in all, the lot of the black slave might be envied by millions of workers in other parts of the world. With the introduction of the "Turk" government, all three classes were considered as "prey"; the slave proper had to work harder so that his master might be able to satisfy the rapacity of *his* master—the official, and the slave knew this; the negroid, who believed in cultivating only so much dourra as was requisite for his needs, found that he had to cultivate enough to feed the soldiers quartered in his province, and to pay taxes not only on what he grew for himself, but on what he grew for nothing for the soldiers. It is no wonder, then, that the three waited the coming of some strong man to rid them of the common enemy.

Although a religious element was introduced into Mohammad Ahmed's movement, many fail to grasp the fact that religion here takes the place of politics in Europe, and when the Arabs rise against the powers that be, they are backed up by some "religious" question, for their laws are based entirely upon the Quoran. Mohammad Ahmed had for years been preaching against the extortions of the Turk officials, and had it not been suggested to him, it is unlikely that he would ever have assumed the *rôle* of Mahdi, though as a holy man only, it is almost certain that his crusade would have succeeded equally as well as it did. The country was ripe for rebellion, and when the followers of Mohammad Ahmed overcame the first "Turk" sent against him, and against whom he had been preaching for years, success was assured, and thousands flocked to him. His crusade, therefore, in the beginning, was not a religious movement pure and simple as we understand such; it was the rising of an oppressed people against a government that had but lately tried to establish its authority over them. It is true that once having had the *rôle* of Mahdi forced upon him, Mohammad Ahmed did his best to act up to it; his miracles—in the way of annihilating successive armies sent against him were very real indeed, and if thousands flocked to his banner in consequence of them, they should not be too severely criticized and charged with fanaticism and unreasoning superstition, for while they flocked to see the worker of these very real miracles, just as many thousands of people in more enlightened climes were making pilgrimages to caves, grottoes and shrines in the belief that the miracles they were praying for would be performed. Nor, considering that the faith in dreams and visions is almost as strong in the east as it was when Pharaoh had his dreams interpreted by Joseph, should Mohammad Ahmed and his successor be blamed for taking advantage of the credulity of the most credulous people on earth in the relating of visions, when but a little time since thousands of people in a highly civilized country were flocking to the doors of one who pretended to be the mouthpiece on earth of the angel Gabriel—a much more mythical being than either the prophet Mohammad or the Mahdi.

Had Mohammad Ahmed lived, there is no doubt but that he would have succeeded in establishing some form of government which, if not better, would certainly have been no worse than the one he had overturned. With the Mahdi's death, Abdullahi found himself with a trust which, as he saw immediately, only a powerful military despotism could enable him to keep. Threatened with attack from all points of the compass, he had also internal dissensions to combat, and met them unflinchingly. While his atrocities have been made much of, he invariably went through the farce of trying people for disobedience during his reign of martial law before carrying out the capital sentence; perhaps, if Abdullahi's atrocities were placed side by side with those associated with revolutions in other countries, his list would be found not the longest. Oppression doubtless was great, but it was concentrated in one place, and being more seen, was as a consequence more felt. Still opinions may be said to be equally divided as to whether oppression was any greater during the worst days of the reign of Abdullahi than it had been under the old government. The foregoing is not written in defence of Mohammad Ahmed or Abdullahi—and I have little reason to say a single good word for the latter, but it is time that the Soudan should be seen through clear glasses. Jealousy of power was Abdullahi's besetting sin, and to this must be attributed the swift punishment meted out to those who in the slightest degree exhibited disobedience of orders. To this jealousy must be added vanity of his power also. I have heard since my release, from people of the Muslimanieh quarter, some of the reasons for Abdullahi's sparing of my life. I had forgotten the incident, but am reminded that when on my arrival at Omdurman I was taken to the gallows in chains to be hanged, I turned to the Emirs and shouted "Has your Mahdi (I used this name at the time) no other way of exhibiting his power but by hanging a bound man before all his soldiers? Take off my chains, and I will fight you, or else get on with your work." Abdullahi was told this while I was still being played with, and said, "A man who will talk like that when he is going to be hanged is a man! He is a big man; I will not hang him; a man who is not afraid of me is not to be hanged; I will keep him." This was said to the Muslimanieh and others. Abdullahi had not made up his mind whether I was a merchant, spy, medicine man or general. Then, again, he kept me alive in order to prove that he was more powerful than my Malek (the Emperor of Germany). I am told that he very often said to people, "You have heard of Abdalla Nufell; he is not afraid of me; his Malek has millions of soldiers like him, but he dare not bring his armies to release him; he is afraid to meet my ansar."

There are other stories of Abdullahi's many references to me, but, as they are of a complimentary nature, I must leave others to relate them; the above are only given for the purpose of affording a slight insight into the man's complex character, and to give an idea of the small actions which could influence him.

The Past of the Soudan may be said to close with the battle of Omdurman; the Present may be given in one word—Transition. Its Future is still in the future; but from what I have written, those intending to make a rush to the Soudan as soon as it is declared open for trade, will understand that a settled government has yet to be established. The Soudan has had but one government, and I have given an idea of what that government was to the inhabitants; the next government established will, as a matter of course, be looked askance at. Although the Khaleefa's army was smashed up at Omdurman, his influence still remains with great numbers, and time must be given for the Soudanese to learn that there are governments *and* governments. All they are conscious of now is, that the Government they turned out has come back again, and they expect from it no better treatment than they received formerly, if they do not expect worse as a punishment for their rebellion. The possession of slaves will be forbidden, and this will give umbrage to the Arabs, while the slaves will no more appreciate or enjoy their freedom than would so many cage-bred birds theirs. There is a considerable amount of ignorance in Europe on the subject of slavery in Mohammedan countries, but I must confine myself to the Soudan on this question. Slave raiding should of course be put down with a strong hand, and there should be, when a raider is captured, no other formality than that of loading the rifles or affixing the rope; the trial might take place at some future date, so that the fact of his execution might be recorded. I wish to speak now only of those who are already *called* "slaves," for, in the majority of cases, it is but a name.

I have remarked that the Black is naturally lazy, and will do no more work than he is compelled to; if liberated unconditionally, he will, unless drafted into regiments, loaf about, and occasionally do a little work for the sake of a meal; but he will refuse to keep to any work long unless some sort of pressure is brought to bear, and he will be only too glad if it is. As a slave, his master must keep him in food and clothes, and also support his wife and children in return for his services, and, being "property," he is well looked after; he is, as I have said, a slave but in name, but the name has an ugly sound to Europeans. The new Government might open a slave register, have a few inspectors to go round and "ask for complaints," and either give an age, or name a date, when all holding of slaves would be a breach of a law yet to be made. Treaties are all very well when dealing with countries boasting a civilized Government, but it is not an easy matter to compel petty chieftains in the heart of Africa to agree to laws which upset the whole political economy of their domains—and this only to please people who know nothing of the existing conditions. However the whole question bristles with difficulties and with arguments for and against leaving matters as they are—only suppressing raiding as I have said already—but as those difficulties do exist, it would be well not to be rash, or to burden the still unconquered and unsettled country with revolutionary laws. Far better to make haste slowly, for laws are of little use unless a breach of them is quickly punished, and the Soudan Arabs have yet to be taught to respect laws emanating from a "Government."

These few remarks on the unsettled state of the country are intended for those who may be going out as entire strangers to the Soudan. They must be prepared to meet with difficulties great and small, disappointments, much discomfort, and many annoyances big and little; but it is to be hoped that they will endure these for a time, and not pester the little and still half-formed new administration with big complaints about petty quarrels or troubles. Any reprisals asked for in case of small annoyances or unpleasantnesses, can but bring in their train much bigger ones; you want but to earn the respect of both Arab and Soudanese to earn his devotion, and you may have both by at least treating him as a man and not as a beast. When speaking of my having borrowed money from the guides whom I entrusted with the arrangements I made for my escape, I drew attention to the strange fact of my borrowing money from them. This was putting the principle I have pointed out into practice; I required their aid. I went further, and gave evidence that I was entirely in their hands—a weakling, but they understood that if they helped me in my weakness, I would help or protect them in my strength; above all, they valued my trust and confidence. There are limits, I know, to both, but you must learn those limits.

The great want of the Soudan at the present time is means of communication; there are enormous tracts of land on which cereals can be raised with the minimum of cost and labour, but without means of transport they might as well not exist. Some talk has been made of a line of rail connecting Khartoum with the Red Sea, and this, certainly, would provide the means of transport and enable the Soudan to compete with almost any other country in cereals, but it is a question whether it would be worth while to construct a railway for the sake of the grain trade, if the trucks which take it to the seaboard have to be hauled back empty, and, maybe, left idle for the greater part of the year. It is possible that during the last fifteen years Nature has to a great extent repaired the enormous damage done to indiarubber and gum trees, when the plants and trees were destroyed in order to obtain a big enough crop to satisfy the rapacity of the "Turk" officials. The forests abound in ebony and other hard woods, but power to saw them into beams or planks of suitable dimensions for transit is requisite before this valuable industry can be developed. From what prisoners from the south told me, in places an almost pure iron is found on or near the surface; this the Shilluks and Dinkas smelt in mud furnaces about six to eight feet high and three to four feet in diameter. The spear heads of the Shilluks and Dinkas, beside their shape being different from all others, are readily distinguishable from their peculiarly deep black shade, while the spear heads made from imported iron are many shades lighter, and in comparison, when polished, have a tinny appearance. If coal is found, and I believe it will be, if the description I was given of "black stones" which took fire is correct, then one might say that there is no limit to the development of the country. Should the Nile and its tributaries be cleared of the "sudd," considerable development would be immediately possible, but the whole country must first be studied, and its present condition with its existing means of transport thoroughly grasped, before people will be justified in subscribing for big ventures, for the failure of one means the failure of others, and a retarding, for want of new capital, of present possibilities in the way of development.

It is quite impossible to compile any statistics of the former import and export trade of the Soudan, that is to say reliable statistics, and as the whole trade of the country was governed by the slave trade—now abolished—a new condition of things has been introduced but not yet established. Barter must, for some time to come, be the medium of trade and exchange, and, here again, new conditions are certain to be met with. Formerly the principal imports were cheap cotton goods, earthenware, ironware, dried and preserved provisions, sugar, perfumes, and such like, which generally came in the category of things which are "cheap and nasty." There are two great reasons why all this must now be changed; with almost 20,000 regularly paid troops in the country, and troops, too, who have, in a measure, been living in the lap of luxury, since 1882, their demands must be met. The sight of well-fed, well-housed, and well-clothed troops, will excite the admiration and cupidity of the Soudanese for similar luxuries, and a demand for articles formerly unknown to them will at once be created. I hesitate to specify some of the goods which I know there will be a demand for, not that I am in any way interested in the subject for the moment, but only to guard against numbers of people exporting large quantities of merchandise of the same class far in excess of the actual demand. I cannot too strongly advise manufacturers to study on the spot the requirements of the people, and to comply with their requirements, whatever the article might be. Disappointment and loss can only ensue if articles they do not want, or which do not meet with their requirements, are attempted to be forced upon them, for while engaged upon this suicidal policy, some one else will certainly be studying the question with the intention of meeting the wishes of his prospective customers. I would strongly deprecate the formation of big syndicates and companies for the exploitation of the Soudan; the country, granted certain facilities for transport, has a great future, but it would be very unwise to lock up large capitals, the greater part of which would be lying unused. Small companies, with all the capital employed, will pay best for the time being, and the pioneers of such companies might be accompanied by a mineralogist, to examine the gold, silver, copper, lead, and other mineral deposits. That gold exists is well known, but the richness of the quartz I cannot speak of; one thing, though, is certain, gold can be obtained with little or no difficulty and labour, otherwise the small bags of gold I saw at Khartoum and Omdurman would not have been brought in. Lead and copper will be found to the west and south-west of Darfur—and possibly silver also, but whether it would pay to work the mines can only be ascertained after an examination of the districts.

To sum up. The Soudan is a country which for nearly a century has been fighting against the establishment of any foreign government; its experience of a "benevolent" administration is of the very worst; the inhabitants sank all or nearly all differences between them when they rose to turn out the hated Turks; their experience of Christians has evidently not been of the best, else why the saying concerning Gordon? Large numbers are still loyal to the Khaleefa Abdullahi, and it will require but a very little mistake to make the inhabitants flock to his banner, or, what is worse, they will retire to the west and leave the country denuded of the population it stands in so much need of. Strangers are not wanted—they will be looked upon with suspicion until they have given evidence of their honest intentions towards the villagers; traders, before they may look for success, must overcome the prejudice of the people against European traders, a prejudice based upon experience of them formerly. And it is necessary for me to say that, after recent experience, it will take some time before the Muslim will believe that the Christian religion is anything but what he believes it to be, and he will be convinced that the boasted superiority of the European over the Arab does not hold good in the Soudan at all events. If those going to the Soudan will bear these points in mind, they will save themselves and others an infinity of trouble, and all barriers will be surmounted, if they keep in mind always the reputation Gordon made for himself for "Goodness and Justice," and make Goodness and Justice their motto.